Lou Grant

The Television Series

Robert Thompson, *Series Editor*

Lou Grant

The Making of TV's
Top Newspaper Drama

DOUGLASS K. DANIEL

With a Foreword by Edward Asner

Syracuse University Press

Library of Congress Cataloging-in-Publication Data

Daniel, Douglass K.
 Lou Grant : the making of TV's top newspaper drama / Douglass K.
Daniel ; with a foreword by Edward Asner.—1st ed.
   p. cm.—(The Television series)
 Includes bibliographical references and index.
 ISBN 0-8156-2675-4 (alk. paper).—ISBN 0-8156-0363-0
(pbk. : alk. paper)
 1. Lou Grant (Television program) I. Title. II. Series.
PN1992.77.L69D36 1995
791.45′72—dc20   95-20141

Manufactured in the United States of America

Contents

Illustrations

Douglass K. Daniel is an assistant professor in the A. Q. Miller School of Journalism and Mass Communications at Kansas State University. He spent eleven years as a reporter and editor with newspapers, magazines, and the Associated Press. As a freelance writer, he has published articles in *American Film*, *Boys' Life*, the *Des Moines Register*, *Exploring*, the *Kansas City Star*, *Quill*, and *Scouting*.

Foreword

Edward Asner

An editor who pleases everybody will be neither sitting nor standing, and there will be lots of flowers around." That plaque hung on my dressing room wall during the time we worked on *Lou Grant*. It not only summed up the feelings of real-life newspapermen but also the attitude of our producers, writers, and actors because we knew we wouldn't please everyone. But where our newspaper, the *Tribune*, was concerned, we stood fast on our principles. No one could deny the show had a conscience; whether you *agreed* with that conscience or not was something else. But it made for five years' worth of meaningful television.

I'd always been interested in journalism, as early as high school in Kansas City, Kansas, when I was feature editor of my Wyandotte High School newspaper, *The Pantagraph*. I loved the idea of being able to annotate history, of helping people visualize history as it's happening. My fellow students praised my writing, so I naturally felt I showed promise in journalism and seriously considered a career in the field. My journalism teacher dissuaded me; he told me I couldn't make a living. I don't know why I thought becoming an actor would give me better odds, but, as fate would have it, I wound up in journalism through my acting.

On *The Mary Tyler Moore Show* I became intrigued by the world of TV news, then, in the hour-long series, investigative journalism. I still follow the inner workings of newspapers and the media, and I formed many lasting friendships with editors and writers from mainstream newspapers to underground papers.

The transition from Lou on *The Mary Tyler Moore Show* to the Lou on *Lou Grant* was hell. The producers had only done sitcoms, and it was the first time anyone had tried to turn a sitcom character into a dramatic one. No one was sure what I should do with the character. As a result of listening to everyone's varying opinions on how I should play the role, I became miserable during the first season.

There were *other* reasons to be miserable, however; MTM was unwilling to spend a lot of money on the show for the first season. The set was so exposed, a man walking by outside could ruin a scene. And instead of fluorescent lights, we had the cheaper kind. The heat was horrible. It was a dry heat, so we didn't perspire much, and the lights consumed our oxygen. They actually had a portable oxygen unit for me to suck on once in a while. Things were different the second year; we finally became an entity unto itself and made a successful transition from comedy into drama while retaining just the right amount of comedy, the right amount of realism versus dramatic license. The show caught the peculiar magic of a modern metropolitan daily and the people in it.

In hindsight, the show is one of the accomplishments I'm proudest of as an actor. I knew, at the time, that we were doing exceptional and *important* work that had the power to make changes in our world. That may sound egotistical; it was, after all, just a television show. Consider, though, that surveys show Americans form their opinions about nearly everything from TV, and the average American watches TV almost seven hours a day. A prime-time show reaches forty million homes. The entertainment industry is America's second largest export, and *Lou Grant* has been seen in seventy-two foreign countries; in many of them, the very idea of freedom of the press is amazing. That kind of power gives my industry an obligation to be responsible for what we produce, and, in that regard, *Lou Grant* was exemplary. The topics on *Lou Grant* covered everything from Latin American dictatorships to nuclear plants to psychological stress in Vietnam vets. After two episodes on *Lou Grant*—on orphan drugs and nursing home conditions—I found myself testifying to congressional panels, which ultimately resulted in legislation on those problems. I even used to hear that members of the Supreme Court would discuss the previous night's show in chambers. Although it was a radically different Supreme Court back then, they probably do the same with topical shows now.

Despite the controversial subject matter we tackled during those years, only a few *Lou Grant* shows were challenged: the Hare Krishna show took static because we tended to condemn the cult deprogrammers more than we did the Hare Krishnas. "Home," the show about abuses in some nursing homes, caused two sponsors—Ford Motors and Oscar Mayer—to threaten to pull their advertising (ultimately, when CBS stood its ground, neither canceled). The producers found only two topics too hot to handle: abortion and school busing.

Lou Grant also presented an ideal opportunity to address First Amendment rights, and it was only because of the First Amendment guarantee that we could *do* so. The Bill of Rights, led by the First Amendment, is a unique set of entitlements that set this nation apart, a priceless assurance to artists that we can express ourselves according to our vision, instead of living in servitude to the vision of the state. I think the national press *needs* shows like *Lou Grant* not only to goose them into action but also so that more people will come to understand why things are done in the press the way they are.

Ben Bagdikian wrote a wonderful book in 1983 entitled *The Media Monopoly*. At that time, he wrote about the "50 corporations that control what America sees, hears and reads." That was a shocking revelation to me back then, but the latest statistics show that only *five* corporations now control most of the sixty-two million newspapers sold daily. We're succumbing to what Marvin Kalb called "herd journalism" (*New York Times*). With few exceptions, investigative reporting seems to be a thing of the past. But we can't afford to blindly accept what often amount to "press releases" in our newspapers, taken at face value without question or investigation. Our task—as editors, actors, citizens—should be to guard America and its freedoms by seeking justice, by questioning authority.

Douglass Daniel has done an exceptional job of tracing the history of *Lou Grant*. "Questioning authority" was what our fictional reporters did on the *Tribune*, and my hope is that, in reading it, even one journalism student or writer or editor decides to blaze a new trail of investigative reporting. Maybe they will focus on the environment or the issues of child abuse or drug abuse or racism. There are enough causes to go around.

Acknowledgments

Dozens of people generously gave their time as I prepared this book. My work would have been difficult if not impossible without their assistance.

I owe a special thanks to MTM Productions. Through the courtesy of Shari Mennell and the office of Mel Blumenthal, I spent nearly four weeks at MTM watching all 114 episodes of *Lou Grant*. The staff of MTM's postproduction office made me feel welcome.

Special thanks also go to those who made material available from their files and agreed to be interviewed. They are Daryl Anderson, who had the only copy of the original character sketches; Edward Asner, who provided hundreds of items from his personal archive; Gene Reynolds, who established the Gene Reynolds Collection at the University of California at Los Angeles; and David Shaw, who provided an original critique of the show.

Interviews with others involved in major and minor ways with *Lou Grant* provided important information. For their interest and time, I thank Mason Adams, Rebecca Balding, Jack Bannon, Arnold Becker, Paul Bogrow, Burt Brinckerhoff, Bill Brink, Allan Burns, George Cotlier, Mel Damski, Kellam de Forest, Seth Freeman, Michele Gallery, Lance Guest, Carol Isaacs, Linda Kelsey, Steve Kline, Peter Levin, Sydney Z. Litwack, David Lloyd, Eric Malnik, Nancy Marchand, Al Martinez, Mark Murphy, Jerry M. Patterson, Alexander Singer, April Smith, Ted Thackrey Jr., Grant Tinker, Leon Tokatyan, Robert Walden, Allen Williams, Patrick Williams, Boris Yaro, Roger Young, and Narda Zacchino.

My visits to Los Angeles were made possible by the hospitality of Holly Daniel, Edye Lerer, Tom Myers, and Jason Schaff. Other friends provided research material, particularly videotapes of *Lou Grant* episodes. Marc Munroe Dion taped dozens of episodes over a four-month period, a feat of diligence and patience. For their assistance, my thanks go to Cort and Linda Anderson, Aaron Biederman, Tim Janicke, Richard O. Linke, Ron Pittman, Mike and Oleta Revzin, and Alan Wild.

Not only did I have help in gathering information about *Lou Grant* but I had help in making sense of it. I owe a special thanks to Patrick S. Washburn of the E. W. Scripps School of Journalism at Ohio University. He is a source of inspiration as a historian, teacher, and friend. I also thank Marilyn Greenwald of the Scripps School of Journalism; David Mould of the School of Telecommunications; and David O. Thomas, director of the School of Film at Ohio University. Additionally, permission to reprint the "Lou Grouch" segment from *MAD Magazine* is gratefully acknowledged. *MAD Magazine,* "Lou Grouch" is trademarked and copyrighted © 1979 E. C. Publications, Inc. Used with permission. All Rights Reserved.

Finally, a few words of thanks are due my family for their unfailing support during my years of graduate study. They provided encouragement and listened with patience and interest to unending stories about Lou Grant and the *Los Angeles Tribune*. I owe a special debt to my sister, Holly, for all her help as I made my way across Los Angeles and, indeed, across the country. My work would have been immeasurably more difficult had she not been so generous. I dedicate this work to her.

Introduction

Seven of the best-known journalists in the United States in the late 1970s and early 1980s worked for a newspaper that never published a single edition. The *Los Angeles Tribune* was only a figment of the imagination, part of a work of fiction broadcast once a week on television in the form of the CBS series *Lou Grant* (1977–82). The *Tribune* staff—publisher Margaret Pynchon, managing editor Charlie Hume, city editor Lou Grant, assistant city editor Art Donovan, reporters Joe Rossi and Billie Newman, and photographer Dennis "Animal" Price—were no more real than attorney Perry Mason or marshal Matt Dillon. Yet each week millions observed their struggle to bring *Tribune* readers the truth about the issues of the day.

Lou Grant exposed the workings of a daily newspaper to a significant segment of the television audience. The series was on the air for five years, longer than any prime-time drama set at a newspaper since the 1950s.[1] Estimates of the number of people who watched the series each week ranged from twenty million to twenty-five million. In addition, between 27 percent and 32 percent of all households watching television when *Lou Grant* aired chose to observe the *Tribune* staff in action.[2] Its audience dwarfed those of the nation's two largest daily newspapers, the *New York Daily News* and the *Wall Street Journal*. Each of those real-life publications had a daily circulation of a mere 1.6 million in 1979.[3]

People within the television industry watched, too. They considered *Lou Grant* one of the medium's best achievements during the period. For two seasons, 1978–79 and 1979–80, the series won Emmy awards as outstanding drama from the National Academy of Television Arts and Sciences. In the five seasons it aired *Lou Grant* received fifty-six Emmy nominations and thirteen awards.[4] The series won numerous other honors, including a prestigious Peabody Award for its "entertaining yet realistic look at the problems and issues which face those involved in the 'Fourth Estate'."[5]

Even more remarkable was its popularity among journalists. Winning over reporters, editors, and critics was a major accomplishment for the creators of the series. Never before had a newspaper drama gained such a following in the press. To many in the profession *Lou Grant* offered the most realistic depiction of newspaper journalism on television. It struck a nerve within the news media because it brought to life their ethical dilemmas and, more importantly, the human side of covering the news in ways that no other television drama had managed to do.

Although *Lou Grant* has been absent from prime-time entertainment since 1982, some television critics still use it as a standard of excellence in the genre of the newspaper drama. Commenting in 1991 on how television has portrayed the news media, Jon Katz of the *New York Times* referred to the "still-missed 'Lou Grant' " as "television's most successful newspaper show."[6] The producers of *Capital News* (1990) learned that the memory of *Lou Grant* still lingered when their newspaper drama aired on ABC. "Turning journalism into prime time entertainment is no easy feat," Marc Gunther of the *Detroit News and Free Press* wrote in an unfavorable assessment of the new series. "Except for 'Lou Grant' . . . newsroom dramas on television have lasted about as long as, well, yesterday's news."[7]

Few television series have been embraced by the public, the television industry, and the professions they depicted. *Lou Grant,* however, gained a loyal following among all three contingents. When the series was abruptly canceled in the spring of 1982, nowhere was the disappointment stronger than in journalism. The *Detroit Free Press* even wrote an obituary for the *Tribune*'s fictional city editor, calling Lou Grant "one of the best-known and most widely respected journalists of his day."[8] Other newspapers, while noting that the series was one of the few on television that dealt with meaningful issues, acknowledged a fondness for seeing their profession depicted realistically. The *Lansing State Journal* in Michigan said in a farewell editorial, "It is one of those rare Hollywood productions that tried to present a picture of the newspaper business as it is today."[9]

Lou Grant merits examination because of its unique place in both the history of television and the history of journalism. Exploring the series on those levels is the goal of this book. In terms of television it investigates the creation of a popular and respected series. As journalism history it reveals how *Lou Grant* portrayed the profession. A variety of sources were consulted, including all 114 episodes of the series. Men and women who played key roles in the history of *Lou Grant* were interviewed, and scores of newspapers, magazines, and books were scrutinized.

To place *Lou Grant* in perspective in chapter 1 I examine the newspaper drama as a genre of television. Twenty-three newspaper dramas aired in the thirty years of prime-time entertainment that preceded *Lou Grant*. Most of these forgotten series were rank failures, unable to sustain a significant audience and generally scorned or ignored by journalists. The newspaper genre had gained little respect within the television industry by the time *Lou Grant* debuted in 1977.

The genesis of *Lou Grant* I explore in chapter 2. The series was designed as a vehicle for actor Edward Asner, who had played Lou Grant on the situation comedy *The Mary Tyler Moore Show* (1970–77). The producers thoroughly researched the state of journalism in the post-Watergate era. They took this unusual step because they were convinced that the success of *Lou Grant* depended on its realistic depiction of the profession. Journalists at several newspapers, particularly the *Los Angeles Times*, played an active role in the research phase.

The information gathered during the research phase was used to create the series's supporting characters. That process and the casting of actors and actresses I examine in chapter 3. Producing, writing, and directing *Lou Grant* I examine in chapter 4. Additionally, in this chapter I investigate the impact of Program Practices, the CBS censorship department. Based on unpublished memos and an interview with the CBS censor in charge of *Lou Grant*, in this chapter I offer a rare look at network censorship of a prime-time series.

In chapters 5 through 7 I examine the series season by season with an emphasis on story lines. In general, episodes focused on journalism methods and ethics, an important social issue, or an interesting character study. In these chapters I also explore changes in casting and characters, reaction by television critics and other journalists, and controversies stemming from specific episodes.

In chapter 8 I review the cancellation of *Lou Grant*, which remains a subject of debate. CBS contended that sagging ratings led to the decision to cancel its most prestigious series. Others, however, argued that Asner's liberal politics, which included sharp criticism of the Reagan administration's policies in Central America, soured sponsors and the network. Indeed, evidence suggests that several factors contributed to the demise of the series.

Finally, in chapter 9 I place *Lou Grant* in context. Its depiction of journalism raises several questions. For instance, what were millions of viewers told about the functions of a newspaper and its staff? What did they learn about the process of gathering news, editorial decisions, and the ethical issues that journalists face? How realistic was *Lou Grant*? What forces, such as the medium of dramatic television, shaped its presentation of the journalism profession?

An examination of *Lou Grant* results in an exploration of journalism and television in the late 1970s and early 1980s. It reflects the post-Watergate era in which the journalism profession was held in high regard by the public. It also reflects the continuing maturation of television as an entertainment medium, which struggled with how it should present society's problems and the human condition. Thus, *Lou Grant* stands as a milestone in journalism and television history. "As a weekly series, 'Lou Grant' brought a distinctive element of substance to the television schedule," *New York Times* critic John J. O'Connor wrote on the eve of the show's last episode. "Television has lost one of its worthier efforts." [10]

Lou Grant

1

The Newspaper Drama
on Television

When Robert Walden arrived at the television executive's office, he was prepared to listen rather than talk.[1] Silence was unusual for the energetic actor. Normally garrulous and eager to share ideas with others, Walden had decided to allow his more experienced companions to pitch. In television jargon "to pitch" was to propose an idea for a production, usually telling the story with a flash of showmanship.[2] Pitching was among the challenges facing nearly anyone hoping to put a project before a camera. Walden's two partners were writers, and together they had shaped an idea for a television series.

The star, of course, would be Walden. He would play a New York City police officer pushed off the force for testifying about police corruption. The character also would be sought by the mob for revealing information about their activities to the government. He was out in the cold, yet he had maintained his integrity. In the series he would be joined by a female reporter. She lacked the ex-cop's street savvy, but she was an incredibly effective journalist. Together, this unlikely pair would uncover scandal in the city and help bring truth to the public. The series would be titled *The Muckrakers*.[3]

The threesome behind *The Muckrakers* took the idea to CBS, which had wanted to develop a series for Walden.[4] At the age of thirty-one he had already acted on the stage and in numerous television series and motion pictures, including the critically acclaimed film *The Hospital* (1971). He had recently costarred in the final season of the NBC series *The New Doctors* (1969–73).[5] CBS had several projects in mind for Walden, but executives had agreed to let him pitch his own.

Nearly two decades after the 1974 meeting with CBS, Walden vividly remembered the executive's sharp reaction to the pitch for *The Muckrakers*. He interrupted one of the writers only minutes into his description of the series. "What the hell are you guys doing here with this?" the executive demanded to know. "Nobody's interested in newspapers. Newspapers are death. It's boring, it's all issues, it all takes place all on the telephone. What are you guys doing here with this?"[6] In effect, the pitch had ended.

Walden was stunned. He had not yet developed the thick skin that enabled writers to shrug off the rejection of a proposal. As Walden and his partners walked through the parking lot at CBS he was surprised to learn that they, too, were shocked by the rebuff. Years later, Walden recalled the intensity behind the executive's swift rejection of *The Muckrakers*. "I thought the sprinkler system was going to go off when we mentioned the word 'newspaper'," the actor said wryly. "He said it's death. That was the word he used—newspaper shows are *death*."[7]

The partners regrouped and took the idea to other executives and other networks. They tried to interest influential producers in backing the project. "Everyone we went to said, 'Listen, we've been wanting to get a show on the air about newspapers for years'," Walden said. "[But] newspaper shows had such a nonhistory of success."[8] Eventually, *The Muckrakers* joined the untold number of ideas for series that never came to be. Walden later would play a reporter on *Lou Grant*, a CBS series. That was three years after the same network's rejection of *The Muckrakers*. Despite the role of the press in uncovering the Watergate scandal, the television industry in 1974 was leery of producing another newspaper series. Behind that judgment was thirty years of attempts to bring newspaper journalism to dramatic television, a string of failures broken only occasionally by success.

★   ★   ★

As a genre of television the newspaper drama is nearly as old as the entertainment medium itself.[9] The first regularly scheduled drama to be broadcast by a network, *Kraft Television Theater*, appeared on NBC in May 1947.[10] Network programming of television grew steadily in the next two years. The first dramatic series with a newspaper setting, *The Big Story* (1949–57), debuted on NBC on September 16, 1949.[11] Two weeks later, CBS aired the first episode of *The Front Page* (1949–50), a weekly series based on the classic Ben Hecht-Charles MacArthur play.[12] Television's initial newspaper dramas represented the spectrum of success and failure the genre would experience. *The Big Story* was broadcast for eight years, longer than any other newspaper drama. *The Front Page* lasted less than four months.

By the time CBS launched *Lou Grant* in the fall of 1977 twenty-three newspaper dramas had appeared—and disappeared.[13] (For a list of newspaper dramas on television see app. A.) Nearly half lasted one season or less; most of the others were broadcast for two to four seasons. Newspaper dramas usually were geared toward action and adventure, featuring reporters and editors as crime-busting sleuths. These efforts ultimately resembled detective and police shows, and the similarities did not escape some television critics. Already tired of the clichés found in many motion pictures about the press, these critics bemoaned the lack of realistic representation of newspaper journalism on television. The lament stretched across the decades that reporters appeared as television characters.

The creators of newspaper dramas probably drew part of their view of journalism from motion pictures. The fast-talking, adventuresome reporter had been a movie staple since the sound era began in 1927.[14] Many film and journalism historians consider the play *The Front Page* (1928) the most influential dramatic portrayal of journalism.[15] The story of cynical reporters who go to any lengths to pursue a story became a classic, meriting a film version in 1931 and remakes in 1940, 1974, and 1988.[16] Hecht and MacArthur, former Chicago newspapermen who became successful playwrights and screenwriters, established the basis of a stereotype that thrived in movies of the 1930s and 1940s and is still felt in the 1990s.

Radio was another potential influence on the television portrayal of the reporter. Programming in the infancy of television reflected the networks' close ties to their radio operations. Many staples of radio, such as *Amos 'n' Andy* and *Your Hit Parade*, moved to the new national medium. Genres popular with radio listeners—the anthology, the quiz show, and the detective show, for example—quickly found their way to television.[17] The newspaper drama had been an ongoing presence on radio. From the beginning of national radio drama in 1926 to the entry of the television dramatic series in 1947 the networks aired ten radio dramas with newspaper settings or reporters as leading characters.[18]

The Big Story was the newest newspaper drama to hit radio. Beginning on April 2, 1947, it aired for eight years, overlapping the television version. Producer Bernard J. Prockter had been inspired by the story of two Chicago reporters whose investigation into a murder case freed a man from a life sentence in prison. He built the series around newspaper stories, usually tales of crime drawn from newspaper files about closed cases. At the end of a show the reporter would be called to the stage to receive a five-hundred-dollar "Big Story Award" from the sponsor. The show gained enough of a following that the rival *Philco Radio Time* with Bing Crosby switched its air time and format.[19]

As a thirty-minute television anthology *The Big Story* followed the radio format of presenting a different cast and setting each week. Episodes were based on actual case histories of journalists, and the reporter received an award from the sponsor.[20] *The Big Story* combined film shot at the actual location of the story with live studio performances. Some critics were impressed by the show's production values during its eight-year run on NBC. At times, however, they were disappointed with the series's penchant for showing reporters as detectives.[21]

One incident questioned the claim that *The Big Story* was accurate. The episode, which aired on June 4, 1954, described how in 1916 an Albany, New York, reporter had helped arrest an armed man suspected of murder and had probably saved a policeman's life. The arresting officer, retired by the time the show aired on NBC, told the *New York Times* that there was no reporter in the area at the time of the arrest and that the suspect was unarmed and did not resist. A spokesperson for Prockter Television Enterprises admitted that although a reporter had aided police in the investigation, the episode's ending had been embellished.[22]

New York Times television critic Jack Gould used the admission to take a droll view of how reporters were depicted on television. In addition to *The Big Story* two other newspaper dramas, *Big Town* (1950–56) and *Foreign Intrigue* (1951–55), were on the air at the time. The revelation that a reporter did not help arrest crime suspects would hurt the image of the Fourth Estate, Gould noted sarcastically.

> Is the reporter now to come home at night and confess to the children that he spends his day covering news? That he isn't Jack Webb [the star of the police drama *Dragnet*] without Jack Webb's money? . . .
>
> The next step will be to show journalists on television who actually take a few notes when they cover a story. This, in turn, might even lead to the suggestion that a reporter sometimes works on a story that does not appear on the front page. . . .
>
> Instead of threatening gangsters and crooked politicians with durance vile, reporters will be expected to come back to the office with some news.[23]

Despite Gould, who was the prominent critic of the time, *The Big Story* remained popular with viewers. The television industry honored the series in 1952 with an Emmy nomination for best mystery, action, or adventure program. It lost to the detective series *Dragnet*.[24]

The television version of *The Front Page* never enjoyed the following that kept *The Big Story* on the air for eight years. Hecht and MacArthur had based their play on their experiences as Chicago reporters in the

1920s, but the half-hour CBS series moved the action to a fictitious, if contemporary, city. Nevertheless, managing editor Walter Burns and reporter Hildy Johnson remained unbridled in their pursuit of news. Burns stayed a misogynist, and Johnson's fiancée, Peggy, still complained about his long hours at the *Examiner*. With a nod toward changes in modern journalism, the producers opened each episode with a title over a city scene: "Center City U.S.A. A last stronghold for the newspapermen of the good old days."[25]

The producers apparently believed the disclaimer permitted their Burns and Johnson to practice the unrestrained, unconscionable journalism found a quarter of a century earlier. Their antics recalled the play and numerous motion pictures about the press from the 1930s and 1940s. In one episode they took a mobster, who was slightly wounded in a gunfight, to the press room of City Hall. Burns primed the hood with whiskey before interviewing him.[26] Another story began with reporters playing cards in the press room and making sexist, sarcastic remarks to a new woman reporter. Burns and Johnson later disguised themselves as doctors to get a scoop from a hospital patient.[27] A different episode began with Burns arranging the theft of records from City Hall.[28] No discussion of journalism ethics passed between Burns and Johnson in any of these programs.

Variety enjoyed the swift pace of the premiere episode of *The Front Page*. Whether it was believable was another matter. "While there is probably no newspaper operating today the way Hecht and MacArthur patterned theirs, it still makes for good drama," the trade journal reported.[29] Gould of the *New York Times* found the first episode to be diverting if implausible. "As is the inevitable way of the show business, the TV series has scant relation to actual practice in the Fourth Estate," Gould wrote, "and might be more honestly described as a straight adventure series."[30]

The producers of *The Front Page* made at least one stab at realism. For the role of Walter Burns they hired John Daly, a news broadcaster for NBC in the 1930s and a news correspondent for CBS from 1937 to 1950.[31] Forty years later, Daly barely remembered his brief career as an actor. He recalled that CBS allowed him to appear in *The Front Page* because he would then write a report about the impact television might have on news coverage. His friend MacArthur also encouraged him to take the part.

"I never wanted to be an actor. I just wanted to get some experience with television cameras," Daly said. "One way to give it [the series] some authenticity was to get a real newsman. In the early days of television they were trying anything. He [MacArthur] told me all you have to do is be yourself. As for authenticity—well, we were only on for thirteen weeks."[32] Daly remained in broadcast journalism, anchoring the evening news on ABC from 1953 to 1960 and serving as vice-president in charge of news during the same period. He is best known, however, as the host of the popular CBS quiz program *What's My Line?* (1950–1967).[33] In a unique arrangement Daly was host of a game show on Sunday nights for one network while guiding the news operations of another.

CBS again turned to radio in creating *Big Town* for the 1950–51 season. On CBS radio from 1937 to 1948 and then NBC radio from 1948 to 1952, *Big Town* had been a Top Ten show. Actor Edward G. Robinson originated the role of Steve Wilson, the crusading editor of the *Illustrated Press*, and continued in the part for five years. A former newsman, Jerry McGill, wrote and directed the early radio episodes. His reporters were serious, hard-working protectors of the public. "Freedom of the press is a flaming sword," according to the *Press's* motto. "Use it justly; hold it high; guard it well."[34]

Big Town was a hit in both media. The television series's six-year run, which included a move from CBS to NBC, is second only to *The Big Story* among newspaper dramas. On television actor Patrick McVey played Steve Wilson (a reporter in the television series) for the four years CBS aired *Big Town*. Four actresses played his girlfriend, *Illustrated Press* reporter Lorelei Kilbourne.[35] The initial episode, which was similar to what followed, concerned Wilson's probe into graft and a murdered police officer.[36] When the series was converted from a live production to film in 1952, *Variety* described *Big Town* as "one of the best in the half-hour crime cycle on television."[37] The first filmed episode was a whodunit about an eloping bride's death.

A major change in the series took place when it moved to NBC in the fall of 1954. Actor Mark Stevens replaced McVey, and reporter Steve Wilson became managing editor of the *Illustrated Press*. In addition, the series became more subdued and realistic in tone and subject matter.[38] Stevens's initial outing as Wilson called for him to track down a child molester. "The situations in which these 'scoop' artists become involved seem somewhat more credible than before," according to a review in *TV Guide*. "The newspaper atmosphere seems more authentic, too."[39]

More changes followed in the 1955–56 season when Stevens took over as producer, director, and half-owner of *Big Town*. Stevens told *TV Guide* he did not like the detective elements of the series and wanted more episodes to deal with issues such as employment, black-market trade in plasma, fixed boxing matches, and low pay for teachers. With the series under Stevens's control, *TV Guide* noted, "the managing editor had calmed down into a newspaperman with a civic conscience."[40] Despite favorable ratings NBC did not renew *Big Town* after the 1955–56 season. Stevens contended the network dropped the show because it did not own it, a charge NBC denied.[41]

Did the changes in *Big Town* sacrifice good drama for realism? Two critics at *Variety* could not agree. In 1955 one critic wrote, "Some purists might protest the spectacle of a managing editor of a metropolitan newspaper doing his own leg-work, but the average m.e.'s sedentary office life is certainly unsuited for the video screen."[42] One year later another *Variety* critic noted that managing editor Wilson "spends so much time in this episode mingling with politicos and Skid Row bums it makes you wonder who's minding the store?"[43] Thus, producers of newspaper dramas faced a dilemma—whether to portray journalism realistically or to make it dramatic and entertaining.

★   ★   ★

In quantity the newspaper drama was at its zenith in the 1951–52 season with six series featuring the exploits of journalists on the air. While *The Big Story* and *Big Town* continued their long runs, four other newspaper dramas debuted. CBS broadcast *Crime Photographer* (1951–52); *Foreign Intrigue* (1951–55) was a syndicated production; and the DuMont network carried both *Front Page Detective* (1951–53) and *Not for Publication* (1951–52). Each of the series, with the exception of *Not For Publication*, featured journalists in dangerous, exciting adventures at home or abroad while pursuing news stories.

Crime Photographer had aired on CBS radio from 1943 to 1955 under various names—*Flashgun Casey*, *Casey, Press Photographer*, and *Casey, Crime Photographer*—before settling on *Crime Photographer*.[44] Both the radio and television shows centered on a newspaper photographer who helped solve crimes. Casey, a character from a series of novels by George Harmon Coxe, could be found at the *Morning Express* or his hangout, the Blue Note Cafe. Actor Richard Carlyle played Casey from April to June 1951 and then was replaced by Darren McGavin for the rest of its run.[45] Although the television series survived just one year, the radio version of *Crime Photographer* continued for another two years.

The production qualities of *Foreign Intrigue* made it unusual for the era. Producer-director Sheldon Reynolds filmed entirely on location in Europe, using an American star and European actors in supporting roles. *Foreign Intrigue* focused on the adventures of an American newspaper reporter as he traveled to various countries on the continent.[46] Actor Jerome Thor played Robert Cannon, a reporter based in Stockholm for the Consolidated News wire service. *Variety* called Thor "extremely competent as the debonair, adventuring reporter."[47] A trench coat and cigarette became synonymous with the character.

Despite the adventure format, *New York Times* critic Gould thought Thor broke away from the stereotype of the foreign correspondent. "He is not the flamboyant exhibitionist customarily identified with Hollywood's distortion of the fourth estate," Gould wrote, "but a quiet, intelligent individual who might actually be found in a newspaper office."[48] The plots of various episodes, however, called for action not associated with journalism. In one episode Thor's character agreed to help a friendly country smuggle atomic secrets out of an enemy nation.[49] In another story the correspondent resorted to jujitsu to save himself from being run through with a sabre by a Prussian youth.[50]

After two seasons actor James Daly replaced Thor, and the lead character of *Foreign Intrigue* became a correspondent for Associated News in Paris. Daly soon found himself in the usual peril. The actor told *TV Guide* that he needed to stay in good physical condition so he could do his own stunts, such as fistfights and dives into water.[51] Daly left the show after two years, and Reynolds instituted more changes for the 1954–55 season. Not only did actor Gerald Mohr replace Daly, but the lead character was no longer a foreign correspondent. Instead, *Foreign Intrigue* featured an American who operated a hotel in Vienna.[52] The weekly adventures in Europe continued unabated. Judging from the final format of *Foreign Intrigue*, journalism was not a critical element to the series. Still, the series gained Emmy nominations for best mystery, action, or adventure series in 1952, 1953, and 1954. It lost every year to *Dragnet*.[53]

As its title suggested the format of *Front Page Detective* combined mystery with reporting. The series featured actor Edmund Lowe as newspaper columnist David Chase. A sign that the idea had become a chestnut came when *Variety* dismissed Lowe's character as "the standard newspaper-columnist sleuth."[54] The trade journal later criticized *Front Page Detective* for weak acting and poor production qualities.[55] The series was aired by DuMont for one year, beginning in July 1951, and then made a brief return to the network from October to November 1953.[56]

A similar fate awaited *Not for Publication*, a DuMont series that aired from May to September 1951 as a fifteen-minute drama four times a week. DuMont claimed the series would feature "vivid but unprinted details of human interest stories" gathered by a reporter.[57] The length of *Not for Publication* doubled when it returned in December for a four-month weekly run on DuMont. One plot had a reporter tracking down a hit-and-run driver based on a tip from a blind man. His sight apparently had been restored by the sound of the car striking the victim. Rather than risk the public accusing the man of having faked his blindness, the reporter omitted that aspect of the story.[58] *Not for Publication* reappeared on DuMont for three months the next spring and then left the air for good.[59]

DuMont tried a newspaper format again two years later with *Night Editor* (1954). In a cost-effective bit of programming the fifteen-minute show featured a single actor playing a newspaper editor. Actor Hal Burdick, who also wrote the scripts, sat at a desk in an unidentified newspaper office and simply told a crime or human-interest story. He moved around the small set as he read, changing his voice for different characters in the script.[60] In reviewing the series *Variety* noted that the peg was an old one: "An editor whose hardboiled veneer shatters when he faces a problem in human interest."[61] The show lasted from March to September 1954.

Before broadcasting *Wire Service* (1956–57), ABC had not yet offered a newspaper drama. The hour-long series rotated three stars—George Brent, Mercedes McCambridge, and Dane Clark—all of whom played reporters for Trans Globe News Service.[62] The premiere aired October 4, 1956, and featured Clark's reporter tangling with uranium hunters in the Colorado desert. *Variety* commented that *Wire Service* producers Don Sharpe and Warren Lewis had offered a more accurate depiction of journalists than previous shows. "All in all," the trade journal stated, "Sharp & Lewis aren't going overboard with the customary melodramatics and hokum involved in the usual newspaperman story, and are playing it for quality and understatement."[63] Gould of the *New York Times* offered a similar assessment, commenting that the first episode "did not fall into the same rut as many fictional dramas about the Fourth Estate."[64] *TV Guide*, however, found less to appreciate. "The show tends to glorify and glamorize the often humdrum life of a reporter for the nation's news services," the magazine reported.[65]

Variety changed its tune while reviewing other episodes of *Wire Service* during the year it aired on ABC. The reviews often noted elements that compromised an accurate presentation of journalism. In the episode "Hideout" McCambridge's character sought a hiding murder witness and was stalked herself by the killer. *Variety* thought a plot focusing on a reporter working harder than the police on a murder case was merely "a dated copy of 'The Front Page' pattern, often bordering on the ludicrous."[66] A candidate for president was the target of an assassin in "Campaign Train," an episode with Brent. "It becomes more the duty of Brent to corner the culprit than keep his syndicate posted on developments," *Variety* noted.[67] Another episode, "Forbidden Ground," took place at an army camp where the commanding general refused to take responsibility after an accident had killed seven soldiers. Brent's character helped the general see the error of his ways. *Variety*, although intrigued by the story, wrote, "Only flaw, and this always seems to pop up in newspaperman yarns, is some of the fourth estaters have an arrogance toward the general which simply wouldn't hold true in real life."[68]

Because NBC had found a winner among newspaper dramas with *Big Town*, which had left the air in 1956, it was not surprising the network wanted to try the genre again. Meanwhile, the western continued to be the most popular genre on television. *Maverick, The Rifleman,* and *Wagon Train* were among a record thirty-one westerns that filled the prime-time schedule in the 1958–59 season.[69] NBC offered *Jefferson Drum* (1958–59), a western with a twist. The title character was a newspaper editor who fought with a printing press as well as a pistol.[70] After his wife was murdered and his newspaper was destroyed in another town Drum and his young son passed through the mining town of Jubilee. When the publisher of that town's paper was killed, Drum decided to remain and resume his career as a crusading editor.[71]

The frontier editor, played by Jeff Richards, was competent with a gun when called on to use one. Yet despite the presence of a newsroom, *Jefferson Drum* held onto the usual elements of the western, including barroom fights and gunplay.[72] *TV Guide* complained that *Jefferson Drum* could have been different from other westerns but was not. "Take away the newspaper and their hero could be just another western marshal," the magazine said, "like most other TV heroes."[73] *Variety* called one episode "a sluggish, undistinguished piece of mediocrity."[74] The series was canceled after one year.

The failure of *Jefferson Drum* did not stop producers from offering a similar series in syndication. *Man without a Gun* (1959) was one of four newspaper shows produced for syndication in 1959 and 1960.[75] It fared no better than the NBC series, lasting only one year. *Man without a Gun,* however, impressed *Variety* by giving its western hero a chance to use his brains as much as his brawn.[76] Actor Rex Reason played crusading editor Adam MacLean, a character described by *Variety* as intellectual and warm-hearted as well as physically imposing.[77]

Deadline (1959) was a syndicated anthology series about journalists. Host and narrator Paul Stewart sat atop a desk in the city room of a newspaper as he introduced each story.[78] Commenting on the episode "Return to Murder," *Variety* judged an actor's performance as a newspaperman to be "in the steely eyed, mythical tradition of fiction."[79] In the syndicated series *New York Confidential* (1959), actor Lee Tracy played yet another crime-fighting reporter.[80] Another syndicated production, *Exclusive* (1960), followed the anthology format but derived stories from experiences of members of the Overseas Press Club of America.[81] The opening episode about the Norwegian underground was based on a story by columnist Bob Considine, who was played by an actor in a role nearly confined to narration.[82] Undistinguished as a group, these independently produced series quickly faded into obscurity.

★　★　★

No newspaper dramas debuted on network television during the 1959–60 season, but the respite from crusading editors and crime-fighting reporters was brief. The three networks—DuMont had folded in 1955—introduced five newspaper dramas over the next four years. ABC broadcast three of them, and NBC and CBS aired one each. Critics and anyone else who had watched the newspaper dramas of the previous decade probably had a sense of déjà vu. Unlike the 1950s, however, there was not a hit on the order of *The Big Story* or *Big Town* among the newspaper dramas of the 1960s. One of the shows lasted two seasons, whereas the other four were finished after one year or less.

While federal agent Eliot Ness protected 1930s Chicago on ABC's popular series *The Untouchables* (1959–63), newspaper reporters in New York chronicled an earlier decade on *The Roaring Twenties* (1960–62) for the same network. Rex Reason, the star of *Man without a Gun*, returned to make-believe journalism as a Prohibition-era newsman battling the underworld for the *Daily Record*.[83] *TV Guide* deemed the series "inaccurate, adolescent, embarrassing and dull. You also may throw in sluggishly written and hamishly acted."[84]

Hong Kong (1960–61) included some location footage for atmosphere but essentially was a studio production for ABC. The heroic reporter assigned to the Asian city, played by Rod Taylor, confronted gold smugglers, border guards, a murderous tycoon, and other exotic characters.[85] *Variety* dismissed it for having "that warmed-over Charlie Chan look—thin, predictable tales of the sinister Orient padded mercilessly to fill an hour and totally devoid of the atmosphere of the pretended locale."[86]

By its creator's account something altogether different was planned for *Target: The Corruptors* (1961–62). It was to be a newspaper drama with a point. Actor Stephen McNally, usually a villain in motion pictures, starred as a newsman dedicated to exposing corruption. Along the way viewers learned about phony charities, protection rackets, bookmaking, and other criminal enterprises.[87] Stirring up problems by exposing them in an entertainment series was a goal of Lester Velie, a journalist and one of the creators of *Target: The Corruptors*. Writing for *TV Guide*, Velie contended that television was ripe for a new type of series. He said he gave the following advice to the producers: "By combining the resources of investigative journalism with the drama of television, a series emerges that marks a transition from the meaningless bang-bang of the Western and the crime shows to a show that is about something and for something. . . . You can have your cake and eat it too. Entertain your audience, of course, but add something no other dramatic series has done: Involve them in current problems that affect lives."[88]

The violence in the first episode, however, put off *Variety*, which called the program "simply another violent brew of killings and maimings, the sort of provocative fare that attracts an instant audience through sheer noise and fury."[89] Velie, in a postmortem for *TV Guide* after the series was not renewed, pointed out that *Target: The Corruptors* changed from the standard crime-show format after its first few episodes. After turning to issue-oriented stories, Velie noted, the series had worked its way up to the top ten shows in the Nielsen ratings. Why ABC had decided to cancel the show, he concluded, was inexplicable.[90]

The newspaper drama returned to more familiar ground with ABC's *Saints and Sinners* (1962–63). Once more, a New York newspaper's star reporter, this time played by actor Nick Adams, was in the middle of the story he covered.[91] In one episode Adams's character went to prison rather than reveal a source of information.[92] Critics at *Variety* and *TV Guide* focused less on that realistic plot development than the overall tone of the series's portrayal of journalism. "The format," *Variety* wrote, "had been established years ago in 'B' movies and in half-hour series when TV was young."[93] Gilbert Seides of *TV Guide*, calling *Saints and Sinners* well-paced and produced, still needled the series for not being original. "No one expects a newspaper in fiction to have more than a faint resemblance to the real thing," he wrote. "You can ask that the newspapermen and women resemble human beings and that is exactly what they do in 'Saints and Sinners'—they *resemble*. They also resemble the old booze-fighting reporter and the old crusading reporter."[94]

Apparently ignoring recent failures in the genre, CBS president James Aubrey decided to add to the shows that featured doctors, social workers, nurses, and other professionals with one about a newspaperman.[95] The task of creating such a series was taken up by Jerome Weidman, the author of several books and stage productions. He soon developed *The Reporter* (1964), a series about a newspaper columnist who was emotionally involved in the stories he reported. Weidman was unconcerned about his lack of experience in newspaper journalism, telling the *New York*

Times that "to write about a subject is to be immersed in it. I've taken it in by osmosis."[96]

To enhance the authenticity of *The Reporter* executive producer Keefe Brasselle bought desks, chairs, and other furnishings from the city room of the defunct *New York Mirror*.[97] That flourish of realism, however, did not impress critics as much as the violent and unrealistic elements of the first two episodes. The premiere featured an attack on a woman and the knifing of her rescuer, who then crawled into a basement and called the columnist for help. Actor Harry Guardino's character joined police in a frantic search to find the man before he bled to death. Not only was the episode violent, complained Gould of the *New York Times*, "The dialogue was of a sophomoric order and the details of police and journalistic behavior in an emergency entirely ludicrous."[98] In the next episode the son of a famous baseball pitcher was kidnapped. The columnist, a longtime friend, helped keep the story out of the paper and off television and radio until the boy was rescued, a situation *Variety* called absurd. "He might as well have been a routine video private eye," the trade paper added.[99]

The speedy demise of *The Reporter*—on and off the air in barely four months[100]—probably cooled any interest the television industry could muster in the newspaper drama. In fact, ten years passed before a network aired another drama featuring a reporter. In the meantime prime-time entertainment focused on situation comedies, police, and spy shows. When television turned once more to journalism for a drama series, it was not in the spirit of *The Muckrakers*. CBS summarily rejected actor Robert Walden's pet project about an ex-cop and an investigative reporter in 1974. ABC decided to revive the newspaper drama in the 1974–75 season but with a truly supernatural approach.

Actor Darren McGavin, who had starred in *Crime Photographer* twenty years earlier, had notched a surprising hit with a made-for-television movie, *The Night Stalker*, on ABC in 1972. McGavin's character, reporter Carl Kolchak, pursued a modern-day vampire in Las Vegas. A sequel, *The Night Strangler* (1973), matched McGavin's reporter against an eerie killer in Seattle, Washington. Riding those ratings successes, ABC ordered a series, *Kolchak: The Night Stalker* (1974–75).[101] Kolchak, now working for a news agency in Chicago, continued to discover werewolves, swamp creatures, and other monsters or bizarre forces. His editor remained skeptical, and Kolchak found it difficult to get his fantastic stories published. *Variety* thought *Kolchak: The Night Stalker* could become a marginal hit if it retained the offbeat humor of the movies.[102] The series left the air the next fall.

Two years later journalism of a more normal vein was practiced by the characters of *Gibbsville* (1976). NBC based the drama, set in a small Pennsylvania mining town in the 1940s, on the short stories of author John O'Hara.[103] The series stemmed from a television movie, *The Turning Point of Jim Malloy* (1975), that had aired one year earlier. In *Gibbsville* actor John Savage played a young reporter for the *Gibbsville Courier*, and actor Gig Young appeared as a renowned foreign correspondent whose alcoholism had brought him back to the paper where his career had begun. The initial episode dealt with efforts of a mining company to cover up an explosion at a laboratory. There also were subplots about romance between the young reporter and an Irish girl and the death of an elderly local playwright. Some critics found the pace of *Gibbsville* too slow and its story lines too complicated to follow with much interest.[104] The series aired on NBC in November and December and then disappeared.

Thus, the CBS executive who had told Robert Walden in 1974 that "newspapers are death" had the bodies to prove it. By the fall of 1975 twenty newspaper dramas had appeared on television since regular entertainment programming had begun almost thirty years earlier. Only four —*The Big Story, Big Town, Foreign Intrigue,* and *Wire Service*—had lasted more than two seasons. Such a high death rate might have led television executives to believe that viewers were not drawn to newspaper dramas as they were to westerns and situation comedies and shows about doctors, detectives, and lawyers. Yet in 1976 NBC broadcast (albeit briefly) *Gibbsville.* More significantly, the networks unveiled three newspaper dramas, including *Lou Grant,* in 1977. What had changed since 1974 when a newspaper series was considered by some to be a death wish?

★   ★   ★

The resurgence of the newspaper drama in 1977 owed less to Bob Woodward and Carl Bernstein's 1974 book *All the President's Men* than to the 1976 film version.[105] Actor Robert Redford, intrigued by the Watergate reporting of the *Washington Post,* had asked the pair about a film based on their investigation before they had written the book. Indeed, his interest in a cinematic telling of the story influenced the book's style and structure.[106] Redford bought the film rights to the book, but Hollywood was slow to embrace a political thriller about Watergate.[107] When *All the President's Men* was published, it became the fastest-selling hardback nonfiction book in American history, eventually totaling nearly three hundred thousand hardback copies. The paperback rights sold for $1,050,000, another record.[108] In Hollywood a movie version seemed like a better idea with each sale.

The film, released in April 1976, met with similar success. It was a runner-up to *One Flew over the Cuckoo's Nest,* a late 1975 release, in ticket sales in 1976.[109] The following spring *All the President's Men* was nominated for eight Academy Awards, including Best Picture. Although it lost the top Oscar to *Rocky* (1976), *All the President's Men* won four others and was named best picture by the National Society of Film Critics, the New York Film Critics, and the National Board of Review.[110]

The book had detailed the painstaking process of gathering information about the Watergate break-in and its ties to the Nixon administration. The film also related the process, with Redford playing Woodward and Dustin Hoffman playing Bernstein. The *Washington Post* newsroom, re-created in a movie studio, radiated realism. There were no women and children to be saved, no confrontations with gun-toting criminals, no arrests by Woodward and Bernstein. *All the President's Men* may have been a detective story, but the methods of detection and disclosure were those used by a reporter, not a policeman. Thus, someone had finally made a popular, critically acclaimed drama that derived its action from the news-gathering process of journalism.

Numerous film critics at newspapers welcomed this new depiction of their profession. Vincent Canby of the *New York Times* focused on that point in the first paragraph of his review: "Newspapers and newspapermen have long been favorite subjects for movie makers—a surprising number of whom are former newspapermen—yet not until *All the President's Men,* the riveting screen adaptation of the Watergate book by Carl Bernstein and Bob Woodward, has any film come remotely close to being an accurate picture of American journalism at its best."[111] Other critics agreed. "In many ways this honest look at the way a major news story is put together is the film's finest achievement," wrote the *Memphis Commercial Appeal.*[112] Richard Cuskelly of the *Los Angeles Herald Examiner* said the film "gives Americans a new journalistic model to relate to [and] avoids sensationalism to concentrate on what constitutes 90 percent of a hard news reporter's daily activities."[113] Critic Roger Ebert of the *Chicago Sun-Times,* however, thought the adherence to reality overwhelmed the narrative. Still, Ebert observed, the film "provides the most observant study of working journalists we're ever likely to see in a feature film."[114]

All the President's Men changed the way critics evaluated movies and television shows about reporters. They no longer had only *The Front Page* as a barometer—and a negative one at that—when gauging a dramatic portrayal of journalism. Instead, they could point to a modern, more realistic, and positive portrayal of the press. The difference probably was not lost on the public, either. There was a stark difference between the Hildy Johnson-Walter Burns reporters of *The Front Page* and the solemn team of Woodward and Bernstein in the newer film. Thus, *All the President's Men* became the yardstick against which future newspaper dramas in motion pictures and on television would be compared.

With its debut in January 1977 *The Andros Targets* (1977) was the first television series held up to this new standard. Critics quickly compared the CBS series to the hit motion picture, which was still playing around the country. The comparison was not uncalled for, considering that the show's creators apparently patterned the fictional *New York Forum* after the *New York Times* and hired a *Times* reporter, Nicholas Gage, as consultant. In the opening episode investigative reporter Mike Andros (played by James Sutorius) probed the suspicious suicide of a young woman who had performed in pornographic films. In future episodes of the series Andros looked into the sordid activities of crooked politicians, crime syndicates, and war criminals.[115] Jerome Coopersmith, the executive story consultant for the series, said he and Gage had disagreed at times over the content of scripts. "I know that a certain amount of fictionalization and dramatic license is necessary to make an exciting script," Coopersmith said.[116]

Perhaps because *All the President's Men* was fresh in their minds, critics were particularly cutting in their assessment of *The Andros Targets*. Tom Shales of the *Washington Post* called the series "just another cop show in disguise . . . [and] part of the price America will have to pay for making a hit movie out of *All the President's Men*."[117] The *Los Angeles Times* called it "standard, predictable television fare" while *Variety* dismissed it as a "potboiler."[118] Gary Deeb, the critic for the *Chicago Tribune*, seemed particularly incensed.

> If it were possible to arrest television producers for creating a fraudulent TV series, the makers of 'The Andros Targets' would be behind bars today. . . .
> I really shouldn't be so upset about 'The Andros Targets.' After all, what makes the newspaper profession sacred? Why should it be different from any other intriguing occupation that has been depicted on TV? Cops. Private detectives. Lawyers. They've all been shamelessly sanitized and melodramatically burlesqued by the bosses of video. . . .
> The life of a real newspaper journalist isn't terribly glamorous. It generally consists of drudgery and a sort of studied cynicism, laced with precious moments of tension, vitality, and 'triumph.' You get none of that in 'The Andros Targets.' And that, my friends, is a crime.[119]

Gage, the *New York Times* reporter who served as a consultant, later wrote that *The Andros Targets* succeeded in some ways and failed in others in depicting realistically an investigative reporter. "It has brought a breath of fresh air to the traditional stereotypes of a newsman," Gage said.[120] Sutorius later said he had been disappointed that many professional reporters had knocked the series as unrealistic. "But we didn't misrepresent investigative reporting in the sense of being cheap. It had class," the actor told the *Los Angeles Times*. "If we did it totally authentic it would be off the air in 15 minutes. We heightened reality; it's supposed to be entertaining."[121]

NBC leaped onto the investigative-reporter bandwagon with *Kingston: Confidential* (1977) the next March.[122] The big news, however, was the return to series television of actor Raymond Burr. Burr had appeared in two of the medium's bigger hits, *Perry Mason* (1957–66) and *Ironside* (1967–75). Now he was back as R. B. Kingston, the Pulitzer Prize-winning chief investigative reporter of a San Francisco-based media group. He had limousines and helicopters at his disposal and lived in a magnificent home. Two assistants performed much of the legwork Kingston needed for his exclusives, occasionally handing out money for information. In the premiere that aired March 23, 1977, Kingston pursued information about the disappearance of a labor leader. Terrorists took over the communications group in another episode.[123]

Labeling *Kingston: Confidential* merely another action show, some critics took pokes at its portrayal of the press. The drubbing meted out to *The Andros Targets*, however, may have been missing from these reviews because *Kingston: Confidential* did not take itself as seriously. "There is little resemblance to the life style of the ordinary working reporter," *Variety* noted. "Burr is a paternalistic, highly ethical practitioner of one of the revered professions, living very high on the hog—with no apparent deadlines to meet or copy to write."[124] John J. O'Connor of the *New York Times* called the series "merely 'Perry Mason' or 'Ironside' equipped with a press card."[125] A critic for the *New Orleans Times-Picayune* wrote, "One would think that *All the President's Men* would have stopped the *Front Page* clichés once and for all, but no."[126] The cancellation of the series in August left Burr with a rare television failure.

As critics panned *The Andros Targets* and *Kingston: Confidential*, MTM Enterprises was busy developing its own newspaper drama. The press already had reported that Lou Grant, a character played by actor Edward Asner on MTM's popular sitcom *The Mary Tyler Moore Show*, would be transplanted to a newspaper setting for the 1977–78 season.[127] Based on nearly thirty years of television programming, the odds seemed against the new series. Large audiences had not tuned into newspaper dramas as they had westerns and doctor, lawyer, and police dramas. Critics had found most newspaper dramas to be average entertainment at best and had pointed out that the shows were seldom accurate in depicting the profession. As the CBS executive had told Walden in 1974, newspaper shows indeed were "death."

The creators of *Lou Grant* were determined to change that perception. They began with the belief that a dramatic yet realistic portrayal of journalism was not only possible but crucial to their success. After rejecting the stereotypes that had developed over decades of films and television, they set out to discover how a modern newspaper functioned and how modern journalists worked and lived. The creators of the new series undertook an investigation—just like a *real* newspaper.

2

From Classic Comedy
to Realistic Drama

A n unusual struggle was under way at the offices of MTM Enterprises in Studio City, California. *The Mary Tyler Moore Show* was going off the air at the end of the 1976–77 season, its seventh on CBS. The production company, however, was not battling the network to prevent the demise of its series. In fact, the producers of *The Mary Tyler Moore Show* had decided to end the hit show while it remained a creative and ratings success rather than wait until the series had sagged enough to merit cancellation by the network.[1] Furthermore, producers James L. Brooks and Allan Burns did not lack a new project to undertake. They already had a commitment from CBS for a new series starring actor Edward Asner, their *Mary Tyler Moore* costar. The difficulty they faced was finding a suitable vehicle for him.[2]

Common practice in the television industry called for a producer to take a series concept to a network. The producer eventually would secure a pilot script and a lead performer as the network edged closer to deciding whether to add the series to its schedule. A commitment usually would not be offered by a network until a pilot episode had been filmed. But in this case the normal process of developing a television series had become skewed by the overwhelming success of *The Mary Tyler Moore Show*. The series already had provided a foundation for MTM Enterprises and had bolstered the fortunes of CBS and everyone involved.

MTM had been formed to produce a series starring Mary Tyler Moore for the 1970–71 season. Moore, the co-star of the situation comedy *The Dick Van Dyke Show* (1961–66), received a thirteen-episode commitment from CBS in the wake of the ratings success of a special, "Dick Van Dyke and the Other Woman" (1969), that reteamed her with Van Dyke.

19

Joining Moore in the formation of MTM, an independent production company, were her husband, television executive Grant Tinker, and her manager, Arthur Price.[3] The president of MTM was Tinker. He had left an advertising firm in 1961 to join NBC as a programmer and then moved to Universal Television in 1968 and to 20th Century-Fox Television one year later.[4]

Tinker hired Brooks and Burns to create a situation comedy for Moore.[5] Brooks had written for CBS News and had written and produced documentaries for Wolper Productions in the mid-1960s. He later wrote for *My Mother the Car* (1965–66), *My Three Sons* (1960–72), and *The Andy Griffith Show* (1960–68).[6] Burns had worked in television since the mid-1950s, writing for *The Munsters* (1964–66), *The Smothers Brothers Show* (1965–66), *He and She* (1967–70), and *Get Smart* (1965–70).[7] Burns also had written for and produced *Room 222* (1969–74), a series Brooks had created.[8] Together, the two men now were charged with finding the right series concept for Moore.

After some false starts—one idea was to cast Moore as a stringer for a gossip columnist—Burns and Brooks created the character Mary Richards. She would be a single career woman in her thirties (CBS refused to allow the character to be divorced) who was hired by a Minneapolis television station.[9] *The Mary Tyler Moore Show* proved to be a television hit, winning twenty-seven Emmy awards over seven seasons and ranking in the top twenty television shows for five of its seven years.[10] MTM Enterprises built on that success with spin-offs such as *Rhoda* (1974–78) and *Phyllis* (1975–77) and an unrelated series, *The Bob Newhart Show* (1972–78), as well.[11] MTM's first series is remembered today as one of the most entertaining and influential television sitcoms.[12]

The Mary Tyler Moore Show also made a star of Asner. Before joining the cast of the series, Asner had worked for years as a reliable, if unheralded, dramatic actor. Born November 15, 1929, Asner was raised in Kansas City, Kansas, the youngest of five children. He played football at Wyandotte High School and worked for the high school newspaper, *The Pantagraph*, as feature-page editor. "I very strongly considered journalism as a career. I thrilled to it and wrote well," Asner recalled. His high school teacher, however, warned him that journalism would not provide much of a living. "So I went on, as you can see, and became an overnight success as an actor," Asner said wryly, "a very secure profession."[13]

Asner's work in drama began at the University of Chicago, which he attended from 1947 to 1949. After dropping out of college, he returned to Kansas City and drove a cab, sold shoes, and worked at other jobs. Then, back in the Chicago area, he worked at a steel mill and an auto plant.

After two years in the United States Army, Asner joined a theater group in Chicago. By the time he took his career to New York in 1955, he had appeared in more than two dozen plays. Asner spent the next several years working in the theater and on local television before moving to Los Angeles in 1961, where he began appearing in numerous television dramas, often as a heavy.[14]

Throughout the 1960s Asner compiled an impressive list of credits, including roles on *Naked City* (1958–63), *Route 66* (1960–64), *Dr. Kildare* (1961–66), *The Fugitive* (1963–67), and *Gunsmoke* (1955–75). Asner also joined the cast of *Slattery's People* (1964–65), a drama about a state legislator in which Asner played a newspaper reporter.[15] He also drew supporting roles in some motion pictures, including *Kid Galahad* (1962) with Elvis Presley, *The Slender Thread* (1965) with Sidney Poitier and Anne Bancroft, *El Dorado* with John Wayne (1967), and *Change of Habit* (1969) with Presley and Mary Tyler Moore.[16]

When Asner read for the part of Lou Grant as casting was under way for *The Mary Tyler Moore Show,* he had appeared only twice in comedic roles on television.[17] At the time Asner and his agent considered guest appearances on hour-long dramas a better way to build a successful career than appearing on comedies.[18] That attitude may have worked in his favor. Ethel Winant, who cast the actors for the series, believed that the role of Lou Grant required an actor with good timing, not a comic, to make audiences see him as a real character.[19] At first, Burns and Brooks wanted Gavin MacLeod for Lou Grant, but both Winant and MacLeod thought he would be better in the role of writer Murray Slaughter, which he then played for the run of the series.[20]

The decision to cast Asner, according to Winant, began with Tinker's suggestion of Asner after seeing him in a television movie. Asner's first reading, by several accounts, was disappointing. Rather than giving an intelligent reading of the part, the producers encouraged him to be imaginative. Asner then showed how inventive he could be in a comedic role, acting crazy and paranoid when the scene called for it. Moore remained uncertain about casting him, but Burns and Brooks assured her that Asner was right for the part.[21] He went on to win three Emmy awards as Mary Richards's gruff boss. Asner later reminded the television industry of his versatility, also winning Emmys for his work in two acclaimed miniseries, *Rich Man, Poor Man* (1976) and *Roots* (1977).[22]

Considering the success of *The Mary Tyler Moore Show,* CBS's quick reception to a new series—any series—starring Asner and produced by Brooks and Burns at MTM is understandable. Burns recalls that CBS President Bob Wood immediately ordered thirteen episodes of the new show. Exactly what the series would be was not an issue. "Very unusual," Burns admitted in retrospect. "No pilot, no nothing. . . . We had the commitment, [but] we didn't have an idea."[23] Over time, Burns and Brooks considered a variety of options for the Asner series, including comedies and dramas. One proposal, according to Burns, came from Bruce Geller, the executive producer of *Mission: Impossible* (1966–73) and *Mannix* (1967–75). Geller suggested that Asner play a character based on his father, Abraham N. Geller, a justice of the New York Supreme Court. At the time of his death in 1969 the elder Geller had been described as a liberal, unpretentious judge.[24] "We were sort of interested in that for a while," Burns said.[25] The producers also considered retaining the Lou Grant character for the new series.[26] The twist, though, would be shifting Lou Grant from a television station to a metropolitan newspaper.

★   ★   ★

As Brooks and Burns weighed their options, a journalist urged them to keep Asner working in the news media for his new series. Sander Vanocur, a former television newsman who was covering the medium for the *Washington Post,* wrote a column about Asner's future. "The easiest thing for Asner and his producers to do would be to move the character of Lou Grant into another journalistic setting," Vanocur wrote. "His fans would follow him wherever he went." Noting that Burns and Brooks were pondering such a move, Vanocur supported the idea and predicted that Asner's believability as a "hard-boiled, bittersweet, honest-to-God editor" was strong enough to make the transition. He also believed that Asner had the talent to make it work. "He is a cult figure among many journalists, who either know editors just like Lou Grant or wish they could work for someone like him," Vanocur wrote.[27]

In retrospect Burns does not recall whether Vanocur's opinion had an impact on the decision to place Lou Grant in a newspaper setting. "We came up with all kinds of approaches for what to do with Ed," Burns said. "But none of them felt quite right. And finally we said . . . why are we fighting this? Why don't we just do another show with Lou Grant?"[28] The character already had a newspaper career established by *The Mary Tyler Moore Show.* Lou Grant, viewers of the series had been told, had worked for newspapers for several years before going to the fictional Minneapolis station WJM-TV. He was a solid newsman, one who valued journalistic integrity and principles.[29]

The decision also increased the chances of a ratings success for the new series. Looking back, Tinker pointed out that production companies favor spinning off established characters whenever possible. "When you're running a production company, the idea is to get shows on networks and keep them on," Tinker said.

> Those characters on the *Mary* show became so vivid and well-seated with the audience that you were tempted to do a show with each of them. *Lou Grant* provided an opportunity. . . . If it had just simply been [actor] Dick Crenna or somebody plopped down in that chair working in that job in that format and for that premise, I don't think it would have worked.
>
> The edge that we got out of Ed coming to it with a character already established and accepted, a character the audience liked and was interested in, was the difference. We came so close to failing as it was, that I think without a known and liked character we wouldn't have made it.[30]

CBS approved of spinning off the Lou Grant character into a new series, probably with a similar eye on boosting its chances of finding an audience. According to Burns, however, the network assumed the format would be another half-hour comedy.[31]

Instead, Brooks and Burns decided to create a one-hour drama with comedic overtones. Part of the reason was the subject matter: newspaper journalism. "We didn't feel we could do newspapers adequately in a half-hour. We wouldn't be able to do justice to it," Burns recalled. "Our feeling was the best movies are usually dramas with comedy in them or comedies with drama in them."[32] The producers also believed that the new series should accurately portray journalism, which they thought no other television series had done. Their decision was influenced by the motion picture *All the President's Men,* which had been released in 1976 to critical and popular acclaim. Burns remembered the impact the Watergate film had on the concept of the Asner series.

> We'd all seen it and we'd all been absolutely fascinated by the depiction of the putting together of a story, the nuts and bolts of how a big-time newspaper operation worked. It was absolutely fascinating to us.
>
> And we said, jeez, we've never seen this before, the budget meetings and all that stuff. . . . And we had to believe that America would be interested in seeing that done right. And who better than Ed Asner in a show about a newspaper where we're really trying to do it accurately, as accurately as we can.[33]

The network was startled by the idea of a drama mixed with comedy in an hour-long format. It "scared the hell out of CBS," Burns recalled.[34]

With the support of Tinker and the earlier commitment by CBS the producers went ahead with their plans.

Burns and Brooks hoped to pursue other projects in addition to *Lou Grant*, and they sought another partner to share the responsibilities of producing the new MTM series.[35] They turned to producer Gene Reynolds. As a young performer Reynolds had appeared in *Boys Town* (1938), *Love Finds Andy Hardy* (1938), *They Shall Have Music* (1939), and other films. After serving in the United States Navy during World War II Reynolds worked in television in New York, appearing occasionally in such Hollywood films as *The Country Girl* (1954) and *The Bridges at Toko-Ri* (1954). By the late 1950s and early 1960s, Reynolds had begun to work behind the camera, directing episodes of *The Andy Griffith Show, My Three Sons, Hogan's Heroes* (1965–71), and other series.[36]

Reynolds became a producer with the pilot for the series *The Ghost and Mrs. Muir* (1968–70). He then worked with Brooks and Burns on *Room 222*. Brooks created the series, Burns wrote for it, and Reynolds served as producer and director. Reynolds later produced the television version of *M★A★S★H* (1972–83), a comedy-drama set at a medical unit during the Korean War.[37] He also wrote and directed episodes of *M★A★S★H* during his five-year stint as producer of the series, winning industry and critical acclaim. He won Emmys for producing in 1974 and for directing in 1975 and 1976.

By the end of the 1976–77 season of *M★A★S★H*, however, Reynolds was looking for other challenges.[38] Brooks and Burns, searching for a partner, recalled Reynolds's penchant for detailed research when they produced *Room 222*. They asked him to join them on the new series about newspaper journalism. According to Burns, "Gene first said, 'Well, we're going to have to do a lot of research'."[39]

Research had been a major element in the production of *Room 222*. Because the men had been out of high school for years, they went to Los Angeles High School to interview students, teachers, and administrators. "Gene did not let anybody start a script on *Room 222* without visiting high schools," according to Burns. "No writer was allowed to just start writing, he said, because you're going to come at it from your own perspective of what school is, and it's not true. It's changed."[40] Consequently, much of the material for *Room 222* came out of such research. Reynolds began to lean on research as a way of finding stories and characters, rather than using stereotypes. "Theater copies from theater. . . . That is why we have a repetition of forms, repetition of ideas in the theater, in motion pictures, and certainly in television," Reynolds said. "I like theater to copy from life."[41] When preparing for *M★A★S★H*, he talked to doctors and nurses who had served in medical units during the Korean War. "Research gave us access to the real problems, to the uniqueness and the variety and the complexity and the ambiguity of life, away from the oft-told stories," he said. "It gave us richness and detail and character and incident, bizarre coincidences, and so forth. It gave us all the stuff that's really going on."[42]

To reach the same goals with *Lou Grant* Reynolds, Burns, and Brooks began researching newspaper journalism. They read books and trade publications about the profession, and Reynolds attended journalism classes at the University of California at Los Angeles.[43] More importantly, members of the *Lou Grant* staff, including writers and story researchers, visited newspapers in Los Angeles, San Francisco, Chicago, New York, and Washington and conducted extensive interviews with reporters and editors. They also visited smaller newspapers in the San Francisco Bay area and in Southern California. Those involved with the series continued to visit newspapers and talk to reporters during the five years *Lou Grant* was on the air.[44]

★   ★   ★

Although men and women at more than a dozen newspapers were asked to talk about their work, the staff of the *Los Angeles Times* became the most important contact for the creators of *Lou Grant*. It was not only a prestigious daily, but the *Times* was only eight miles from the MTM studios. Thus, it was practical for the producers and others with the series to visit the *Times* and remain in touch with the journalists they had met.[45] "I went down constantly," Reynolds said. "They had a little room for us. I'd say we interviewed between twenty and thirty of their people, editors and reporters."[46]

For Reynolds, Burns, and Brooks their initial meeting at the *Times* was with senior assistant managing editor George Cotliar.[47] Writers had often asked the *Times* for help as they worked on journalism-related projects. Cotliar remembered being dubious when he heard about plans for yet another television series to be set at a newspaper. He had been disappointed with previous efforts to dramatize journalism, and he was not sure he wanted to participate in the creation of a new one. "If your feeling is that you go to a movie or turn on TV and you see a newspaper person being portrayed as a lowlife or a drunkard or an incompetent, it gets to you, just as doctors would think a number of the doctor shows would be demeaning," he said. "Whatever it was we saw really didn't portray journalists in any way, shape, or form that approximated what we do."[48]

Cotliar then was told that the latest request was coming from those behind *The Mary Tyler Moore Show* and *M*A*S*H*. That changed his mind. "I thought, well, if anyone could get it right, these people seemed like they could be the ones," he recalled.[49] Later, he was impressed by the three producers and their associates: "Their credentials were impeccable. They were highly articulate. It was worth the shot."[50] Thus, he asked the *Times* staff to cooperate with the producers. Cotliar was interviewed for four or five hours over a few days, and he allowed *Lou Grant* personnel to attend news meetings at the *Times* to observe how coverage was planned each day. "They were all very sharp, very concerned people, concerned in that they wanted to portray journalists as best they could," he said.[51]

Other editors and reporters at the *Times* shared Cotliar's initial disdain of television's latest effort at turning journalism into entertainment. One was Mark Murphy, the metropolitan editor of the *Times*. Print journalists had little respect for the broadcast medium, Murphy remembered. "Like all newspaper editors, especially of that era, I thought television was pretty shitty and took a very dim view of it," he said. "We had a very arrogant attitude toward television. When *Lou Grant* first came on, even when it was first proposed, we all pretty much pooh-poohed it, that it would come nowhere near capturing our business. That, once again, it would be reporters with little things in their felt hats chasing ambulances."[52]

Murphy agreed to meet informally with the production team, and, as they took notes, he related anecdotes, revealed inside stories about activities at the *Times*, and answered questions about his job as metropolitan editor. "I told them some great stories, battles we'd had in the newsroom, things I had done to other editors, coups we'd pulled off, how we managed people, how I'd handled stories," Murphy said. He eventually was won over. "It was fun talking to them. They were bright, interesting people."[53]

Not long after the interview, Murphy became further convinced of their efforts to make *Lou Grant* more realistic. Robert Walden, the actor who had been cast as aggressive reporter Joe Rossi, was observing activities in the *Times* newsroom. While chatting with the actor, Murphy noticed Walden was carrying some typed sheets of paper. To Murphy's amazement and chagrin the papers were the transcript of his interview. "It really stunned me that those people had been that careful listening to me and had taken down so much information," Murphy recalled. "I thought, my God, I don't want that to be distributed all over this newspaper." He told Walden not to let other *Times* people see the transcript.[54]

Many other *Times* journalists were interviewed by the producers of *Lou Grant*. Narda Zacchino, a young reporter for the metro section of the *Times*, recalled having a lengthy lunch with Reynolds and Burns. "They

wanted a woman reporter. There weren't many of us then, two or three,"
she said. "I was flattered that they were spending so much time with
me."[55] The producers also met over lunch with *Times* media writer David
Shaw, who also had agreed to help. "They were quite clear about what
they were doing. They were going to do this series about the city editor of
a Los Angeles daily newspaper. They wanted to make it as realistic as
possible," Shaw said.[56]

Times reporter-photographer Boris Yaro allowed Leon Tokatyan, who
developed the series and wrote the first episode, to ride along with him as
he went out on assignments. Walden later joined Yaro as he interviewed a
federal agent for a story. "I was tickled pink," Yaro said, "because this
was a kind of break from my routine."[57] Yaro allowed the prop staff of
the series to look at his car, which had an array of police and fire radios
and a radio telephone. The photographer's car in the series would contain
a similar arsenal of equipment. The car used by the photographer in the
series, however, was old and dumpy, whereas Yaro's was just the opposite. The difference in image did not bother Yaro, he says, because he
understood that the series was creating its own character. "I'm a scriptwriter on my own," Yaro added, "and that's the show's business. If that's
what they want this guy to be, that's it, that's the end of that."[58]

Several *Times* journalists recalled that stories they had related to
Reynolds and others later appeared in episodes. For example, Cotliar had
told the producers about seeing an expense account from a reporter that
included a bill for a "class reunion." After telling the reporter that the
Times was not paying for his class reunion, Cotliar was informed that the
bill was for drinks with a source at a bar called "Class Reunion." A similar
exchange appeared in a *Lou Grant* episode, Cotliar remembered. "Even
little tidbits, throwaway lines, whatever," said Cotliar, "they picked up
on a variety of things."[59] Murphy said that a *Lou Grant* writer would call
sometimes and ask what he as an editor would do in a particular situation
involving ethics or coverage of the news. "Then later I would see something like that on television," he added. "I saw things I was familiar
with."[60]

★   ★   ★

In another effort to make the series credible and realistic the producers hired technical advisers for *Lou Grant*. Once more, they turned to the
Los Angeles Times. Al Martinez, a *Times* reporter, had written scripts for
television, including the pilot for the police series *Bronk* (1975–76), and
he had created the police series *Jigsaw John* (1976). He and Reynolds also
shared the same agent, who suggested Martinez to Reynolds as a *Times*

contact.[61] Martinez remembered that he did not expect to work on *Lou Grant*, but he wanted to help Reynolds develop an understanding of the profession. At a long lunch they talked about various aspects of journalism from relationships between reporters and editors to how Martinez got story ideas. "He asked an endless amount of questions. I felt it was in the best interests of all of us in newspapering just to have the series a good one," Martinez said. "If there was going to be representation, then I wanted it to be accurate. Well, not necessarily accurate. Portrayals on television are never exactly accurate, but I wanted it to be sort of representative of what we did on newspapers and destroy some of the myths."[62]

Concerned that they considered the *Times* representative of all newspapers, Martinez took Reynolds and other *Lou Grant* staff to the *Oakland Tribune* where he had worked before joining the *Times*. "They got a good look at what a smaller, more active, old-school newspaper looks like," he remembered. "San Francisco journalism is different than L.A. journalism—a little faster, a little harder kind of journalism, a little tougher."[63] For the next few months Martinez continued to help the production staff, answering questions on the phone and talking with some of the cast.

Later, his agent called with an offer from Reynolds to be a technical adviser for the series. For three hundred dollars a week, Martinez read scripts for accuracy and commented on them.[64] He occasionally visited the set and continued to answer questions from writers. Not all his suggestions for changes were followed, however, and he sometimes clashed with Reynolds regarding his comments about the quality of the scripts. Martinez maintained that the scripts lacked the wry humor of the newsroom and that the characters were stiff. Reynolds, according to Martinez, pointed out that commenting on the quality of the writing and injecting humor into scripts were not part of his job. Still, Martinez was not disappointed with the series. "I was pleased. In most cases the technical errors were very minor in terms of nomenclature—you know, what you call somebody or something and terms used around the city room to describe things," he said.[65] At the end of the first season, however, Martinez was told by his agent that his option for another season had not been picked up.

Another *Times* reporter, Ted Thackrey, Jr., also served as a technical adviser on *Lou Grant*. He had worked on other television series as a writer and was among the journalists interviewed before production began.[66] He worked with *Lou Grant* for all five seasons, appearing on the newsroom set for three or four hours a day for a few days each week while scenes were shot. He would answer questions and help actors look as though they were writing stories, talking on the phone to sources, and performing other actions relating to activities in the newsroom. After watching film shot that day he would leave the studio by early afternoon and go to work at the *Times*.[67]

After the first few episodes Thackrey also began reading scripts and commenting on them. Whenever he found a problem, he would offer a solution that would bring the story closer to reality. Common problems with scripts, Thackrey recalled, dealt with the chain of command at a newspaper.[68] For instance, he pointed out that Lou Grant would not assign his reporters national or foreign stories. A real city editor also would ask the composing room rather than the press room for more time during a breaking story. In addition, he told writers that the chief photographer, essentially an administrator, would not go on assignment with a reporter. "Not huge stuff," Thackrey recalled, "but stuff that made a difference." He remembered winning more points than he lost—"not because of my great force of personality, but because they really wanted to get it right."[69]

Research was a crucial element in the look of the newsroom set. Tokatyan, who developed the series, remembered that the newsroom of the *Los Angeles Times* was quite different from his concept for that of the fictional *Los Angeles Tribune*.[70] The *Times* newsroom resembled an insurance office, he said, rather than the rustic newsrooms depicted in old movies. The *Times* was only one of many papers the creators of the series visited as they interviewed journalists and took note of their surroundings. The newsroom at the *Oakland Tribune*, however, caught Tokatyan's eye.

> We found a real old newspaper office up at the *Oakland Tribune*. Everybody hung out at the bar around the corner with the prizefight pictures on the wall, which we of course used in the show. The city editor had a scanner going on behind him and his desk looked like mine, only worse. And he had a bottle and he drank, you know. It was a real old black-and-white newspaper movie. . . . My own personal concept was built from old-time movies and, my god, it still existed, at least in a couple of places.[71]

Designing the *Tribune* newsroom and other sets for *Lou Grant* was the job of MTM's art director, Sydney Z. Litwack, whose career in films and motion pictures dated back to the 1950s.[72] To prepare for *Lou Grant* Litwack visited four papers in the area—the *Los Angeles Times*, the *Los Angeles Herald Examiner*, the *Valley News* (a suburban paper in Van Nuys, California, now called the *Daily News*), and the *Long Beach Press-Telegram*. "What you'd do is give yourself a crash course and steep yourself in the atmosphere," he recalled. "You do an awful lot of observing, and you take hundreds of photographs to record those impressions and the detail."[73] Litwack noted during his visits that each office or desk reflected the personality of the occupant, from slobs and precise organizers to liberals and conservatives.

When creating the newsroom set for *Lou Grant* Litwack borrowed from each of the newsrooms he had visited. "What I ended up with was basically a mixture. I didn't replicate any one room that I saw," he said.[74] The *Tribune* newsroom eventually appeared to be older and a bit run-down, which Litwack contended was justified because the script had established that the *Tribune* was not the city's top newspaper and was struggling to stay afloat. While he designed the newsroom set for accuracy, he also had to make the set meet the demands of cameras and other elements of the television production. "You bend reality to fit the context," he said, "but base it always on as much reality as you can. The brief given us all was that we wanted to be as authentic as possible."[75]

For example, the fact that many newspapers had large, open newsrooms worked well for the television set. Duplicating such a setting for the series would be realistic, yet it also would give directors numerous ways to stage scenes. "A variety of directors would come in," Litwack said, "and you'd have to give them as many ways to play a scene as they might have the opportunity."[76] He placed two other sets—the managing editor's office and the conference room—just off the main newsroom set. Both rooms featured lots of glass, giving a clear view of the activity in the newsroom even as scenes within the rooms were played out.

"Sometimes that's reality and sometimes not," Litwack admitted. "There's no sense shooting them in a fourteen-by-twenty-foot room that's got four walls to it and you can't see anything but black walls behind every person's head. So you have a series of office partitions and open glass. You locate this particular room in a way such that when you shoot it, you background yourself with the main room and have the action and traffic going on behind you. You have depth and focus and atmosphere and all types of stuff going."[77] Another set was designed for a bar called McKenna's, the hangout for the *Tribune* staff. Litwack visited the Redwood Bar, a watering hole in downtown Los Angeles favored by the *Times* staff. Rather than duplicate the Redwood, Litwack simply noted the decor and character of a bar popular with *Times* journalists.[78]

Scripts had placed the *Tribune* building downtown, and a suitable building had to be found for exterior shots. In numerous episodes a brief shot of the outside of the *Tribune* would establish the location of the upcoming scene. The building that served as the exterior of the *Tribune* was located at Fifth and Hill streets off Pershing Square. The art-deco style of the structure was appropriate for the age of the newspaper, Litwack said, and the nearby square allowed the building to be filmed in longer shots than would have been possible had it been surrounded by other structures.[79] One corner of the building housed a Thrifty Drug Store. When an exterior scene was shot, the store's sign was covered with one for the *Los Angeles Tribune*.[80]

Examining the genesis of *Lou Grant* reveals that two major factors contributed to its inception. First, and more important, were its ties to *The Mary Tyler Moore Show*. The gamble CBS agreed to take was based primarily on the belief that Burns and Brooks could, with Asner's help, re-create the magic of the earlier series. Yet audiences are fickle, making nothing certain in television production. One series that seems destined for greatness often fails while another series with low expectations becomes a sensation. CBS hedged its bets on this new series for the 1977–78 season by employing three men who had beaten the odds before. The decision to retain the character Lou Grant was an afterthought, but it, too, played on the success of *The Mary Tyler Moore Show*. As Tinker has suggested, *Lou Grant* may well have failed had viewers not already been familiar with Asner's character from the old series.

Second, Brooks, Burns, and Reynolds built a firm foundation in reality by committing themselves to researching modern journalism. Unlike casting Asner as Lou Grant in the new series, conducting research on journalism was not a decision that guaranteed an audience. There was no compelling evidence to show that viewers cared that television series were accurate in the way they portrayed journalism, law enforcement, law, or other professions. The series's creators acted on instinct, believing that authenticity would help them create a series with a ring of truth. That, they believed, would win over viewers. Only time—and ratings—would establish whether they were correct.

3

Characters and Casting

Jack Bannon was known as a "day player," an actor who worked for a few days on a television series and then moved on to another role.[1] Dining at a restaurant with a friend in 1977, he noticed actor Edward Asner sitting at a nearby table. Bannon, an admirer of Asner's work on *The Mary Tyler Moore Show*, walked over and thanked him for "a lot of wonderful nights," a compliment Asner graciously accepted.[2] Bannon had not yet heard of Asner's new series or of the role of assistant city editor Art Donovan that he soon would be hired to play. "I went back to my table and sat down," Bannon recalled, "and three weeks later shook hands with him on a set and did that show for five years. It was amazing."[3]

Such stories of coincidence abound in Hollywood. Yet for Bannon and the five other actors who were cast in supporting roles in *Lou Grant* the experience remained fresh in their minds after more than fifteen years. That is understandable because *Lou Grant* would prove to be a milestone in their careers. Long before the actors set foot on the MTM lot in Studio City, however, the roles of Lou Grant and his colleagues at the *Los Angeles Tribune* were carefully defined by the series's producers and writers. With their research into modern journalism well under way, they began to use the information they had gathered to create the fictional characters for the series.

Once they were selected, the actors had three sources of information about their roles. Foremost, of course, were the scripts supplied by the series's writers. In addition, two-page sketches provided background for each character and a sense of his or her attitude and place in the *Lou Grant* world. (The sketches appear in App. B.) Only one copy of the character sketches appears to have survived, and it is unsigned and undated.[4] The sketches probably were the work of series developer Leon Tokatyan, who devised the *Lou Grant* family in consultation with producers Jim Brooks,

32

Allan Burns, and Gene Reynolds.[5] Finally, the actors themselves were encouraged to research journalism, especially by spending time with reporters and editors. Taken together, the character sketches and the recollections of the series's creators and actors and the journalists they consulted show how the staff of the *Los Angeles Tribune* came to be.

No character sketch was written for Lou Grant, and none was needed. One hundred sixty-eight episodes of *The Mary Tyler Moore Show* had provided Lou Grant with a history as well as a personality. Television historians Tim Brooks and Earle Marsh offered a concise description of Lou Grant as he appeared in the comedy series: "An irascible, cantankerous, blustery man whose bark was much worse than his bite. Underneath that harsh exterior beat the heart of a pussycat."[6] In the beginning viewers of the comedy series knew that Lou was a family man, married with two daughters. After a painful separation depicted in the first year of *The Mary Tyler Moore Show* Lou and wife Edie divorced in the series's third season. Professionally, Lou was depicted as a dedicated newsman at a mediocre television station, one whose commitment to good journalism seemed tested at WJM-TV. On tough days Lou turned to the bottle of whiskey he kept in his desk.[7]

Most of those traits would carry over to the new program. Looking back, Reynolds described Lou Grant as "a very earthy diamond-in-the-rough. Tough, smart, vulnerable, not a terribly sophisticated guy. A good newsman, a very experienced newsman—canny, shrewd—a tough newsman."[8] Although the character may have changed little from one series to the next, the context in which Lou existed changed significantly. *Lou Grant* had its comedic elements, but it was essentially a drama about a professional editor on a respected newspaper. The character would need to change accordingly. "There is behavior that is acceptable and believable in a sitcom that you can't do in an hour drama," Reynolds noted. "The parameters are much narrower."[9] Keeping a bottle of whiskey in the desk might work for a comedy, but such an action would have damaged the credibility of *Lou Grant* as a realistic look at journalism. "If he pulled a bottle from the bottom of his desk, it becomes an entirely different thing," Tokatyan said. "Now he has an alcohol problem."[10]

Not only had the character shifted from comedy to drama, it had been placed in a completely different context in the production of a television series. *The Mary Tyler Moore Show*, on the one hand, was a half-hour situation comedy filmed with three cameras before a live audience. *Lou Grant*, on the other hand, was a one-hour, single-camera series filmed over seven days without an audience. It is difficult to comprehend the immense challenge that faced Asner. Although he would no longer be playing an overtly comedic character to a live audience, he would continue to play the same character, one already known to millions of viewers, in a far different setting.

"I regarded it as the most impossible task in the world," Asner recalled. "It was the most ridiculous order of the day."[11] Reynolds also noted that the acting style for *Lou Grant* was quite different from that for *The Mary Tyler Moore Show*. "You can be much broader in a sitcom. You can go for the gag, you can go for the laugh," Reynolds said. "I know that it was, for a long time, an adjustment for Ed Asner, of what he could do as Lou Grant in the hour drama."[12] Asner remembered receiving little aid in deciding how to make that transition. He recalled being encouraged by producers and directors to "remember who Lou Grant is," but the vague advice was not much help.[13] He would have to find his way once production of the series began.

During the development of *Lou Grant*, the creators considered making Lou the assistant city editor at the *Tribune* rather than the city editor. The lower position, they thought, would be more believable for a journalist who had not worked on a newspaper for a decade. That change, however, would have put three people over him instead of just the managing editor and the publisher, and it raised concern that Lou's stature would be diminished.[14] Indeed, Grant/Asner was at the center of the series. Dramatically, he was required to have a pivotal role in the newsroom. "He had to be the city editor," Reynolds said. "You've got to put your guy at the helm. You've got to make your guy the quarterback."[15] To make the hiring of Lou believable Tokatyan included a storyline in which the publisher, Margaret Pynchon, was such a tyrant that no one wanted to work with her.[16] The first episode, "Cophouse," established that Lou replaced a city editor who could not handle the pressures of the job or deal with Mrs. Pynchon.

Some actors prefer to do their own research as a way of gaining insight into a role. Having worked on his high school newspaper in Kansas City, Kansas, Asner knew how a story was edited. The role of city editor would demand no technical skills beyond handling a pencil or typing on a computer terminal. "I could always fake that when I'm working at my desk," Asner said. "There's nothing to that. There ain't much else."[17] Throughout the series Asner relied on the show's technical adviser and the research that guided the writers.[18] He read about journalism but made only a perfunctory visit to the *Los Angeles Times*. Unlike the other actors on the series, Asner was a star. He believed he would have been asked more questions about himself than he could have asked *Times* staffers about journalism. In fact, he considered such a visit a waste of time.

"When all was said and done, when the producer-writers had done all their research, when the advisers had given all their expertise, there's nothing for me to do," Asner said. "My job is to act and to get the greatest meaning out of the simplest line. And if I do that well and interestingly, then I will have done my part for journalism."[19]

Beyond creating a believable circumstance under which Lou Grant would be hired as city editor at the *Tribune*, little time was spent developing the Lou Grant persona, which already existed. The task of surrounding Lou with believable characters was more urgent.

★   ★   ★

The concept of *Lou Grant* was fairly simple. Reynolds described it this way: "Lou Grant working on a big-city newspaper with a little family of people—an assistant city editor, a managing editor, a couple of reporters, and a boss. Those are the basic characters."[20] To create the members of Lou's "little family" Tokatyan and the producers of the series relied heavily on their journalism research. Their visits to the *Los Angeles Times* and other newspapers, the books and trade journals they had read, and the journalism classes they had taken contributed to their sense of what kinds of people would be working in the *Tribune* newsroom. "Things come out of research that you can't make up," Tokatyan said. "Some of our characters grew out of research."[21]

But research alone did not dictate the creation of *Lou Grant* characters. Just as important as accuracy, and perhaps more important, the dramatic framework of the series had to be served. The staff of the *Tribune* would be created and cast for contrast and conflict. Each character would have an inherent dramatic conflict with other characters in the series. "Drama and conflict are synonymous," Tokatyan said. "You want a mix of interesting people. You don't want two, three characters to be the same."[22] The creators of *Lou Grant* also sought to reject the journalistic stereotypes they believed had flourished for decades in motion pictures and television.

The series would feature two *Tribune* reporters who worked for Lou Grant, one male and one female. The male reporter was given the name Joe Rossi, Tokatyan remembered, in part because the writer's agent was named Ross.[23] In the character sketch Rossi is described as a twenty-seven-year-old general-assignment reporter certain that he is bound for greatness. He is a crack reporter—perhaps the best in the city—abrasive, rude, and obnoxious, and not at all modest about his talents. "But behind his brashness, there is a dark and sparkling charm; and above everything else, he is one hell of a newspaperman," the sketch stated. "Wherever there is a free press, he would be at home. Wherever there is a balloon filled with hot and pompous air, you'll find him sharpening a needle. He was born cynical, and nothing he has encountered since has mellowed that cynicism."[24] Rossi also hides a vulnerable humanity, the sketch added, but it is exposed only rarely. The sketch concluded: "He is neither liked nor understood, which is—he insists—fine with him. But he is respected."[25]

Reynolds recalled meeting reporters like Joe Rossi. "We wanted a hot, ambitious, ruthless, understandable, and likable character," the producer said. "Reporters can be very assertive, they can be monomaniacal, very focused, myopic, distrusting, skeptical."[26] Making an audience warm to such a personality might seem difficult, but Reynolds maintained that Rossi did not turn off viewers because he was a recognizable character and was human. "You can still like a character and even admire a character who has to be that way to get his job done or who has those kind of human characteristics."[27] Tokatyan describes Rossi as "an abrasive smart-aleck who has talent but who is so full of himself that he needs to be guided."[28]

The Rossi character was influenced by David Shaw, the media critic of the *Los Angeles Times* and one of the reporters interviewed during the research process.[29] As the character of Rossi was being conceived during the initial stages of research Tokatyan remembered someone at the *Times* describing Shaw as "an arrogant little prick."[30] That description eventually was applied to Rossi. The sketch noted that Rossi's colleagues at the *Tribune* consider him "that arrogant, little creep" and added: "Their assessment of him won't change, even after the Pulitzer Prizes he is sure he will win. And Rossi couldn't care less."[31] Interestingly, Shaw was awarded the Pulitzer Prize for criticism in 1991.

Sometime after the producers had interviewed Shaw, the journalist met actor Robert Walden in the *Times* newsroom. According to Shaw, Walden introduced himself and said: "My character is supposed to be young, cocky, aggressive, abrasive, not much liked by his peers. People tell me I should follow you around for a few weeks."[32] The back-handed compliment amused Shaw. "He may have overstated it some," Shaw recalled, "but the basic elements were accurate."[33] He recalled spending a great deal of time with Walden over the next several weeks as the actor learned how journalists worked. On one occasion Walden witnessed a verbal donnybrook in the newsroom. "I got in a huge fight with an editor that actually, in retrospect, was my fault," Shaw remembered. "I'd said something stupid. Bob was sitting there wide-eyed watching me fight with this editor."[34]

At times during the run of the series Shaw noted that Rossi's dress and mannerisms mimicked his own. For instance, Shaw preferred using a headset rather than a hand-held receiver when talking on the phone. In some episodes of *Lou Grant* Rossi could be seen wearing a headset. Shaw pointed out, however, that the character played by Walden was not a replica. "He ultimately told me that they decided they really wanted him to be a somewhat younger, scruffier, less-established reporter than I was because they wanted Lou Grant to be able to read him the riot act," Shaw recalled. "They wanted him to make some mistakes, excesses of enthusiasm and so on."[35] The journalist does not recall anyone making a serious comparison of Rossi to him. "It was different enough from me," he said. "I think that, by and large, most people who watched it did not see that as being me."[36] Shaw and Walden became friends, attending sporting events together and even double-dating a few times.[37]

Walden's interest in research was markedly different from that of Asner. In fact, Shaw was not the first person he had shadowed to learn about a profession he would depict on film or television. For his role as senior resident in the film *The Hospital* (1971) Walden read medical books, interviewed doctors, and almost lived in hospitals. He took a similar approach when he played lawyers, police officers, and junkies.[38] "I want to know the language of my character," he told *TV Guide* in 1978, "the attitudes, the tools, the clothing, the atmosphere. I want to feel natural—confident—in front of the camera."[39]

Walden, born in New York on September 25, 1943, had studied with Lee Strasberg at the Actors Studio while attending City College of New York.[40] By the early 1970s Walden was appearing frequently on television and in films. He was a regular on "The New Doctors" segment of the series *The Bold Ones* in 1972, and his other television work included roles on *The Rookies* (1972–76), *The Streets of San Francisco* (1972–77), and *The Rockford Files* (1974–80).[41] Walden's film assignments included acting with Shelley Winters and Robert De Niro in *Bloody Mama* (1970), George C. Scott in *The Hospital* (1971), and Woody Allen in *Everything You Always Wanted to Know about Sex* (1972).

As *Lou Grant* was being planned Walden was on movie screens around the nation in *All the President's Men* (1976), playing political trickster Donald Segretti. He first heard about Brooks and Burns's new series when he appeared in an episode of their MTM sitcom *Rhoda* in December 1976. "They wouldn't tell me what it was, just that it was an hour show," Walden said.[42] The actor decided not to take a film role to make certain he would be available for the series, which he later discovered was a newspaper drama. "They were writing the role with me in mind, I was led to believe, and they were," Walden added.[43] Other actors and people at MTM even referred to the part as "the Bobby Walden role," he said. "All these people were coming up to me saying, 'Listen, I just read for the part, and it's absolutely tailor-made for you.' They didn't know it was written with me in mind."[44]

Yet when Walden read for the role in the spring of 1977, he was not immediately offered the part. He was asked to read a second time, which was emotionally trying because he had heard from friends that the role had been offered to another actor. Walden then learned that a second actor had been offered the part after the producers' first choice had declined. "I was pretty shattered," he admitted. "My ego was really bruised, to say the least."[45] The news came at a difficult time for Walden. His longtime manager had just died, and his mother underwent cancer surgery the same week.

As Walden left town to visit friends in northern California, his agent passed along better news: the actor to whom the part had been offered could not accept it because of another commitment. Although he was the third choice, the role was Walden's if he wanted it. "I didn't know what to say," he recalled. "I just felt totally rejected, and I didn't know at that moment if I could do a good job, I had so many mixed feelings. . . . I wound up saying yes and found a way to Scotch Tape my damaged ego."[46]

Was the abrasive Joe Rossi written with Walden's personality in mind? "I hope not!" he declared. "They just knew I could play characters that hard-nosed, that willing to be obnoxious, stand alone, you know, tunnel-vision types of guys who aren't scared to be seen a certain way. Most actors want to be heroes. . . . You don't necessarily want to become an actor to play an asshole. Generally, that's not your motivation."[47] Walden read the character sketch for Rossi and devoted time to observing Shaw at the *Los Angeles Times*. "He was a real iconoclast, and proud of it. A real maverick," Walden said. "He said, 'I may not be loved around here, but I'm respected'."[48] It was a key part of the attitude Walden incorporated into his portrayal of Rossi as the series began production.

★   ★   ★

When they developed the character of the woman reporter in the city room of the *Tribune,* the creators of *Lou Grant* sought a stark contrast to Joe Rossi. The character sketch for reporter Carla Mardigian compared her to Rossi ("unlike him, sensitive to her fellow human beings") and established her as a counterweight to his presence in the newsroom. The Mardigian sketch also described her as "stunning and talented" and "an enigma to many, a paradox to all."[49] It focused as much on the sexuality of the twenty-eight-year-old character as her prowess as a reporter. "A tough competitor in what is still basically a man's field, there is no one who has ever called her by that stock male business put-down: a ballsy chick," the sketch claimed. "Because Carla is first and last, that fantasy figure in the very curvaceous flesh: a totally feminine woman not above using her femininity when going after a story or a man she wants, yet who knows her own real worth and is quite comfortable with it." [50]

In casting the role of Carla, Reynolds placed Linda Kelsey at the top of his list of potential actresses. He had worked with Kelsey on $M*A*S*H$ and thought the red-haired actress would be perfect for the part. "Somehow, it got scratched by somebody," Reynolds recalled, unsure whether Kelsey simply was not available or whether someone thought she was not suitable for the role.[51] Lack of interest on Kelsey's part might have been the reason. At that time in her career Kelsey did not want to join the cast of a television series. "I'd been adamant to my agent about it," she said.[52] She thought that the best roles for women on series television were in guest appearances, not regular characters. "I was the one who the plot was about because I was the guest actor," she said, adding that in many series, "all the woman got to do was say, 'You can do it, honey,' or run down a hallway with a gun out." [53]

For the role of Carla Mardigian the producers hired Rebecca Balding, a relative newcomer to television. Balding, born September 21, 1948, was a theater arts graduate of the University of Kansas, had come to Los Angeles in 1976 from Chicago, having worked for four years in Equity theater.[54] She surprised herself by finding work and an agent almost immediately. For *Lou Grant* Balding relied on the scripts for guidance about the character she was playing. She does not recall reading a character sketch for Carla. "In television casting, you are essentially cast for who you are, and there's not a whole lot of character work done, particularly if you are the female lead," she said. "What you are, who you are, is what they get and generally why you're cast." [55]

Balding remembered spending part of one day with reporter Narda Zacchino of the *Los Angeles Times*. "I sat next to this lady . . . and watched her work," Balding said. "I was just amazed how much of it's done on the phone." [56] Zacchino offered Balding a chance to check some information by phone, but Balding declined. "I'm an actress, I'm not a journalist," she said. "If I had words written for my mouth to say when I picked up the phone instead of me having to make them up, then I might have been able to do that. But I felt very uncomfortable doing that." [57] Still, the visit to the *Times* helped Balding see what a reporter did and how a newspaper operated. "I was really impressed," she said. "It was just like in *All the President's Men*." [58]

How closely was the character Carla Mardigian based on Zacchino?

At first the *Times* reporter was flattered that the producers and others with the series valued her experiences as a woman journalist. "One of them, somebody related to the show, told me they were modeling this woman reporter after me," Zacchino said. "In fact, and I remember this explicitly, he said in the scripts her name is Narda."[59] An incident early in the production of *Lou Grant* changed her attitude. Zacchino saw a script that included an incident between the reporter and her boyfriend. She was shocked to realize the scene was taken from a personal incident Zacchino had related about her ex-husband. "And I mean down to all the details of what we had said to each other and what had happened and everything," she said. "I really felt violated."[60]

Following the advice of a lawyer, she requested compensation from the *Lou Grant* producers for basing the character on her life, but they refused. Zacchino said she was more interested in stopping such personal references from appearing in the show than receiving money.[61] The relationship between the producers and Zacchino ended without animosity, both she and Reynolds contended, but she was no longer consulted for information and advice.[62] The incident apparently carried over to other people consulted at the *Times*. Shaw recalled Walden telling him that cast members had been told to stop spending time at the newspaper or with its reporters and editors because of a fear of lawsuits.[63]

Balding played Carla Mardigian in the first three episodes of *Lou Grant*. The producers, unhappy with her work, replaced Balding with Kelsey, who had appeared in a guest role as *Tribune* reporter Billie Newman (the change is discussed in a later chapter). Was Balding's firing related to Zacchino's concern that the character had been too closely linked to her? That was the story that made the rounds at the *Los Angeles Times*, according to Ted Thackrey, Jr., and Al Martinez, *Lou Grant* technical advisers and *Times* journalists.[64] Reynolds and Tokatyan, however, adamantly denied any link between Zacchino's complaint and the dismissal of Balding.[65] The actress was replaced, Reynolds contended, because she was not convincing in the role. "In relationship to the material, to the issues, it was all just not quite believable that she would have that kind of maturity to be given the job," he said.[66]

★　　★　　★

The creators of the series had decided to have a woman publisher preside over the *Tribune*, in part because they wanted a female hero on television. "If we'd had a male publisher, except for Billie Newman, we'd have an all-male cast," Reynolds recalled. "We just liked the idea. And there is the precedent of women publishers."[67] The name Pynchon was chosen, according to Tokatyan, for its seventeenth-century quality and Restoration ring. He perceived the character as a cross between Dorothy Schiff and Katharine Graham, two of the most prominent women publishers in the United States.[68] Schiff published the *New York Post* from 1942, when owner and husband George Backer became ill, until she sold the paper to Rupert Murdoch in 1976.[69] Graham's father, Eugene Meyer, bought the *Washington Post* in 1933, and control of it shifted to her husband, Phil Graham, in 1948. When he died in 1963, his widow became publisher of the *Post* and *Newsweek* magazine. Katharine Graham became a national figure in the wake of the paper's prize-winning coverage of the Watergate scandal.[70] The Pynchon character, Tokatyan added, was "an amalgam, nothing at all like the real people."[71]

Yet the character sketch for Margaret Pynchon did not refer to Graham but mentioned Dorothy Schiff by name, noting that Pynchon shares her penchant for trivia and affection for gossip.[72] Mrs. Pynchon's father had bought the paper, according to the character history, but in the series it was suggested that her husband had died and left her to run the *Tribune*. The two-page sketch established a quirky older woman whose constant companion is a yapping Yorkshire terrier, but also one who is devoted to a newspaper that is foundering in a highly competitive news market. She is described, in part, as

> a woman of great charm and power, somewhat eccentric. She can be capricious, arbitrary, maddening. But it is her paper and she has the right to run it any way she sees fit. . . . She can and does rise to situations that call for insight, fairness, and decisiveness.
>
> And if she is capricious and at times arbitrary, there remains always an underlying strength of purpose. She believes in this newspaper her father founded and her dearest wish is to have it return to the days when it was synonymous with reason, objectivity, truth.[73]

One of the actresses considered for the part was Nancy Marchand. Born June 19, 1928, in Buffalo, New York, Marchand earned a bachelor of fine arts degree from Carnegie Institute of Technology in Pittsburgh in 1949.[74] In the next three decades Marchand devoted much of her career to the theater, but she also appeared frequently on television.[75] Her work in television's "Golden Age" included the role of the plain girl who falls in love with a butcher in the classic drama *Marty* (1953). Marchand acted in several daytime television dramas, including *Love of Life* from 1970 to 1974, and then played the grand dame of a Boston family on the prime-time series *Beacon Hill* (1975).

Marchand was suggested for the part of publisher Margaret Pynchon by Asner and flew to Los Angeles for a reading at MTM.[76] After the reading she realized she had left her glasses at the studio. They had been placed in an envelope for her, and Marchand slipped the envelope into her purse without opening it. "When I needed my glasses for something and I opened the envelope," she recalled, "there was a little note in there that said, 'Congratulations, you got the part.' So that was all very exciting to me."[77] The flight to Los Angeles became the first of many for Marchand. She commuted from New York to Los Angeles for the five-year run of the series, usually working only one or two days on the show and then returning to New York.

Marchand was forty-nine when *Lou Grant* first aired; she wore a gray wig for the part of the sixtyish publisher. To prepare for the part of Margaret Pynchon Marchand read extensively about journalism and women publishers, but she did not visit newspapers or meet with Graham or Schiff. She also does not remember reading a character sketch of Mrs. Pynchon.[78] Thackrey, the show's technical adviser, contends that Marchand based Mrs. Pynchon's upper-crust accent on Schiff, his step-mother.[79] Marchand, however, remembered that the accent was a way of suggesting Mrs. Pynchon came from money. As for the basis of the character, Marchand admitted she made no great effort to research the part. "I know that their research was enormous and very thorough," she said. "They really cared about making it as realistic as possible."[80]

Dramatically, Mrs. Pynchon provided conflict for Lou Grant and other members of the *Tribune* staff. "Ed was the star of the show. He had that pressure from upstairs, from the old lady upstairs," Marchand noted. "He wasn't necessarily completely in charge, and that gave him a much more interesting dimension."[81] Disagreements with Mrs. Pynchon also allowed for different points of view to be expressed in an episode. "I was sort of a linch pin," Marchand said of her role. "I either began the story or I ended the story or I made a simple announcement of the point of view the paper was going to take in the middle of the story."[82] Mrs. Pynchon also was called on to deal with emotional issues facing her staff, a dramatic device for telling a story if not a realistic function of a publisher. "She was a titan. She could do everything," Marchand said. "I don't think that most publishers have to deal with all of that."[83]

★   ★   ★

Unlike Mrs. Pynchon, the qualities of *Tribune* managing editor Charlie Hume came in part from a *Los Angeles Times* journalist interviewed by the producers. George Cotliar, the assistant managing editor of the *Times*, was the first *Times* person the *Lou Grant* team had met; he had allowed the show's producers to talk to reporters and editors for background information. To Reynolds, Cotliar represented the opposite of the managing editor who had appeared in the play and film versions of *The Front Page*, which featured a tough, aggressive loudmouth. "He really surprised me," Reynolds said of Cotliar. "Here we have this very soft-spoken, gentle guy. I really liked the idea of not going with what we've seen in the movies. Here was a guy who was very bright, very sharp, very capable." [84]

The character sketch for Charlie Hume, however, described a cautious, insecure person who feels pressure from several sources: the publisher, his family, and Lou. "A careful man," the sketch said, "with a surface ease belied by two very sweaty palms. A good man, with a very nervous stomach." [85] A graduate of Dartmouth, the sketch said, Hume worked briefly for Random House before joining the *Philadelphia Inquirer* as a cub reporter and moving from paper to paper in his career. "He was a hungry reporter for too long. Whatever it is that makes a newspaperman eluded him. He feels he landed in his present job through a series of lucky mishaps and moves, and he does not want to lose it." [86] Still, the sketch maintained, Hume is not incompetent and does his job well, even if he has "lost his nerve." [87]

The part went to Mason Adams, another New York native with a background in the theater. Adams, born February 26, 1919, earned a master's degree in theater arts from the University of Wisconsin. [88] Although Adams worked primarily on the stage, his voice was known to millions through numerous radio dramas, including a seventeen-year stint in the title role of *Pepper Young's Family*, which ended in 1959. [89] When Reynolds and Burns were casting Charlie Hume, they remembered Adams from a television movie, *The Deadliest Season* (1977). [90] He had played the nasty head of a hockey organization, a change of pace for an actor who usually was not cast as a villain. "I assume that he saw a certain hard-edged quality that would match up with a normal gentleness in my personality so that it would be a good combination for Charlie Hume," Adams said. [91]

Reynolds, who had been impressed by the laid-back personality of Cotliar at the *Times*, cast against the *Front Page* stereotype by hiring Adams. Reynolds and Burns also made the unusual decision to cast the first person who read for the part. "We thought, 'We can't hire the first guy'," Reynolds later told *TV Guide*. "But why not? We were charmed. Mason plays Charlie with humanity, humor, authority." [92] The new series would be Adams's first as a regular, and he was dubious about moving from the East Coast to Los Angeles to be one of seven characters. Assured that Charlie Hume would be an integral part of the show, Adams joined the project and, at age sixty, took what turned out to be "the part of my life."[93]

Except for his work as drama critic for the high school newspaper, Adams had no knowledge of journalism. In addition to reading the copious amount of research gathered by the *Lou Grant* staff Adams conducted his own research into the role of the managing editor.[94] While riding a commuter train to New York from his home in Westport, Connecticut, Adams was introduced by a friend to another Westport resident, Bill Brink. Brink, managing editor of the *New York Daily News* since 1974, invited Adams to visit the *Daily News* and learn about the newspaper business.[95] "He sat in my office quite a bit and talked things over with me," Brink remembered.

> [Adams] was kind of interested in what kind of day you spend and how you approach the news, how you deal with the staff and so on. But he was more interested in the news conferences we had, and I'd have one major one in the morning. He would sit in and all my sub editors—city editor, suburban editor and that sort—would come in and discuss the day's news. We sort of figure out what we're going to do that day.
>
> The rest of my day consisted of jumping from one thing to another, principally back and forth between personnel matters and eventually ending up on the news desk monitoring the papers that came together to go into the first edition. He stayed around for that, too.[96]

Editorial meetings—called budget meetings at some newspapers—would be an important element of Adams's work as an actor on *Lou Grant*. Charlie Hume presided over such meetings in nearly every episode.

Spending about one week watching Brink at work was important to Adams. "My main education was at the *Daily News*," Adams said. "I really got a sense of what it was like to preside over a news conference. . . . This was a whole new world to me, and I got some insights from it."[97] Brink's personality also impressed Adams. "Bill Brink was a managing editor's managing editor. Very, very quiet, knowledgeable, forthright, very much in command of himself and what was going on there," Adams said. "He was above the fray but part of it. And in command." Had the chance meeting with Brink not taken place, Adams is certain he would have learned about the duties of a managing editor from another source. "We've all seen *The Front Page* . . . but to see it actually happening was sort of valuable," Adams said.[98]

★   ★   ★

Two other roles were created for *Lou Grant,* those of an assistant city editor and a photographer. Lou Grant's assistant served an important dramatic function on the series: he allowed Lou to leave his desk when a script called for his presence outside the newsroom. "We put him there to take over the desk so Ed could be doing things in the field," Tokatyan said.[99] Consequently, the assistant city editor had to be highly competent to assure viewers that Lou's absence would not harm the paper. The character sketch described assistant city editor Arthur Donovan, Jr., as happy and satisfied with himself and his job. An important aspect of his personality was his pursuit of women, a trait elaborately described in the sketch. Donovan's hitch in the Navy during the Korean War was a period in which he spent "a credible number of hours in Seoul, Tokyo, and San Francisco learning his craft: coition."[100] He became a newspaperman, according to the sketch, after he saw some pornographic pictures of a movie queen taken by a staff photographer for the *Los Angeles Times.* Noting that the photographer had stayed past his allotted time for the dalliance and then had billed the newspaper for overtime, the sketch concluded: "Obviously, this was a milieu made for Donovan."[101]

Donovan also is a sharp dresser, a connoisseur of food and wine, and one who juggles one deal after another in pursuit of a condominium in Tahiti, a fifty-four-foot sloop, or anything else that catches his eye. In his heart he loves being a newspaperman but insists to others that the job is only a convenient base from which to operate.

> He is forever disappearing for "coffee" returning an hour later smelling of expensive perfume, smiling his Errol Flynn smile, and picking long silken hair of varying shades from between his Errol Flynn teeth.
> But when Lou must leave the desk, Donovan takes over the Desk with a verve and competence that gives him away. (He could be brilliant, but that might blow his scene. They just might give him a more responsible, better paying, higher ranking job. God forbid.)[102]

Donovan and Lou get along, according to the sketch, even though Lou's style of dress makes him wince. He is summed up in the last sentence of the sketch: "Donovan—full of stories and that great Irish charm—is a hell of a lot of fun."[103] The character's natty appearance was based in part on some editors Reynolds had noticed wearing cuff links, tailored shirts, and vests.[104] "We needed a contrast," added Tokatyan. "Ed was supposed to be very sloppy, puts on mismatched socks, and things like that. The assistant city editor was in a white collar, striped shirt, always a vest, extremely well-dressed."[105]

Actor Jack Bannon, who was hired to play Donovan, had worked in television during the 1960s and 1970s. He was born into a show-business family on June 14, 1940, in Los Angeles. His father, Jim Bannon, was a radio announcer and an actor best known for his work in the *Red Ryder* series of western films. Bannon's mother was actress Bea Benaderet, the star of the comedy series *Petticoat Junction* (1963–70).[106] The younger Bannon opted for an acting career while at the University of California at Santa Barbara, graduating in 1963.[107] At age twenty-four he was hired as dialogue coach on *Petticoat Junction*. Bannon performed at times on that series as well as *The Beverly Hillbillies* (1962–71), *Green Acres* (1965–71), and *Daniel Boone* (1964–70).

Bannon moved to New York in 1971 but found little work in the theater. Returning to Los Angeles, he began making the rounds on various television series, including *Kojak* (1973–78), *The Rockford Files* (1974–80) and *Charlie's Angels* (1976–81).[108] In 1977 Bannon was encouraged by his agent to read for a part in a new series that would star Asner. All he knew about the character was the name, Donovan, and that he was Irish. When Bannon went to read, he did so in an Irish brogue, but the producers immediately asked him to drop it.[109] Reynolds then offered Bannon the chair behind his desk, a familiar setting for a desk-bound assistant city editor. Bannon went through the scene not once but, at the request of Burns, twice. It was a good sign, Bannon thought, and he left the studio with a positive feeling about the audition. In four days he was offered the role.[110] Bannon later was given a sheet of information about the part, probably the character sketch.

Bannon spent a few days at the *Los Angeles Times* observing assistant editors, particularly Eric Malnic, the night city editor. Malnic remembered enjoying those evenings in part because Bannon was a pleasant person who asked intelligent questions about the job. The night of the actor's first visit, Malnic recalled, would have given anyone the wrong impression that a newspaper was always bustling.

> The first night he was here, we had something like a plane crash at LAX [Los Angeles International Airport]. I can't remember what it was. He walked in the door and all hell broke loose. It was one of those nights you dream about as a newspaperman. I was night city editor that night.
>
> The shit was hitting the fan, and people were flying all over the place, and it was terrific. And he thought, 'Gee, that's the way it's going to be every night.' Of course, then for the next two weeks absolutely nothing happened. That gave him a much more realistic look at what it was really like.[111]

During his visits to the *Times* Bannon noted the pressures on editors, from constant phone calls to complaints from reporters about how their stories had been edited. "I tried to look at the way people handled things —phones, those pencils with no erasers," he said. "I tried to get a feel for that rather than just make a complete pretend out of it. It's probably a job that not as many people would know as much about as they would about reporting. You see reporters, you see them on television. You don't see assistant city editors, generally."[112] The visits helped Bannon understand the role of an editor at a newspaper. When the series was in production, Bannon relied on the advice of Thackrey, the show's technical adviser, for advice about what an editor would do in a particular situation.[113]

To round out its fictional staff *Lou Grant* needed a photographer. The character sketch noted that his name was Dennis Price but immediately pointed out that he is called The Animal. "Twenty-six years old," the sketch said, "with very long blonde hair pulled back in a pony tail, he is a consumate slob in everything except his work and anything related to his work."[114] The sketch continued to focus on two aspects of the character, his brilliance as a photographer and his disdain for personal appearance and, at times, hygiene. "He is unique," the sketch concluded, "and only his press card saves him at times from being hauled off for questioning."[115]

Unlike the sketches for the other *Lou Grant* characters, the description of Animal includes references to unethical behavior. Although colorful, this aspect of Animal's background raises disturbing questions about his integrity and that of the profession of photojournalism.

> In the trunk of his car, in addition to the zippered bags of lenses and related photo equipment and the fireman's helmet and heavy clasped coat, is an assortment of props that helped earn him his sobriquet: a pair of baby shoes, worn and scuffed; a child's doll, sad and broken; a blind man's white cane, splintered. He is not above tossing them in the foreground of a freeway accident he is photographing, according to the station of the victims involved.[116]

Interestingly, Animal never sinks to such actions during the series. In fact, the character is a highly ethical, sensitive photographer. Had Animal manipulated an accident scene as described in the sketch, the series's efforts to be realistic would have been damaged. Dramatically, such an incident could take place, but with an actor in a guest role rather than a character the audience liked and respected. That segment of the character sketch for Animal, it seems, is more a throwback to the *Front Page* stereotypes the producers sought to avoid.

The actor chosen for the role of Dennis "The Animal" Price was Daryl Anderson, born July 1, 1951, in Seattle.[117] He studied acting at the University of Washington and the Seattle Repertory Theater. A role in *Sweet Revenge* (1977), filmed in Seattle shortly after he graduated, gained Anderson membership in the Screen Actors Guild. He moved to Los Angeles and appeared in some theater productions before auditioning for *Lou Grant*, which became his first television job.[118] Tall and lean with dark hair and a stubble of beard, Anderson was not the embodiment of Animal as envisioned by Tokatyan. "I remember Allan Burns coming in and saying, 'We've just cast Animal and you're going to fall in love with him immediately,' and I did," Tokatyan said.[119] The contrast between old-school Lou Grant and Animal was "humor personified," Tokatyan added. "He was hysterical. Sort of slouching through with his cameras. But he was a brilliant photographer."[120]

A major source of information about photography for Anderson was Nikon, the camera manufacturer that provided equipment for him to use in the series. He attended a seminar sponsored by Nikon and was later instructed on how to use equipment by a Nikon representative.[121] Anderson learned more about photojournalism from Boris Yaro, a reporter-photographer for the *Los Angeles Times*.[122] He went on assignments with Yaro, shooting pictures and seeing how a photographer functioned within a newspaper. Their first day together showed Anderson the realities of news photography. The pair drove to a brushfire, Yaro recalled, but it turned out to be of little news value. On the way back to the *Times* Yaro shot a feature photo, but it was not published in the newspaper.[123]

More importantly, Yaro helped the actor learn how to use the camera he had loaned him. They talked about how to hold the camera properly, how to look for angles when photographing, and other aspects of a news photographer's job. Yaro also had Anderson take pictures, and he critiqued the actor's work. "The concept, the ability to see something, was there," Yaro said. "One slight flaw is that he didn't realize he had to focus a camera, which was funnier than hell. We get back and here are all these great images that are out of focus. We cured that in about thirty seconds. I just said, 'Daryl, this is how you focus a lens.' It wasn't just point and shoot."[124]

Yaro led Anderson through the process of going on assignment, taking pictures and developing them, and taking photographs to the editor. They also discussed the ethics of news photography. "We spent a nice, long leisurely day. It was a lot of time to talk about things," Yaro said. "And he was conscientious. He asked about things."[125] The time with Yaro enlightened Anderson about a photographer's job, the actor recalled.

I picked up very quickly the photographer's feeling of being slighted, the awareness that the picture on the front page is what sells the paper to someone who's not a subscriber, and that that's not recognized. And that reporters look at photographers as illustrators. They don't know each other. When they go to a news event, part of the tension is to what degree the reporter is going to instruct the photographer as if he's the assistant. Photographers are very resistant to that. They're also telling a story, just through a different method.[126]

There was one major difference between Yaro and the character Anderson portrayed. Whereas Animal wore grubby clothes, Yaro dressed in a jacket and tie unless the assignment called for jeans and a work shirt. "You can't walk in looking like a damn bum," Yaro said. "You just can't do that, not working for the *Times*."[127] Martinez, the *Times* journalist who served as technical adviser, contended that Animal was drawn in part from a rough-and-tumble photographer with whom he worked at the *Oakland Tribune*.[128] Whatever the origins of Animal, many news photographers later would take great offense to Animal's slovenly appearance, even writing the producers of *Lou Grant* in protest.[129] Yaro, however, remained pleased with the spirit the character conveyed in the series. "Daryl Anderson, in his role as Animal," Yaro said, "was a conscientious photographer who felt very deeply about things."[130]

★ ★ ★

The creation of the fictional staff of the *Los Angeles Tribune* leads to a guessing game about who was the basis for which character. Tokatyan objects to suggestions that individuals can be cited as models for the characters he helped create. "It's ridiculous," he said. "It all came out of my head. I don't know who these other people are who say it's based on them, or based on this, or based on what."[131] Given the research involved in preparations for *Lou Grant*, the point is debatable. Without question, Shaw influenced the characterization of Joe Rossi, and Cotliar's personality influenced that of Charlie Hume. Citing Katharine Graham of the *Washington Post* as the model for Mrs. Pynchon, however, ignores the fact that other women, including Dorothy Schiff of the *New York Post*, were publishing newspapers.

Other claims that a *Lou Grant* character was based on a specific person also seem weak but have an almost mythic stature. For instance, Zacchino insisted that Lou Grant was based upon the *Times* metropolitan editor of that period, Mark Murphy. "Everybody knew it," she said. "Ask anyone here who was the model for Lou Grant and they'll all say Mark Murphy."[132] Murphy, however, was equally adamant that he was not the model for Lou Grant although he was interviewed at length during the research process. "I don't know how that got started," Murphy said, adding that the connection followed him to the *Fort Worth Star-Telegram* where he worked as features editor.[133] Of course, the argument that Murphy was the model for Lou Grant ignores the fact that Lou Grant had appeared on *The Mary Tyler Moore Show* the previous seven years.

Ultimately, the influence of real people on these fictional characters becomes a matter of perception for those involved in the process. "I think what's really at the heart of everything is identification with the character," Tokatyan said.

> There are things in these characters that strike a chord in the people who are watching. I think if a character is successful, he or she will have some kind of universal beam that will set off these things. If the characters are right, it will resonate with a viewer. And if they have been talked to, that compounds the belief that they are the ones being depicted on the screen. The only one who didn't was the photographers across America, who hated it.[134]

Thus, the six supporting characters of *Lou Grant* were carefully slipped into place as the series moved toward production. They were designed to represent a mix of personalities, each clashing in some way with the others. In their initial conception, all the *Lou Grant* characters were given strengths and weaknesses that journalists could recognize. The next step, then, would be to produce, write, and direct episodes that would place the staff of the *Tribune* in realistic but compelling situations.

4

Series Production and Censorship

There was no question who was in charge as the production of *Lou Grant* began. With the series's premise firmly set and its recurring roles created and cast the creators of the new series could turn their attention to the actual production of episodes. In their roles as executive producers Jim Brooks, Allan Burns, and Gene Reynolds remained the creative force behind every aspect of *Lou Grant*. In broad terms that meant hiring producers to help oversee daily operations; assembling a staff of writers to develop scripts; and hiring directors to turn those scripts into television episodes. The three men participated, to varying degrees, in story conferences, script rewriting, casting, and other aspects of production during the first season.

Reynolds would prove to be the most active and have the strongest influence of the three creators of *Lou Grant*. He wrote or cowrote five episodes, directed eleven episodes, and served as executive producer during the five seasons the series aired. Burns's title changed from executive producer to executive consultant after the first season, but he remained involved in the production on an almost daily basis. After *Lou Grant* began its first season Brooks left the production to turn his attention to a new comedy series, *Taxi*.[1]

The producers kept tight control over the process that shaped each episode. The premise—a realistic drama with comedic overtones about the people who worked at a daily newspaper—could not change without their consent. In addition, the quality of the writing and overall production remained in their hands. Supported by MTM President Grant Tinker and guaranteed thirteen episodes in its maiden season by CBS, the producers now faced the challenge of making *Lou Grant* a smooth, efficient, and creatively satisfying production. Journalists who hoped that this new television series would portray their profession realistically

51

and still succeed dramatically could not have hoped for a stronger foundation.

★　　★　　★

Brooks, Burns, and Reynolds had solid experience in writing for television. Consequently, they valued good writing and understood that any chance of success for *Lou Grant* began with developing excellent scripts. More importantly, they guided a staff of writers in focusing an idea, outlining a story, evaluating a script, and rewriting scenes. Their vigilance at the script stage resulted in consistently well-written episodes. "It was considered the premiere show in terms of writing," according to Seth Freeman, a writer who became a producer and director on the series.[2] Awards showed the television industry's respect for the writing on *Lou Grant*. The series won two Writer's Guild of America awards and two Emmy awards for dramatic writing during its five-year run.[3] For two seasons *Lou Grant* dominated the Emmy nominations for dramatic writing. Three of the four nominations in 1978–79 and four of the five nominations in 1979–80 went to *Lou Grant* scripts.[4] (For a list of major awards earned by the series see app. C.)

For many members of the writing staff the systematic process by which a *Lou Grant* script was conceived, outlined, and written was unlike that of any show on which they worked before or afterward. Scripts began with subjects from three basic sources: research into journalism issues, current events, and the production staff. Freeman recalled that many subjects for stories came from the interests of staff members, their experiences, or the experiences of people they knew. The staff avoided drawing ideas from other television shows or motion pictures, preferring instead a foundation in real life. "There would be a lot of truth to a good show," Freeman said. "The source material was the world, not the latest hit movie."[5] In drawing from sources grounded in reality *Lou Grant* seemed unusually relevant and timely for a dramatic series at that time.

A script often contained subjects from all three of the basic sources. The 1980 episode titled "Goop" was such a hybrid. It evolved from Freeman's interest in the dilemma of the undercover journalist who becomes involved in people's lives while using deception to gain information. Articles and interviews with journalists showed the *Lou Grant* staff how a reporter could become friends with the people on which he was spying, a situation that ultimately could lead to betrayal. The writers then chose the illegal dumping of toxic waste as the issue the fictional reporter would investigate because it was a problem that had been in the news. Thus, "Goop" shows *Los Angeles Tribune* reporter Billie Newman working undercover at a chemical plant suspected of dumping toxic waste. Gaining the trust and friendship of a young woman, Billie begins to feel uncomfortable in the ruse. Her investigation confirms the company's illegal dumping but also results in the arrest of the young woman's boyfriend. When Billie's identity is revealed, the young woman bitterly rejects her.

Once a subject had been suggested for possible use in a *Lou Grant* story, the series's researcher began a file or notebook for information about the subject and related topics. Michele Gallery, a receptionist at MTM, had been hired as researcher for the series because she had a master's degree and knew how to gather information about a subject. In addition to interviewing journalists and collecting information about the profession Gallery went to libraries in the Los Angeles area to find material on subjects that might be used in episodes.[6] Reynolds kept a list of subjects, many culled from newspapers, for which research material had been collected. "When we'd try to come up with a new story, which was always, I'd run down that list," Reynolds recalled.[7] After he had chosen a subject the staff reviewed the clippings and other material in the subject file. "The story and the characters and how they would relate to our people would eventually emerge," Reynolds said, "and then we could tackle it."[8]

Eventually, research notebooks used by the *Lou Grant* staff contained a broad range of subjects under consideration for episodes. One notebook included these subject headings: infertility, teen suicide, university corruption, gambling, disarmament, discrediting reporters, investigative reporters, troubled kids, personalities, prisons, violent crime, Armenians, cults, human interest, American Indians, architecture, and freedom of the press.[9] Another notebook listed health, anthropology, evolution, television, government programs and policies, technology, insanity and the law, terrorism and radicals, urban ills, Chinatown, and civil rights.[10]

Some of the newspaper and magazine stories placed in the research files focused on single incidents or investigative reports. In files Reynolds donated to the University of California at Los Angeles several finished scripts were accompanied by such research material. For example, a file for the 1980 episode "Blackout" contained articles about the 1977 New York blackout.[11] For the 1981 episode "Boomerang" the file included a lengthy *Mother Jones* article about U.S. companies that sold products overseas even though they had been banned domestically as unsafe.[12] A file labeled "Boys on the Bus," the title of a classic 1973 book on campaign reporting by Timothy Crouse, was created for a 1980 episode titled "Pack"; the file included an outline of the book.[13]

Clippings, anecdotes, and personal experiences were important to the development of *Lou Grant* episodes. Gallery noted, however, that those sources provided only ideas for stories. "We were always interested in not just being topical," she said. "We were always interested in what is the point of that story, and then building our own story that would speak to that point. The show really operated on a good principle. If you see a story that engages you . . . ask yourself, 'What's that saying about how human beings react or what it's like to live in the 1970s or 1980s'?" [14]

After reading the research material collected on a subject the producers and staff writers met. Reynolds used a blackboard to outline the story in the standard one-hour television format of four acts, each with five to six scenes. These sessions usually lasted several hours a day for as long as a week. They were open forums for ideas and points of view about the subject and how the story should be told. "We'd be arguing, giving and taking, pushing and shoving, staring at the wall," Reynolds remembered. [15] At issue was the order of scenes in the script, what scenes provided transitions to move the story from one point to another, and how characters could be used to tell the story. Such issues were addressed in the context of the theme or subject of the episode and how they would provide a dramatic story that would engage a viewer.

Steve Kline, a newspaper reporter who became a story editor and writer on *Lou Grant*, realized that outlining a story made the creative process of writing it much easier to handle. "A creative problem is almost impossible to solve. A creative problem is just daunting," he said. "But if you break a creative problem down to a mechanical problem, any mechanical problem can be solved. And that is what you are doing by putting a story on a blackboard. You're making it a mechanical exercise." [16] Outlining stories and exchanging ideas in a group also helped the staff develop a closeness that made working on *Lou Grant* stimulating. "What bound us all together was an intellectual curiosity, a desire to figure out what these issues meant," recalled April Smith, a staff writer on *Lou Grant*. "The process was . . . exploration for us. It was exciting." [17]

Before outlining a story, the producers assigned a staff writer or an outside writer to an episode. With a staff of four writers handling about four scripts per season, the producers usually needed about six free-lance writers to meet the demand of twenty-two to twenty-four episodes per season. The writer assigned to an episode wrote a first draft of the script from the story outline. The staff critiqued the draft, suggesting revisions. The writer then worked on a second draft, which the producers polished further as they saw fit. [18]

The producers rarely showed scripts to people outside the television production, such as experts on a particular subject. [19] In one instance the director of a rape-treatment center in Santa Monica, California, reviewed the script for the 1981 episode "Rape." In a letter to Freeman the director suggested several changes in scenes at a hospital emergency department "to demonstrate the nurse's sensitivity to the victim's needs."[20] Another time, the producers asked a Los Angeles attorney to review the authenticity of the Armenian subplot in the 1980 episode "Inheritance." The attorney pointed out misspelled words, offered suggestions on accurately depicting an Armenian wedding, and offered to help the actors correctly pronounce foreign words.[21]

In one case script approval was essential to gaining technical assistance. The 1978 episode "Sect" depicted managing editor Charlie Hume's struggle to understand his son's decision to join Hare Krishna. Reynolds wanted permission to film inside a Hare Krishna temple in Los Angeles. "Had we not gotten their script approval, they never would have allowed us in there," Reynolds said. "There was a great deal of negotiation. The only thing we had to assure them was that we wouldn't have the kid departing the movement at the end of the show."[22]

The *Lou Grant* cast saw scripts for the first time during weekly readings over lunch. The actors read the script aloud, which allowed the writing staff and others to hear how the script sounded. "I've never seen that happen anywhere on any other show," director Peter Levin recalled. "I would just sit there and sort of watch, listen and occasionally make a comment."[23] After more polishing the script was ready for production. "When they finished working on that script," Levin added, "it was just beautifully done."[24]

★   ★   ★

Despite the critical role directors played in the production of *Lou Grant,* they did not have the creative power over their work that was common to motion-picture directors. The hierarchy of nearly all television productions of the late 1970s and early 1980s was markedly different from that of motion pictures. Film directors generally exercised creative control over a project. In episodic dramatic television the producer was the creative force behind production. Television directors were hired as needed, moving from series to series during the busy production season.[25]

"You are a free-lancer," noted Alexander Singer, a director of episodic television since the 1960s and, having directed eighteen of its 114 episodes, the most prolific *Lou Grant* director. "The director's role is very considerably constrained. Someone who directs well in series television has displayed a level of resource, courage, and professionalism that is not understood. . . . That good work is done directorially under those circumstances is a triumph."[26] The difference owed in large part to the fact that the producer handled the day-to-day operations of a series throughout its existence. Often, he or she was the creator of the series and served as a writer. Understandably, a producer would want to retain control.[27] "In TV," Burns told an interviewer, "you do not want someone as director who has his own vision of the show."[28]

Once a story for *Lou Grant* had been outlined the producers sent copies to the art director and the heads of departments that prepared sets, costumes, and the various elements of the production. The director of an episode saw the first draft of a script. Directors, however, were hired much earlier. Months before the beginning of a season, the producers reviewed the weekly production schedule and assigned directors to episodes according to their availability. "There was no matching of script with director," Reynolds recalled. "Whatever script was ready fell to the director whose time had come."[29] He tried to hire four accomplished directors each season to serve as his "front-line pitchers."[30] Then he filled in the schedule with other directors, some of them promising beginners.

With a draft of the script in hand directors did not have an opportunity to shape the story or its theme. Instead, the challenge they faced came in guiding actors through the script and meeting the production schedule of seven shooting days. "Directors are journeymen," said Roger Young, the associate producer of *Lou Grant* who became a director on the series.

> In episodic television they're mostly sort of craftsmen. . . . They [the producers of a television series] are not really interested in his creative input from the standpoint of what the show should be about. They're interested in his creative input from the standpoint of how the show can get done in the seven days they have to shoot it. And how it can look as interesting as possible. . . . Alex Singer said to me one time, "We're like the gunfighters in the Old West. They want us to come in, shoot the sheepherders and get out of town."[31]

Of course, the contributions of directors could not be ignored. They were in charge of turning the script from mere words on paper into a dynamic visual form. "As writers," Freeman said, "you know that it doesn't matter what you write. . . . It dies if the director doesn't pull it off."[32]

Compared with other producers of dramatic series, Reynolds was unusually supportive of the directors hired for *Lou Grant*.[33] He valued their contributions and allowed them as much involvement in the editing of episodes and other postproduction work as they chose. "Gene always encouraged the directors to be involved, more than just coming in and telling people where to stand," director Burt Brinckerhoff remembered.[34] Young added: "Gene really respected the director. On a lot of other episodic television the director has to fight like hell to say anything about the editing."[35] The reputation for efficiency *Lou Grant* earned over time also reassured directors. According to Levin, "You walked in to start your shooting day with complete confidence that you had a script that worked, that the writers knew what they were doing, [and] the actors knew what the writers were doing."[36]

Under Reynolds's system a director was largely free to develop a style for telling the story, which included such elements as camera location and movement and how a scene was paced as well. "They did not try to predetermine the stylistic questions that might be a director's choice," Singer said. "They tried only to clarify the content and the level of message they wanted to be delivered."[37] Moreover, Reynolds did not limit the series to a particular look, Brinckerhoff recalled. "He liked for the show to be fluid," the director remembered. "Gene was always encouraging the directors to come up with different styles that were more applicable to the situation, rather than *Dragnet* style—you know, once you saw one show you'd seen them all. These were much more dramas dictated by situation, atmosphere, and time constraints within the stories themselves."[38] Reynolds encouraged younger directors to try different things as long as they met the production schedule. Mel Damski had directed only a handful of television episodes before receiving a *Lou Grant* assignment. Yet Reynolds respected Damski's status as a director and deferred to him. "He gave me a lot of guidance," Damski said, "but he never dictated to me. He gave me the creative freedom to bring a different kind of style to some of my episodes."[39]

Although they came to an episode after it had been written, directors understood what the producers sought in the series. They knew that *Lou Grant* was striving for a realistic portrayal of journalism, human relationships, and current issues. "The general instruction was to treat reality as seriously as possible," Singer said.[40] To ensure as much journalistic realism as possible within the drama the directors often consulted with the show's technical advisers. "If I was insecure about whether so and so would do this or not do this, we consulted," Brinckerhoff said. "There was always someone there trying to keep it in the realm of reality."[41] Singer added, "Very few shows were as careful and attentive to technical advisers as *Lou Grant* was."[42]

At least two directors, Young and Damski, had studied journalism or had worked as reporters. They brought to their work a personal sense of what was realistic. Young had earned a master's degree in journalism and theater at the University of Illinois and had directed news, sports, and documentaries for television before working in dramatic television.[43] Before pursuing a film and television career, Damski had worked for three newspapers and taught journalism in graduate school at the University of Denver. "I had instant credibility with the actors even though I was only thirty years old, much younger than a lot of directors, because they knew I had been a reporter," he said.

> I did a very good job of getting a lot of movement into the show. I knew how chaotic a newsroom was and all the different kinds of behaviors that reporters do. Instead of having Ed do a scene at his desk, I rarely let him sit at his desk. I had him ripping some copy off the AP wire, walking to the coffee machine. . . . I just got the people on their feet a lot more because I knew that's the way it actually was in a newsroom.[44]

Judging from the directing awards bestowed on the series, directors flourished in the *Lou Grant* system. Directors of episodes won the Directors Guild of America Award in 1978, 1979, and 1980.[45] They dominated the Emmy nominations in 1978–79 with three of the four nominations and again in 1979–80 with four of the five nominations, winning the prize that year. Directors gained two nominations in 1980–81 and another nomination in 1981–82.[46] If awards were any measure, the television industry apparently viewed *Lou Grant* as a well-written and well-directed series.

The film shot under the director's guidance was edited into a tightly crafted episode that ran about forty-seven minutes. In other postproduction activities such elements as sound effects and music were added. The quality of the music composed for *Lou Grant* went unheralded outside the television industry. Those within the industry, however, took notice. Composer Patrick Williams, who wrote the *Lou Grant* theme and the music for most of the 114 episodes, was nominated for an Emmy four of the five seasons the series aired, winning the award for the 1979–80 season.[47] A Grammy Award-winning composer, arranger, conductor, and recording artist, Williams was almost the house composer at MTM Studios. He wrote music for *The Mary Tyler Moore Show, The Bob Newhart Show,* and other MTM productions and for numerous other television series and motion pictures as well.[48]

The *Lou Grant* producers permitted Williams to compose music he thought would be appropriate for individual episodes. "In my experience, very, very few shows work that way," Williams said in retrospect. "The lack of creative interference on *Lou Grant* was just wonderful. I didn't have to deal with bureaucratic types who have to show up and get in the way."[49] His work began with a "fine cut," a version of the episode that was nearly ready for broadcast. First, Williams attended a spotting session to determine where music would be placed in the episode and what style of music should accompany scenes. Within seven to ten days of the session, he composed music for the episode. Then, he added the music with a studio orchestra, a process called "scoring."[50]

Intuition guided many of Williams's compositions. As he wrote, he considered the message of the episode and each scene, their underlying themes, and their dramatic impact. "That gives you the keys you need to open the doors where music can enhance the subtext of a film," Williams said. "It can deal very effectively with the emotional content of the piece."[51] Williams had long recognized that his work should accompany the drama rather than stand on its own. The vast differences in the subjects of *Lou Grant* episodes, which changed from week to week, made Williams's work challenging and exciting. "It was really like little movies, one-hour movies," he said.[52]

Music for episodes ranged from ethnic sounds to jazz to classical notes, depending on the content of an episode. In the 1981 episode "Hometown" Lou returns to his boyhood home with a sense of nostalgia warmly conveyed by the music. Set in a Hispanic section of Los Angeles, the 1977 episode "Barrio" features Latin-style rhythms. The music took on a film noir tone when Williams scored 1979's "Hollywood," in which the *Tribune* reporters investigate an old murder mystery tied to a reclusive actress. "It never got into some kind of boring rut that a lot of shows do," Williams said of the series. "It had a freshness about it."[53]

★   ★   ★

A review of a *Lou Grant* script by the Program Practices department at CBS was a routine part of producing the series each season. At the time Program Practices wielded significant power over what the network broadcast to millions of homes. Similar departments, commonly called standards and practices, operated at all three networks. Their staff viewed every commercial and every non-news program to determine whether it conformed to network policies. Because they judged what was appropriate for the television airwaves, standards and practices personnel were commonly referred to as network censors. Indeed, they had the authority to require changes in words, scenes, or entire episodes at various stages, from script to finished product.[54]

After a story for an episode had been discussed, outlined, written, and revised, the series's production office at MTM forwarded the script to the network.[55] The Program Practices editor assigned to the series read the script, noted potential problems, and sent a report to the *Lou Grant* production office. If the producers disagreed with changes suggested by the editor, they called the editor and discussed the problem. If the disagreement could not be resolved, the producers contacted a higher executive at Program Practices to appeal. This process was followed for revised scripts and "rough cuts" of episodes, which lacked music, sound effects, and other elements.[56]

Nearly all the Program Practices reports for *Lou Grant* were written by Carol Isaacs, the editor assigned to the series for most of its five seasons. Isaacs joined CBS in New York in 1969 and moved to the network's Los Angeles office in 1973.[57] Rather than a censor, Isaacs considered herself "just one of the troops" assigned to ensure that what CBS broadcast would not embarrass or upset its affiliates.[58] Although most of the reports were addressed to Reynolds, communication between Program Practices and the *Lou Grant* production office usually involved Isaacs and Freeman, who produced the series in its second through fifth seasons.[59]

Looking back on the relationship between Program Practices and the *Lou Grant* staff, Isaacs and Freeman agreed it usually was cordial but adversarial. Although unable to recall specifics, Isaacs remembered having "pitched battles" with Freeman. "I thought we had a pretty tense kind of relationship," she said. "I thought we always were in some state of disagreement."[60] Freeman, too, recalled "some times when we really lost patience" in dealing with Program Practices. "It was definitely not a help," he said of the censorship division. "I don't think that in any case they ever improved a show. It was annoying most of the time."[61] Isaacs, however, said she hoped that her work did not have a negative impact on the quality of the series. "At the same time, I don't know that I was making any positive contribution," she said. "I was probably hoping to . . . tread lightly and not leave a trace, not have it evident that the heavy hand of the censor was at work."[62]

People who worked in television, particularly for the production companies that created programming, sometimes had intense feelings about Program Practices. "There were those production company folks who loved to hate us," Isaacs recalled, "and then there were those who admired us or enjoyed working with us or thanked us for saving them from themselves."[63] Although some producers believed that censors stifled their creativity, Isaacs contended that she and her colleagues were attempting to ensure the broadcast acceptability of material to prevent problems for affiliate stations.

Not everybody is as hip and happening as folks are in New York or ・ L.A., and stuff they thought was acceptable wasn't necessarily going to be well-received by certain segments of the audience. We didn't want to bland their stuff away, but we wanted to make sure it was kind of acceptable nationwide. It was kind of hard to do, you know. You just hope that shows will find their audience and people who don't like it won't tune in and complain. Know what to expect and move on or know what to expect and stay tuned.[64]

During the years CBS aired *Lou Grant* Program Practices did not have written guidelines for its editors. Areas such as profanity, sex, and violence obviously warranted careful consideration. Isaacs remembered that learning what to allow and what to exclude in *Lou Grant* and other programming involved more than the "gut" feeling of the editor. Decisions also were guided by what other editors in Program Practices were doing, particularly the veterans. If she happened to be unsure of a line of dialogue or a scene, Isaacs read reports on other series or talked to her colleagues. "It was an informal way of picking up the guidelines, which were not installed anywhere until 1986. It was handed down verbally, and every now and then we'd have a staff meeting and many topics would be covered from various perspectives," she said. "After you were here a while, if there was a new person in the department, you might just sort of make yourself available, take them under your wing."[65]

Program Practices reports for *Lou Grant* and other shows were not made public by CBS. When executive producer Reynolds established an archive in his name at the University of California at Los Angeles, his papers included Program Practices reports for 50 of the 114 episodes of *Lou Grant*.[66] The typed reports are one to two pages and bear the signature of Isaacs or another editor. There are no copies of responses from the *Lou Grant* production office. Both Reynolds and Freeman remembered dealing with Isaacs and other editors most often by phone or in person.[67] Although they represent less than half of the reports written for *Lou Grant*, the Program Practices reports in the Gene Reynolds Collection appear to focus on the areas in which censorship by CBS was most active.

Two "routine production cautions" were consistently noted in the reports. First, producers were reminded that all names of businesses and characters should be fictitious. Second, commercial identification of products or services was to be avoided. The reports often cited specific names of characters in scripts. In a report on the 1978 episode "Renewal" Isaacs wrote: "The name Tyler Armitage should be fictitious."[68] A report on the 1978 episode "Sect" said, "Dr. Henderson should be a fictitious name for the L.A. school board member."[69] These and other standard cautions were repeated by Isaacs in every report because different directors and production personnel might be used from week to week.[70]

To determine whether names of businesses or people in *Lou Grant* scripts might coincide with real institutions or people in similar occupations the producers employed a research service.[71] De Forest Research in Los Angeles reviewed every script and, by checking reference materials, cleared names for use. When a name was too similar to that of a real business or person, it was changed to avoid possible defamation or other legal problems.[72] For example, the script for the 1978 episode "Mob" called for a character named Anthony Falcone. "There is only one man by this name in the L.A. area," the de Forest Research report noted. "To avoid any possible conflict suggest: Louis or Mark Falcone."[73]

Commercial identification involved products or services. Understandably, CBS was not inclined to give free advertising in its entertainment programs or to risk alienating advertisers whose products were not featured.[74] The memos from Isaacs often warned that products should be treated with care in scenes. "In Lou's kitchen," Isaacs wrote in the "Sect" memo, "please avoid commercial identification on food containers, etc."[75] The memo for the 1978 episode "Renewal" noted, "At the newsstand, please avoid commercial identification."[76] The report for an episode in 1977 titled "Housewarming" dealt almost exclusively with product identification. It listed numerous items that should be treated generically, including paint cans, breakfast cereal, a clock radio, and laundry detergent.[77]

The memos also noted whether dialogue or direction in scripts referred to specific products. "Please delete 'Coke' mentions," Isaacs wrote in a memo for the 1977 episode "Barrio." "A generic reference should be used."[78] In the 1978 episode "Schools" an exchange between characters Lou Grant and Charlie Hume concerning old cars was cited by Isaacs. "The three Ford mentions create problems for us. Since Lou and Hume are reminiscing about old times, please consider substituting one of the following, now defunct, automobile names: Studebaker, DeSoto, Nash, Hudson."[79] Similarly, she requested a dialogue change in 1980's "Coverup": "Instead of 'Buick,' please have Rossi use an expression like 'big car'."[80] In another report Isaacs said all brand names for medication should be fictitious in the 1978 episode "Pills."[81] The medication was being distributed recklessly by a physician, a storyline to which the drug makers would not want to be linked, Isaacs recalled.[82]

Organizations were subject to similar considerations. To avoid a potential complaint and legal action from the Ku Klux Klan Isaacs suggested that a fictional group be cited in a 1977 script focusing on the leader of an American Nazi group.[83] Although not mentioned in any of the reports in the Reynolds papers, Isaacs remembered overlooking a Red Cross sign on a wall of the newsroom set until someone pointed it out. "I guess I always thought the Red Cross sign was no big deal, but United Way or somebody probably complained, so we probably asked them to take that down eventually," she said. "Maybe we wanted to put up something of a different public-service nature, you know, like conserve water or don't smoke in the forest or Smokey the Bear. Something generic."[84]

Commercial identification dominated Program Practices reports. "I would say that was what they were mostly concerned about," Freeman said in retrospect. "We couldn't use the word *coke* to refer to the drug cocaine. Not because it was in bad taste but because Pepsi would object and say you have given Coke free air time."[85] Looking back, Isaacs noted that commercial identification went directly to CBS's function as a business.

> Suppose Coke is interested in the *Lou Grant* series, or any other series, and they see that Lou Grant is just busily mentioning Pepsi. "Oh, Billie, would you like a Pepsi?" "Hey, Rossi, did you bring any Pepsis over?" Then we'd not be able to sell any time to Coke, for instance. We'd try to avoid that so that the sales department could sell the time. They wouldn't have to go out and explain why Coke or Pepsi or Ford or Chevy was getting free time while they, General Motors or 7-Up, would have to pay for it. It was mostly that.[86]

In another area the use of profanity consistently was cited by Isaacs and other Program Practices editors. Although *damn* and *hell* were permissible in scripts, the words were not to be overused. "The usage of casual profanity, as listed below, needs to be greatly reduced," editor Holly Traister said in a memo for the 1977 episode "Hoax."[87] The script contained, by her count, four uses of the word *hell* and seven of the word *damn*. Casual references to God also were subject to editing. "By at least half, please reduce the six casual usages of 'God,' " Isaacs requested in a report on the 1978 episode "Scandal."[88] Some profanity that appeared in *Lou Grant* scripts was rejected outright. *Bastard* and *goddamn* were two words that were unacceptable for broadcast in any context.[89]

Isaacs recalled that there was a "floating number" for the amount of profanity, depending in part on the series, the time at which it aired, and who spoke the words. Decisions also were based on whether the point could be made with dialogue that did not include the offensive language. "As for the God stuff, we'd get grief from the Bible Belt," she said. "They weren't amused, they just thought that was beyond the pale . . . even though on either coast we probably talk that way."[90] Other words, phrases, and descriptions that were potentially offensive to viewers also merited deletion. A line by character Joe Rossi in the script for 1978's "Spies" caught Isaacs's attention. She wrote in her report: "Rossi's 'Go spit in your hat' too closely resembles a crude expression which is unacceptable for broadcast. Please rework. Something like 'Stick it in your hat' would be acceptable to us."[91] The use of the words *whore* and *whorehouse* was unacceptable, Isaacs noted in reports for 1978's "Hooker" and 1981's "Execution."[92] The ban on *whore* was because of a Program Practices executive's dislike of the word. "Sometimes those things were just personal," Isaacs said.[93]

Humorous dialogue was targeted when it was deemed too racy. In the script for 1977's "Aftershock" a reporter dies in the arms of a prostitute. Reporter Billie Newman cracks, "He died with her boots on," and another character comments, "I guess that's not the worst way to go." Isaacs requested that both lines be removed.[94] She asked for a similar change in 1978's "Babies." "We would appreciate your providing a different porno movie title—one that is less suggestive than the currently proposed 'Four Girls and a Sailor'," she wrote. The title was changed in the final draft to "Swingin' in the Rain."[95]

Sex also was treated with care with actual or suggested nudity forbidden. A reference to pornographic magazines in a 1978 scene merited a caution from Isaacs that the covers of the magazines should be acceptable for broadcast.[96] Similarly, a 1979 reference to women in swimwear also resulted in a caution that they be appropriately attired.[97] When the script for 1977's "Henhouse" called for Rossi to grab Billie's leg, Isaacs asked that "it should be apparent that his hand is on her lower leg."[98] Decisions regarding sex, according to Isaacs, often were based on reaction from viewers who called or wrote CBS. "I guess we tried to take our cue from those who bothered to complain," she said. "We didn't just follow everything they said, but they gave us a notion about how people felt, what they found acceptable, what they disapproved of, what they might tolerate."[99]

Violence was another area that drew particular scrutiny from Program Practices. *Lou Grant* was not an action-adventure series, but it dealt at times with rape, murder, and other violent incidents. Network policy at the time may have called for counting violent acts in an episode and limiting them to three or four, according to Isaacs. Violence also was sanitized, she recalled, with cautions issued about blood and sound effects as well as slow motion or any other effects that tended to sensationalize or heighten violence.[100] One report for *Lou Grant* noted that network policy forbade violent acts in teasers and openings.[101] "We didn't at that time want to use violence as a hook to get people to watch," Isaacs remembered. "That, of course, has since vanished." [102]

In the *Lou Grant* reports Isaacs often cautioned that confrontations between characters should be accomplished without violence. "The action involving the hardhats and Earl should result in no physical harm to Earl," she wrote in response to the 1978 script for "Renewal." [103] Lou Grant discovers he has been misled by an old friend in the 1977 episode "Hoax," but Isaacs cautioned that "Lou should not throw Jack into the sand more than once." [104] In her report on the episode "Barrio" Isaacs suggested restraint in another confrontation: "The following action should be accomplished non-violently: 'Lou grabs Henry by the collar. Lou pushes Henry against the wall'." [105]

Graphic violence was another matter. Isaacs responded to another scene in "Barrio" with this note: "Please avoid gory or sensational aspects of the injured woman '. . . her bruised body lying uncomfortably on sheets, stained brown, here and there, with dried blood'." [106] The violence in the 1978 episode "Prisoner" was problematic. The story involved managing editor Charlie Hume's flashbacks to the time he was tortured in a Latin American country during his tenure as a foreign correspondent. The story also dealt with protests of a visit to the United States by officials of the same nation, fictional Malagua. References to acts of violence in the Program Practices report on "Prisoner" included:

> We caution that when "the noose is dropped around his neck and tightened" Hume should be terrified but he should not be in pain.
>
> In the interest of minimizing depictions of violence, please avoid showing any unnecessary rough handling when we see slides showing "a man being shoved into a car."
>
> Under our current standards, we feel that Bazan's speech contains elements which are too graphic and explicit to be acceptable for broadcast. Please delete the following portions:
>
> "they told her that in a few minutes, when their hands began to roam between her legs, she would sing like a nightingale."
>
> "they attached wires to her *toes* and *her ear*" (delete underscored words).
>
> "woke up and she was lying in a pool of dirty water and her own blood. Then the head man stood on her back and with the help of another man forced a truncheon." [107]

The episode "Rape" presented similar problems for Program Practices. In the story a *Tribune* reporter is raped at knifepoint at her home. Isaacs wrote in her report:

We prefer that the assailant not hold the knife at Sharon's throat and that he not graze her neck with the weapon. And, please do not feature the weapon's glint and gleam.

"I'm not prejudiced or anything. I always get cleaned up." "You liked it, didn't you? Didn't you?"

"You didn't act like you liked it?"

"Do you want to do it again?" "This time you're going to act like you like it."

We feel that the preceding graphic dialogue should be trimmed. Talk of doing it again seems excessive. We prefer to end the scene without that conversation. And, please avoid any action which would suggest repeated rape.

Unfortunately the explicit, "He was in me" is not acceptable for broadcast.[108]

Program Practices at CBS was concerned with racial or ethnic stereotyping as well as sexism. In reaction to complaints that television usually portrayed criminals and other undesirables as members of an ethnic group or minority Program Practices sought balance through other roles in the same episode, Isaacs recalled.

We would try to get positive portrayals elsewhere in the piece, even if they weren't major speaking roles or featured roles. If it was some incidental character—maybe a shopkeeper, maybe a judge, maybe a civil servant, maybe a policeman in the background—just to show these ethnic types in other roles. We wouldn't say no, you can't have any blacks and Latinos as whores, hustlers, murderers, rapists, robbers, whatever. But try to incorporate elsewhere in the piece some positive portrayals as well.[109]

In response to the 1979 script for "Slammer" Isaacs expressed concern in her report that portrayals of ethnic groups in the prison story lacked balance. "Please ensure that ethnic minorities are also shown in significant positive roles," she wrote.[110] When a scene in a 1980 script called for a Mexican busboy, Isaacs suggested that another character representing that ethnic group be added for balance.[111] The script for 1982's "Suspect" included scenes with prostitutes, bringing a similar request: "As scripted, ethnic balance is lacking among the hooker and pimp population (which is all black). Since there is no favorable black character in the story, we urge some adjustment to remedy the situation. Nothing less than a mini-U.N. delegation will do. As always, we trust that the too-short-and-too-tight dresses provide adequate coverage in all respects."[112]

One *Lou Grant* report in 1977 suggested avoiding Italian names for mobsters, and another requested the deletion of the term *Okies* in a script about an itinerant family.[113] On another occasion in 1978 Isaacs suggested changing a reference by publisher Margaret Pynchon to a female reporter from *the girl* to *her* or *the woman*.[114] The word *fag* was cited for removal from a 1979 story about a homosexual police officer, and Isaacs asked that the term *beaner* be deleted from a 1979 script about a prison.[115] Although such words as *fag* and *beaner* probably would be uttered by people with homophobic or racist tendencies, they were considered unsuitable despite the context.

In addition to these policies the Program Practices memos pointed out miscellaneous concerns. Offensive actions, such as the character Dennis "Animal" Price scratching himself, or objects, such as urinals in a men's room, were to be avoided.[116] In a 1977 script Animal throws a half-eaten hot dog out of his car window, an action Isaacs asked to be omitted.[117] It was, she admitted in retrospect, a strictly personal decision.

> I hate littering, I can't stand it. And this is just personal. And they [her colleagues] would always say as I'm sending these notes out, "Oh, come on, Isaacs, you think they're going to do that?" And I said, "Well, I've got to give it a shot." If we show this on television, some people will think it's OK. And it doesn't advance the story, as far as I'm concerned. . . . If I can get rid of it, I'm going to try. They'd say you're out there on your own, we're not going to back you on this one. So I'd send the note. Sometimes it would work, and sometimes it wouldn't.[118]

The Program Practices reports also stressed that procedures by police and other agencies should be portrayed accurately. For example, Isaacs asked in a report on the 1982 episode "Recovery" that "the Assistant Attorney General and his raiding party should depict accurate procedures."[119] Isaacs also requested that information related by dialogue be accurate. Publisher Margaret Pynchon discovers in the "Recovery" episode that her late husband profited from the relocation of Japanese Americans after the Pearl Harbor attack. In her report Isaacs wrote, "Please ensure the accuracy of all figures cited and statements pertaining to relocation/internment policies carried out in 1942."[120]

★   ★   ★

Even though CBS had final say on the content of programs it broadcast, the censors were willing to discuss their concerns. Potential problems were negotiable, and the Program Practices reports reflected this in their language. Most changes were termed "suggestions," and relatively few were deemed "unsuitable for broadcast." The willingness to discuss the proposed changes, according to Isaacs, stemmed from recognition that the department at times misread things. "Sometimes I might speed through this stuff and completely miss what was intended and get the wrong impression and issue some erroneous notes and they'd call me on it," she said. "We weren't always sure we were right."[121] Freeman added: "They could give the most lurid interpretations to things just because of their mind-set. It was very frustrating for us."[122]

The fact that items might be negotiable, however, led to suspicion that some material was included in a script only as a negotiating tool. Isaacs said some television producers would add material they expected to be objectionable, thus allowing them to save the material they really wanted in the episode. "Everybody was playing a game," she contended. "They'd put in more than they wanted so they could get what they wanted. I'm not necessarily saying with these folks, the Lou Grant folks, but sure, there was a lot of that. They probably engaged in it, too, and we knew it, they knew we knew it, and we all played along."[123] Freeman denied playing that game. "They would assume that our script was a negotiating document designed for Program Practices," he said. "And that was frustrating, too, because this is the script and how we think it should be."[124]

Considered in toto, the Program Practices reports indicated that discussing the merits of profanity, sex, violence, stereotyping, and other content issues was a regular part of producing *Lou Grant*. Freeman, however, was unhappy that time was taken away from other elements of the production to deal with Program Practices. In addition, he did not think anything positive resulted from the work of the censors.

> We put so much work into these stories, and when we'd solved them and went through the rewrite process and we felt it was working creatively, it seemed like we had accomplished so much. And then the Program Practices concerns just really seemed like an annoyance when you've done the hard things. Just something that was there to diminish what we'd accomplished, because in a lot of cases the piece just wouldn't be as good. We'd have to use a softer word, change a joke, or not show something that was going on in the world.[125]

Isaacs, however, viewed her role in the process of creating television series with an assembly-line mentality. She served as Program Practices editor for several other programs in addition to *Lou Grant*. For her, the award-winning series was one of many assignments at CBS: "It was just another widget to me." [126]

Program Practices played an important role in the fictional world of *Lou Grant*. Although the creators of the series were firmly in control, CBS censors set boundaries that had a significant impact on what viewers saw during the five years the series was broadcast. Unlike the creators, however, Program Practices was largely unconcerned with such issues as how the series presented journalism. To the censors at CBS, *Lou Grant* was merely a product that needed to be checked lest it dissatisfy merchants or consumers; it was one of many products manufactured by an entertainment factory.

No new television product had a more promising production team in place when *Lou Grant* began filming in the summer of 1977. Presiding were Reynolds, fresh from producing, writing, and directing the hit series *M*A*S*H*, and Brooks and Burns, who had just ended *The Mary Tyler Moore Show*, one of the medium's most acclaimed comedies. Their vision for their new series was clear, and their commitment to it was unshakable. They had assembled a strong production staff and a fine cast, and they were working within a major studio under a network commitment. Yet, a crucial question remained: Would the public tune in once the series began airing? Despite months of preparation and attention to quality, *Lou Grant* remained essentially a gamble.

5

First Season, 1977–1978

Television viewers may have been unsure of what to expect from the new fall series called *Lou Grant*. The situation comedy that spawned it, *The Mary Tyler Moore Show*, had been off the air only two weeks when *Lou Grant* premiered on September 20, 1977.[1] When the cover of the Sunday television section of the *Los Angeles Times* featured a photograph of its star, the cover line read, "Ed Asner in a New Comedy."[2] The *Indianapolis Star* headlined its review, "Grant Even Better in Semi-Serious Show."[3] Even David Shaw, the *Los Angeles Times* reporter who had served as a model for the character Joe Rossi, asked at the time, "Why is it being advertised by CBS as a comedy?"[4] Many viewers probably expected another laugh-filled series from the makers of *The Mary Tyler Moore Show* and *M*A*S*H*. Yet the subjects depicted in the first season were scarcely amusing: American Nazis, terrorism, murder, earthquakes, ghetto life, and wife beating.

Audience expectations were just one of the problems the producers of *Lou Grant* faced that first season. They decided the role of the woman reporter had been miscast and replaced Rebecca Balding ("Carla Mardigian") with Linda Kelsey ("Billie Newman") after just three episodes. The concepts of two other characters proved flawed. Asner, the series's strongest feature, was unsure how to play Lou Grant in a drama. Ratings were so lackluster by midseason that CBS wanted to change the direction of the show to make it more action oriented.

Combined, these problems could have overwhelmed the series and doomed it to cancellation. But there was one bright spot: *Lou Grant* became a hit with television critics. Reviewers across the nation called it one of the better shows, if not the best, on the air. Many applauded the series for its realistic portrayal of journalism, intelligent scripts, and human characters. But critical accolades could not ease all the troubles the series faced in the fall of 1977.

Lou Grant aired Tuesday nights at ten o'clock eastern time. It competed for viewers with ABC's *Family* and NBC's *Police Woman*. In its first full season, *Family* depicted the life of a middle-class California family. Considered well written and well acted, the drama had been a favorite of critics as a six-episode miniseries and had been nominated for a 1976–77 Emmy Award as television's outstanding drama. Its young supporting cast, Gary Frank and Kristy McNichol, had won Emmys for their work.[5] *Police Woman*, in its fourth season, starred Angie Dickinson as a sexy undercover cop.[6]

The first thirteen episodes of *Lou Grant*, which CBS had guaranteed on the strength of the people creating the series, established a content pattern that would be followed for five years. (For a synopsis of each episode of the series, see app. D.) The story lines of all 114 episodes fit into three broad categories: journalism, social issue, and human interest. Journalism episodes focused on the practice of the profession, often dealing with ethical dilemmas or challenges in covering news. Social-issue episodes depicted an important problem facing society, such as hunger or poverty. Human-interest episodes told stories that were compelling but without lasting consequence, much like a feature story in a newspaper. Some episodes were hybrids, their story lines fitting two or all three categories. By drawing on different subjects the series avoided the stale nature of detective, medical, and other single-formula programs. "You want to orchestrate," producer Gene Reynolds said. "It's ideal to have that kind of variety."[7] In the beginning episodes firmly established *Lou Grant* in the context of journalism.

Nearly all *Lou Grant* episodes told two story lines over the hour. By structuring scripts with more than one story line the series mixed its subjects, featured more than one character, matched drama with humor, or counterposed ideas. Contrasting elements often created a deeper level of meaning in an episode. In later seasons the structure of episodes became more sophisticated in their use of subtext. But no matter what the subject, *Lou Grant* told its stories through people. "Every story has got to be a person story to work," Reynolds noted. "That's what drama is all about: some person in the middle of the storm fighting his or her way out of it."[8]

A clever title sequence showing the making of a newspaper introduced each episode of the first season. It began with a lone bird singing in a tree. A logger cuts a tree with a chain saw, and it falls in the forest. Machinery pulls away the logs, dumps them in a river, and sends them along a conveyor belt. Another machine produces large rolls of newsprint, and a truck delivers the rolls to a building. Asner then appears in shirt and tie, signaling the beginning of the titles. A shot of the *Los Angeles Tribune* newsroom appears as the series title is displayed in pica type, the characteristic typeface usually used by newsroom typewriters. Close-up shots introduce the cast: Robert Walden, Rebecca Balding, Mason Adams, Jack Bannon, Daryl Anderson, and Nancy Marchand. The sequence then shifts to a newspaper press room as a conveyor belt carries papers to a bundling machine. The driver of a Volkswagen passes through a quiet neighborhood, tossing a paper in a mud puddle and throwing another on the roof of a house. A man in robe and slippers picks up a paper from his front yard and begins to read it at a breakfast table over coffee. A pair of hands tears off the front page and slips it beneath a bird cage. The camera then pans upward to reveal another singing bird, a wistful reminder of the transitory nature of the daily newspaper (and allowing a bird revenge for chopping down the tree in the first place).[9] In this twenty-seven-shot, sixty-second sequence the producers quickly established the locale of the series and set its wry tone.

★   ★   ★

The first episode, "Cophouse," introduced the cast, established Lou Grant as the series's moral voice and conscience, and showed the newspaper budget meeting as a place where editors debated issues and made news decisions.[10] Before it explored journalism or anything else, the series explained why the *Los Angeles Tribune* hired an unemployed television news director from Minneapolis as its city editor. "Cophouse" opens with a jetliner landing at a Los Angeles airport. Through the terminal walks a surprisingly trim Lou Grant (Asner had lost forty pounds since *The Mary Tyler Moore Show* had ended).[11] Rather than hire an expensive cab with an obnoxious driver, Lou rides a bus downtown. He stops at a row of newspaper racks to buy a copy of the *Tribune*. The rack is open, and Lou hesitatingly takes a newspaper without paying for it. As he walks away he stops and shakes his head. Returning to the rack, Lou drops a coin in its slot. (Viewers may have wondered whether the Lou Grant of *The Mary Tyler Moore Show* would have been so honest.)

In the *Tribune* lobby a guard treats Lou rudely. When the guard asks Lou why he has written his name on a notepad, Lou sarcastically replies, "My Christmas list." Sitting at a newsroom desk while waiting to see managing editor Charlie Hume, Lou is brusquely ordered to move by reporter Joe Rossi. When Lou asks his name, Rossi tells him, "Bella Abzug," the name of a noted New York congresswoman. Scruffy photog-

rapher Dennis "Animal" Price tosses photos on the desk of reporter Carla
Mardigian, belching when Lou tries to introduce himself. "They call
me the Animal," the photographer says. "I can't understand why," Lou
remarks. Rossi yells to Carla, "Hey, gorgeous!" She ignores him and
then says, "Oh, when you said 'gorgeous' I thought you were talking to
yourself." To Lou's amusement Rossi complains that the editors had
"butchered" his story in the morning edition.

Finally, Lou is ushered into Charlie's office. Looking at his trim
friend, Charlie remarks, "I liked you better fat." They reminisce about
old times in the newspaper business (establishing Lou's prebroadcast career as a newspaperman) before Charlie asks Lou why he thinks he can
hold down the job in the *Tribune* city room. Lou replies confidently that
he can handle anything but then is shocked when Charlie tells him the job
is city editor. Charlie, however, is convinced Lou can bring the necessary
leadership to the job. The only problem is Margaret Pynchon, the publisher. After going through three city editors in eight months Charlie is
afraid to hire Lou without taking him to her office on the top floor. "Let's
go to the tower," Charlie says. Lou replies, "I feel like Anne Boleyn."

As they walk to Mrs. Pynchon's office, Charlie warns Lou not to tell
her he has worked in television because of her disdain of the medium.
Instead, he says, "tell her you were in jail." Seated at her desk with a
Yorkshire terrier in her lap, Mrs. Pynchon appears upper-crust and icy.
She and Lou do not hit it off. Stroking her diminutive pet, Mrs. Pynchon
asks, "Do you like dogs?" "Yeah, I like dogs," Lou replies, "big dogs."
Although Charlie is clearly afraid of her, he urges Mrs. Pynchon to hire
Lou. She reluctantly agrees. Back in the city room, Lou meets the affable
assistant city editor, Art Donovan. Pulling out his notepad, Lou asks to
see Rossi, Animal, and the lobby guard. He loosens his tie and prepares
for work.

The sixteen-minute sequence deftly established Lou's credentials as a
journalist and showed why he would be hired after so many years away
from the newspaper business. This exposition was achieved in a humorous
and entertaining way, a testament to a fine script by Leon Tokatyan. It
also gave the first glimpse of the personalities of the regular characters.
Rossi is talented but arrogant, Carla feminine and strong, Animal slovenly, Charlie weak, Donovan friendly and funny, and Mrs. Pynchon
strong-willed. All the characters would change over time, showing different sides of their personalities, but "Cophouse" introduced them much as
they had been outlined in the series's character sketches.

The rest of "Cophouse" explored the problem of divided loyalties for
reporters who cover a beat for many years. George Driscoll, the *Tribune*'s

police reporter for thirty years, has refused to report a sex scandal involving teenage girls on a youth soccer league sponsored by a police department. When Rossi develops the story with his own sources, Lou demands that Driscoll stop covering up for the police. The veteran cophouse reporter sees the officers as friends who would be hurt and angered by the public disclosure of the scandal. Driscoll tells Lou, "My only worth to the paper are my contacts. You take them away from me and I'm finished."

Bias was another issue raised in "Cophouse." Although Lou puts Rossi on the story, he fears that Rossi is not objective. Reading his story later, Lou remarks, "You're really mad at these guys, aren't you? I can tell. . . . I shouldn't be able to tell." He orders Rossi to rewrite the piece, making it more accurate and less sensational. Driscoll eventually writes a story about the scandal and his involvement in keeping it unreported. In a news budget meeting Lou pushes to have the Driscoll story on the front page, but Charlie says Mrs. Pynchon would not approve. The publisher tells Lou she does not want more criticism that the *Tribune* is antipolice. "You mean that we're not going to run the story just because you don't happen to like it?" Lou asks. Mrs. Pynchon replies, "We don't print everything that happens. . . . We often hold back stories I don't like." Furious, Lou reminds her that deciding what is news is his job.

At the time the show aired the conventions of television drama demanded that Lou's point of view win out in the end. Thus, Mrs. Pynchon approves publication of the story, which Lou is surprised to find on page one. Her change of heart probably came because the *Lou Grant* producers did not want to weaken Lou's authority, not because a publisher would recognize the wrongness of her own bias. In fact, Lou seldom lost an argument with Mrs. Pynchon or Charlie, almost always bringing them around to his way of thinking. "You can't set up Lou and then kind of chop him down by saying he's wrong and she's right," Reynolds admitted. "Your hero, to have the story satisfying, carries the day." [12] Although essentially unrealistic, Lou's dominance over his superiors was a necessity if audiences were to respect him.

"Cophouse" also introduced the budget meeting, which appeared in nearly every episode of the series. In the operation of large daily newspapers key editors meet each day in budget meetings to discuss the top news stories and determine where they will appear in the paper. Not only did the budget meetings in "Lou Grant" add realism to the series, Reynolds noted, they were useful for exposition. "You've got a whole bunch of people in there discussing what's going to go in the newspaper," he said, "some happy about it, some unhappy about it, selling, losing, selling, winning, somebody trying to run the thing, making judgments, making decisions. . . . It was a wonderful device of telling the audience, without looking into the lens, what the hell's going on." [13]

When episodes focused on journalism or social issues, the budget meetings often were used to introduce opposing arguments. The meetings also allowed Lou to be the voice of reason without giving an unwarranted lecture on a subject. Charlie Hume's character gained strength from the meetings because he usually presided over them.

Other early episodes of *Lou Grant* portrayed ethical and moral dilemmas that face many journalists. How news is reported and the responsibilities of the news media were primary elements of the episodes "Hostages" and "Nazi." [14] In "Hostages" a young man, Andrew Martin, angered by news coverage of his brother's shooting death in a holdup, takes Rossi at gunpoint to the newspaper office. He holds *Tribune* staffers hostage until they agree to write a story that vindicates his brother, whom he claims was murdered by a store clerk who owed the youth money. As the staff tries to meet his demands television coverage of the incident becomes sensationalized and inaccurate. One television reporter describes Andrew as "heavily armed" and leading a "daring daylight raid" into the newspaper.

Lou agrees to print a story that meets Andrew's terms, but he does not reveal that it will appear only in the first one hundred copies. Television reporters, however, broadcast the ruse, enraging the gunman. He surrenders only after Mrs. Pynchon assures him that a detailed story about his brother's death will be published. Later, Mrs. Pynchon directs the staff to publish the story on inside pages to play down the incident. "We're not going to glamorize terrorism," she says. "I don't want it to be possible for every sorry person with a gun to come in here, [and] use my paper to grab his little moment of pathetic glory."

While probing why a Jewish man would become the leader of an American Nazi group, "Nazi" looked at news coverage and its impact. Charlie is concerned about publicizing the Nazi group's demonstrations, even though one has resulted in a riot. Lou disagrees, stating that "news is news." When Billie is assigned a feature on the leader of the group, Donald Stryker, she discovers that he is Jewish. Stryker threatens her and then pleads with her (and later with Lou) not to report his background. On the day the story appears Lou gently tells Billie that Stryker has killed himself. She is shaken, but Lou assures her it is not her fault. "We can't weigh each story and say maybe we shouldn't print it because somebody might get hurt," he says. "Sometimes people do get hurt. Sometimes careers are ruined, governments are brought down. But if the story is there, we have to print it. It's our job. If you're going to be in this business, you'll have to learn to handle it."

Three episodes examined the pitfalls of news gathering. In "Hoax" an old friend of Lou's named Jack Riley leads the *Tribune* on a wild-goose chase for a missing industrialist.[15] Riley takes Lou and Rossi to the Caribbean for a promised rendezvous with the industrialist. When the man's body turns up in a car accident in a remote part of Los Angeles, Riley admits he was lying to bring fun and excitement to his life. Lou later proposes that the *Tribune* write about being hoaxed. "Write your story, Mr. Grant," Mrs. Pynchon says. "But at the *Tribune* we insist on accuracy. Be sure you make yourself look like a complete ass."

In "Scoop" Rossi makes errors in breaking-news stories because he is in such a hurry to beat competitors, especially television.[16] At one point Lou and Charlie reminisce about the days when reporters would do almost anything to get a story. "We've grown up now," Charlie says. "The scoop mentality is dead. I mean, today it's more important to be right than be first. And that makes our whole profession more respectable." Lou adds, "And a lot less fun." Nonetheless, Rossi pays a man fifty dollars to use his telephone and then cuts the cord so a competing reporter cannot call in a story. Then, his scoop about a motorcycle policeman's fatal accident turns out to be wrong; the officer survived. An angry Mrs. Pynchon declares, "I want truth, not speed. I want good reporting, not good fiction."

The *Tribune* staff followed two stories in "Christmas," both of which took unexpected twists.[17] Billie's feature about a poor family camping beside a Los Angeles highway results in nearly five thousand dollars in donations from readers. Then, Billie discovers the family makes a living going from city to city, drumming up publicity and cash from sympathetic readers. Rossi, meanwhile, discovers that a low-level state official is a bigamist with two families, one in Los Angeles and the other in Sacramento. In a rare display of sympathy apparently fueled by the holiday season he decides not to reveal the chicanery to readers or his editors.

Newsroom sexism was revealed in "Henhouse."[18] The episode, which introduces Billie as a feature writer, hinges on the sexism of Lou and Rossi. Lou refers to the *Tribune's* Today section as "the women's section" and even calls its offices "a henhouse." Neither he nor Rossi seems to believe a woman can cover a hard-news story as well as a man. Rossi says, "I can't picture a reporter named Billie." He grudgingly works with her on the mysterious death of a prominent playwright. By the end of the episode Billie has proved herself a match for Rossi in reporting skills. Lou also admits he was wrong about her and offers her a job covering news on the city staff.

The story lines of "Psych-Out" touched on two issues in journalism: undercover reporting and the chilling factor caused by lawsuits.[19] Without his editors' knowledge Rossi checks into a mental hospital suspected of overmedicating patients and other abuses. After he gathers firsthand evidence he is prohibited from leaving and becomes an overmedicated patient himself. Meanwhile, the *Tribune* is threatened with a lawsuit by an antiobscenity crusader unhappy with coverage of the issue. When a *Tribune* lawyer begins to edit Billie's stories to remove anything that might offend the crusader, Lou and Charlie become concerned that the threat of litigation is hurting the *Tribune*. Charlie argues, "The point is whether we can allow him to dictate what we print by threatening to sue us." Noting that defending a libel suit costs money regardless of its merits and outcome, Mrs. Pynchon says, "The point is whether we can afford to go to trial. . . . The First Amendment does not pay court costs." Lou comes to Rossi's rescue and later spends the evening with the *Tribune* lawyer going over Rossi's expose.

Although journalism issues dominated the early episodes of *Lou Grant*, three shows depicted social issues. "Barrio" explored youth gangs in the Latino district of Los Angeles,[20] "Housewarming" portrayed wife beating, and "Judge" examined the problem of incompetent judges.[21] Only one early episode, "Aftershock," took a human-interest approach to its story lines.[22] The widow of a *Tribune* staffer relies on Lou for guidance and emotional support in the aftermath of her husband's death. Meanwhile, a series of mild earthquakes leads to a story in the paper about a researcher who claims his cockroaches can be used to predict impending tremors. The episode is played mostly for comedy as Lou tries to distance himself from the clinging woman and learns to live in earthquake-prone Los Angeles.

The producers of *Lou Grant* prided themselves on developing stories that stemmed from actual incidents. Episodes often had their roots in well-publicized events or anecdotes told by journalists to series researchers. For instance, the plot of "Nazi" is nearly identical to a 1965 incident involving a *New York Times* reporter whose story led to the suicide of a Jewish Nazi. The anecdote was reported in *The Kingdom and the Power*, a book about the *New York Times* that was read by series researchers.[23] "Hoax" drew its inspiration from a similar incident in which the *Los Angeles Times* was hoodwinked into following a tip that kidnapped newspaper heiress Patty Hearst was being held in Hong Kong.[24] A sex scandal cover-up by a police reporter, similar to that depicted in "Cophouse," was related by *Times* reporters who talked to *Lou Grant* researchers.[25] The bigamy story line depicted in "Christmas" may have stemmed from a similar incident that occurred in South Dakota in 1976. Unlike the television version, however, the real incident was reported by a newspaper (which then was sued after the official died of a heart attack).[26]

Research did not guarantee a totally realistic portrayal of journalism because realism often conflicted with the dramatic requirements of the television series. Hence, journalists pointed out instances in which story-telling superseded reality. Shaw, the *Los Angeles Times* reporter, viewed the first five episodes of *Lou Grant* before they aired. The producers had asked him to critique the episodes, and his five-page memo to Reynolds cited twenty-six actions he thought "didn't ring true." Shaw's points ranged from unrealistic dialogue by reporters to unlikely actions by news sources and a newspaper publisher.[27]

For instance, he contended that a reporter who refused an assignment as Driscoll did in "Cophouse" would be fired immediately. The first episode, he believed, also gave the impression that a publisher dictates news coverage and slants it to fit her views, which he said was not accurate. No city editor would be unaware of what stories were appearing on the front page, he continued, as Lou had been at the end of "Cophouse." Shaw claimed that a hostile subject would have smashed a reporter's tape recorder instead of returning it as the Nazi had done in "Nazi." In addition, he did not believe a young reporter would have shared the old-fashioned view that women were not cut out to be news reporters, as in the plot of "Henhouse."

Despite his sometimes sharp comments (he called one plot development "bullshit"), Shaw assured Reynolds that he had enjoyed the episodes enormously and termed his criticisms "mostly nitpicks." Other reporters at the *Los Angeles Times* did not share his enthusiasm for the first episode. He told Reynolds that eight of the ten people he queried thought the opening episode was "dull, slow-moving, not funny enough, filled with hoary old newspaper cliches."[28] He dismissed their criticism, concluding, "There is much sour grapes and envy there, methinks."[29]

Judging from the reviews of numerous television critics, the under-whelmed *Times* reporters were in a minority in their low opinion of the show. Several critics around the country called *Lou Grant* one of television's best series and praised its efforts to be accurate in its depictions of journalism. "It is not only the best thing to hit the television screen this season," wrote *Washington Star* critic Judy Flander, "there's nothing else that's even close to it."[30] Tom Shales of the *Washington Post* agreed: " 'Lou Grant' is the best new show of the season. . . . There's not a prime-time network entertainment series more intelligently crafted or more demonstrably concerned with human nature."[31] Associated Press television critic Jay Sharbutt called the series "a happy surprise—a well-acted, reasonably realistic depiction of modern, big-city newspapering."[32]

Despite favorable reviews, some critics cited what they believed were inaccuracies in the newspaper drama's portrayal of the profession. They contended: Lou was not grumpy enough to be a city editor, Rossi's character was a cliché, Lou's desk looked too neat, the *Tribune* had too few staffers for a metropolitan newspaper, what passed as good writing at the *Tribune* was actually bad, and Lou spent too much time away from the newsroom.[33] Yet most were forgiving of these and other unrealistic moments in *Lou Grant*, acknowledging that the medium could not be completely accurate. "Who are we to complain?" asked Marvin Kitman of *Newsday*. "TV does every profession wrong. . . . Are we asking them to show the routine drudgery?"[34] Mike Drew of the *Milwaukee Journal* wrote, "On commercial TV, 'Lou Grant' is as close to what happens around here as you're likely to get."[35]

Other critics were impressed that *Lou Grant* brought out the human element of a newsroom and treated its audience with respect. "In the one episode, there were dozens of little decisions, dilemmas and dastardly deeds that newspaper people see constantly," claimed *Austin American-Statesman* critic Ray Mariotti. "*The American-Statesman* newsroom was buzzing the next day over the remarkably human picture drawn by the show."[36] Gary Deeb of the *Chicago Tribune* wrote, " 'Lou Grant' not only is a triumph for intelligent programming, it's also proof that TV can stray from its tested formulas and still present a gripping story with mass-audience appeal."[37]

★   ★   ★

The positive reaction of critics was welcomed by a television production shaken by several setbacks during its first summer and fall of production. Although *Lou Grant* premiered in September, the series had begun production in late June.[38] Almost immediately, the creators of the series were concerned with Balding's portrayal of Carla Mardigian. "From the very first day of dailies, I said, 'This is not working'," recalled Tokatyan, who developed the series and wrote the first episode. "Walden chewed her up. She looked like she was going to break into tears any second. She was taking it too seriously."[39] Indeed, Balding appeared almost delicate in the first three episodes. Reynolds saw the problem not so much as Balding failing to hold her own against Walden but as being unconvincing in the role of a woman reporter.[40]

While the character sketch had contended that Carla would not be put down as a *ballsy chick*,[41] Balding used the term to explain, in part, why she was fired from the show after three episodes. For the first episode filmed, "Hoax," she followed director Jay Sandrich's suggestion to be more cute than tough. "I honestly think that maybe I got off on the wrong foot with the first show," she said in retrospect. "I wanted to go in a different direction, which essentially is going against type, going against the way I look."[42] She met with the producers after the filming of "Hoax," which would be aired after the pilot, "Cophouse," and another episode, "Hostage." "The producers called me into the office and talked to me and said, 'You know, what you did in this isn't why we cast you'," she recalled. " 'You had a different quality in your reading we'd like to see . . . more gutsy, ballsy'."[43]

By the time "Hostage" was filmed in mid-July[44] the producers had decided to replace Balding. She had played a minor role in each of the three episodes filmed by then—none had yet aired—and she wondered when a script would showcase Carla. She remembered the producers asking to meet with her after the day's shooting. They insisted that they come to her trailer at MTM Studios rather than meeting her at the production offices, which made her nervous.

> They came to the trailer and I just looked at their faces, the three of them. I said, "Oh, my God, you guys are going to fire me." And they said, "Well, we don't like to think of it that way, we just like to think of it as letting you go." . . . I know how badly they felt. I mean, God, what an awful thing to have to do, come tell some poor little girl who thinks she's got the world on a string she doesn't, that she's not part of this thing anymore.[45]

The producers told Balding, then twenty-eight, that she had poor chemistry with Walden and appeared too young and vulnerable, which might cause the audience to be concerned for her when she got into tough situations.[46]

Reflecting on her work on *Lou Grant*, Balding acknowledged that she had been too self-conscious in her first major television role. "Working in the newsroom set, there were jillions of people and I was obsessed. I was thinking all the time, 'You can't screw up, Rebecca, you've gotta . . .' and I think that stopped me from doing my best work, certainly."[47] Not only was she fired that day, but a tree on the MTM lot fell on her roadster and a toothache resulted in a root canal.

"Well, I cried all night," Balding remembered. "I was very well-behaved when they were firing me. I heard later they were so relieved."[48] Although hurt, she tried not to be bitter and made a point of attending some *Lou Grant* parties to show there were no hard feelings. Her career continued with a television movie and a horror film, and she went on to appear in the series *Soap* for three years. "Your first series is like your first love affair," she said. "It just always will have a special place in my heart. Plus Ed. Ed and I got along really well."[49]

Finding a replacement for Balding concerned the producers when they looked for an actress for the role of reporter Billie Newman in the episode "Henhouse."[50] To play Billie, Reynolds wanted Kelsey, who had worked on *M*A*S*H*. She had been his first choice for the role of Carla, but she had been scratched from the list of actresses while Reynolds was out of town.[51] Kelsey's agent called her about reading for a guest role on Asner's new series, and she did so without knowing that the producers were looking for a replacement for Balding. She was surprised to find several other actresses reading for the part. Then, she was asked to read again for the producers and other studio personnel. "I thought, 'Boy, they're really careful how they cast these guest parts'," she remembered. "And then they asked me all these questions—'This is kind of comedic, but do you have experience doing heavy drama'?"[52]

To the producers Kelsey brought to the role of a woman reporter what Balding had lacked. "Linda Kelsey somehow had the maturity, the intelligence, the point of view, the kind of sentiment that was very believable," Reynolds said.[53] Her agent called on a Friday with the producers' offer for the part in the episode and a continuing role in *Lou Grant* as well. Although she asked for the weekend to consider the offer, Kelsey decided within hours of the call to accept. " 'You jerk'," she recalled telling herself. " 'You have to do this. This is MTM, this is Ed Asner, this is brilliant writing. This is a wonderful part. What are you waiting for'?"[54] Kelsey, who had appeared in a guest role in *The Mary Tyler Moore Show* three years earlier, thus became *Tribune* reporter Billie Newman. Kelsey, born in Minneapolis, Minnesota, on July 28, 1946, had appeared on *The Rockford Files, Barnaby Jones,* and several other series and in television movies.[55]

No character sketch had been created for the character Billie Newman; one was never written. The "Henhouse" script described her only as "an attractive woman in her late twenties."[56] Set to begin work on the show in a week, Kelsey immediately began researching journalism. The producers showed her the film *All the President's Men*, but she was not comfortable with her lack of firsthand knowledge.[57] She traveled to San Jose, California, and was granted permission to "hang out" at the local newspaper. While making the rounds on the police beat, Kelsey was introduced as a cub reporter for the *Los Angeles Tribune*. She then visited the *San Francisco Chronicle*, talking to reporters and editors and gaining a sense of the activity in a newsroom. "I work from various ways, but I need to know what it feels like and what the sounds are and what it looks like," the actress said. "I wanted just to sit quietly and watch the paper go through deadline."[58] Kelsey returned to Los Angeles and began what would become a five-year stay on *Lou Grant*.

The characterization of Charlie Hume posed another problem for the producers. Charlie's cautious and insecure nature came across clearly in the first episodes, so much so that his change from a weak-willed managing editor to a stronger character was an obvious change in the first season. "We saw him as being totally under the thumb of the publisher," Tokatyan said, "someone who was desperately afraid of losing his job because he had a family."[59] Adams did not like playing Charlie as a buffoon or wimp, and he lobbied against that characterization. "This guy was managing editor of a newspaper. He's the major general. You don't have a wimpy managing editor," Adams said. "He didn't remain a nervous, nail-biting fellow too long."[60]

Charlie's spineless nature also hurt the character's usefulness in episodes. "After a while it got in the way," Tokatyan said, "because we needed someone on Ed's level being able to talk back and forth."[61] These problems were spotted quickly, according to Reynolds, and a stronger side of Charlie soon emerged.[62] By the episode "Scoop," the eighth to air, Charlie was standing up to Mrs. Pynchon and offering forceful arguments to support positions he and Lou favored. In "Sports," the fifteenth episode to air, Lou and Art Donovan describe Charlie as an evenhanded but firm boss. "When Charlie gets through working you over," Lou says, "you never know if you've been assaulted or massaged." Donovan adds: "I'd hate to get chewed out by Charlie 'cause he's kind and calm. You almost hate yourself for putting him through it."[63]

If Charlie's weak-willed ways embarrassed or angered senior editors around the country early in the series, they did not protest to the producers. Many photographers, however, complained bitterly about the use of Dennis "Animal" Price to portray their profession. In the five-year run of the series the only consistent note of unhappiness among journalists appeared to revolve around a news photographer perceived by many as a sloppy, unshaven, unreformed hippie. "Of all the complaints from America, that was the predominant complaint," Reynolds recalled. " 'Why do you call my noble profession this guy, this symbol of my profession, Animal'?"[64] The root of the problem, the producer believed, was the nickname. "If he'd been called Benny, I don't think anybody would have said, 'How dare you dress this way'," he said. "I think the word colored the appearance."[65]

News Photographer, a magazine published by the National Press Photographers Association, received numerous letters of complaint about Animal's nickname and slovenly appearance. Several appeared in the April 1978 issue, which was published as the first season ended. "One of the most disgusting things about television . . . is the Lou Grant show's portrayal of a newspaper photographer named Animal," one photographer wrote. "Collectively and individually we cannot stand by and watch our image be so defamed."[66] Another photographer asked, "Long after Lou Grant leaves the network will we carry the stigma his show has given us in the public eye?"[67] In letters published in subsequent issues of the magazine some photographers pointed out that they had worked with similar breeds. "As far as I am concerned," one wrote, "some of them actually do look like him!"[68] One photographer admonished his colleagues: "It is a fact of life that such an animal exists and is alive and well in the field. . . . If we don't like it, we should get our own act together by cleaning up our dress and appearance before we condemn CBS."[69]

Among the letters of complaint sent to the *Lou Grant* production office was one from the Professional Photographers Society of New York expressing "our deep feeling of resentment" toward Animal. "In no way does your character resemble any professional photographer I know," stated J. Robert Mantler, a spokesman for the New York group. "It is cruel and thoughtless to take away a person's dignity in so general a manner."[70] Mantler contended that the seventeen-thousand-member Professional Photographers Association of America would be urged to write the program's sponsors to complain. In the history of the series it would not be the only call to pressure sponsors of *Lou Grant* because of something viewers disliked about the show.

Daryl Anderson recalled: "For every one of those [negative letters] I got lots of letters asking for pictures. I got one that said, 'We'll hang it maybe right next to David Kennerly [a Pulitzer Prize-winning photographer]'."[71] Reynolds dismissed the criticism from photographers as petty and small. "We never did play the guy grotesque," he said. "We never had him spilling food out of his mouth and so forth. He was a very good guy and always doing a good job, very professional, very capable and respected."[72] Reynolds contended the complaints had no impact on the series or the Animal character. Anderson, however, recalled that the other characters stopped referring in scripts to Animal as being dirty, his clothes became less ratty, and his stubble became a full beard by the fourth season.[73]

★   ★   ★

Replacing Balding and retooling characters paled in comparison to the most serious problem *Lou Grant* faced midway through the season. Its weekly rating, which was the measure of how many households watched the show, was disappointing. The first episode had scored a promising 19.9 rating and a 34 share.[74] According to the A. C. Nielsen Company, the firm that tracked television audiences, each rating point represented 729,000 homes. A share represented the percentage of televisions in use that were tuned to a particular program.[75] Thus, 14.5 million households, or about 1 out of 3 households watching television that evening, had seen the first episode. That was good enough for *Lou Grant* to beat its head-to-head competitors and rank as the nineteenth-most-watched television show of the week.[76]

Lou Grant, however, failed to remain in the top twenty programs. Unusually stiff competition from special broadcasts may have hurt the show's ability to build an audience. In weeks four and five of the new season *Lou Grant* competed with the first and final games of the World Series.[77] In week nine *Lou Grant* lost its time period to the final installment of NBC's four-part presentation of *The Godfather,* the top box-office movie of that time.[78] Through November 20, the end of the ninth week of the new season, *Lou Grant* had a 16.4 average rating, ranking forty-sixth out of seventy-three television series. The only good news was that *Lou Grant* was the sixth-most-watched of twenty-three new television series. Meanwhile, its competitor on ABC, *Family,* had averaged a 19 rating to rank twenty-ninth. NBC's *Police Woman* was just below *Lou Grant* at forty-eighth with an average rating of 16.[79]

The weak ratings midway through the season concerned CBS executives, and they called a fall 1977 meeting with MTM President Grant Tinker and the *Lou Grant* producers.[80] The network executives, Allan Burns recalled, did not think there was enough action in the series. The solution they offered was to turn Lou Grant from an editor to a reporter, Burns remembered. "They told us all the mistakes that we were making, that we had to get Lou out from behind that desk and get him on the streets and make him more of a Kojak [the title character of a popular CBS police series]," he recalled. "We said, 'Wait a minute. Newspaper editors don't do that. They don't go out and investigate things on their own. It would violate everything we were trying to do.' "[81] The series's subtle, unsensational tone also concerned the CBS executives. "They said, 'What you are giving us is the *New York Times*, and what people read is the *Daily News*'," Burns said.[82]

Tinker and the producers listened to the criticism and suggestions. "Their real complaint was that the thing wasn't attracting enough audience," he recalled. "That, to a network, means you must not be doing what you should be doing, so let's do something else."[83] But Tinker believed the producers, whom he considered the best in television, were doing the series as well as it could be done. Thus, he told the executives that the producers would continue doing the show as they had and that CBS could cancel the series if that was not satisfactory. In retrospect Tinker thought the possibility of losing the creative minds behind *Lou Grant* to another network forced the CBS executives to drop their demands. "They backed down, which is a rare pleasure, if you're a producer, to cow a network," he said. "It was kind of like playing with fire to talk to a network the way we finally did that day."[84]

Despite his support Tinker had doubts about the series. He had been disappointed by the transition of the Lou Grant character from *The Mary Tyler Moore Show* to an hour-long drama. The series seemed thin to him and barely suggested the operations of a real newspaper. "My bravado at CBS in that meeting came more out of my confidence in the guys than my judgment at that moment about the show," he said.[85] Had the series not starred Asner as Lou Grant, a character audiences had enjoyed for seven years, Tinker doubted the show would have survived.[86]

Ratings remained a problem through the end of the year. In the first thirteen weeks of the 1977–78 season *Lou Grant* averaged a 17.1 rating to rank forty-fourth of seventy-eight television series. *Family* was twenty-fourth with an average rating of 19.8, and *Police Woman* fell to forty-ninth with an average rating of 16.5.[87] Had *Lou Grant* not had the thirteen-episode commitment from CBS (nine more were subsequently ordered), it might have been canceled by November along with six of the network's other new shows.

Asner was among those feeling the pressure of working hard on a series that was faring poorly in the ratings. He remembered attending a CBS party about that time and seeing Bud Grant, the network's top programming executive. Grant asked him why he looked sad, and Asner admitted he was worried about the series. "He said, 'Ahh, don't worry about it. If it doesn't work out, we'll do something else,' " Asner recalled. "And I thought, 'Jesus Christ, he didn't understand'."[88]

Throughout the first half of the season Asner struggled with his old comedy role and new dramatic setting. Having lost forty pounds to create a different image, he was physically weak when the series began. The set was chaotic, he said, with Balding being fired, crew members being replaced, and MTM groping its way with its first hour-long drama. "I must say, I'm very proud of what the shows looked like, as much agony as I was in," Asner said.[89] In the middle of the season he hit on a way to cope with the acting challenge before him. He had drawn on the image of his fun-loving brothers to play the comedic Lou Grant. "For the hour Lou Grant," Asner recalled, "I said, 'I've got to play this with my own soul.' So I went and worked. You're not going to notice any difference . . . but I relaxed. Somehow, I got myself to relax, to use myself more intensively."[90]

As Asner subtly changed his approach to the role CBS changed its scheduling scheme. The network announced in December that *Lou Grant* would move from Tuesday night to Monday night in January. Its new competitors would be ABC specials and NBC movies.[91] Even before the move, *Lou Grant* began to rise in the weekly ratings. The series won its time period in week fifteen of the season (the first week of the new year), and it ranked as the eleventh most popular show the following week, its best showing so far.[92] " 'Lou Grant' has really caught on," *Variety* reported in January 1978, "and the thought is that it is a hit show now (and it's obvious that CBS is placing sizable stakes that this evaluation is correct)."[93] In its new time period of ten o'clock eastern time on Mondays, the series soon tied for twelfth place in the weekly ratings.[94]

Why had more viewers suddenly "discovered" the series? Asner believed the show's stories were faster paced and its characters stronger and more appealing by the second half of the season.[95] Reynolds thought that viewers, irritated because *Lou Grant* was not a comedy in the *Mary Tyler Moore* vein, may have begun to accept the series on its own merits.[96] Without the special programs that had competed against *Lou Grant* in the first months it aired viewers may have settled into the habit of watching the series. Fans of *Police Woman* also may have tuned into *Lou Grant* when the crime drama moved in December to another night. Moreover, when *Lou Grant* moved to Monday night, it no longer faced competition from *Family*, a show that attracted the same type of viewer. Continuing critical acclaim and favorable word of mouth also may have prompted the public to watch.

★ ★ ★

The so-called "second season" in television began in the first week of 1978. The three networks had reworked their schedules, canceling some programs and moving others to new time periods. Five of the remaining nine episodes of *Lou Grant* that aired in the first three months of 1978 drew heavily on the journalism setting. The other four shows were divided evenly between social-issue themes and human-interest stories.

Staff dedication and the excitement of covering a breaking news story fueled the episode "Airliner."[97] In the story *Tribune* reporters and editors break away from their personal activities one evening when an airliner bound from Paris to Los Angeles cannot lower its landing gear. The possibility of a disaster and its impact on the news spurs an exchange between Charlie and Lou about the nature of news and the journalist. "On the way down here," Charlie admits, "I caught myself thinking we had such a slow news day, now we'd have something decent for the front page. And then I thought, 'How ghoulish'." Lou replies, "That's this business. We don't stop to think about how much of it is dealing with other people's tragedies." The event becomes personal (and the episode more dramatic) when they discover that Charlie's daughter is aboard.

The *Tribune* staff divides the chores of covering the event. Within hours the newsroom is buzzing with activity. Mrs. Pynchon, surveying the newsroom, marvels at their dedication. "Here it is, almost midnight, and all those people out there working, doing their jobs, just as if it were another normal deadline," she says. "Mr. Grant said most of them didn't need to be called in. They came in when they heard. No histrionics, no big to-do. At their desks working, doing whatever is asked of them. I think it's at times like these that I love this business best." The plane lands safely, Charlie and his daughter are reunited, another edition of the *Tribune* is finished, and the weary but proud journalists go home.

The episode "Scandal" was not nearly as complimentary about all journalists, but it indicated the importance of integrity for a newspaper.[98] The story shows a new *Tribune* reporter, Liz Harrison, gaining inside information about a city supervisor's campaign for reelection by sleeping with him. Lou sees the relationship as a conflict of interest. "Here you are," he tells her, "with emotional reasons to be loyal to the guy, and he's giving you information." Later, Lou quotes what he calls an old editor's saying: "You can get romantically involved with elephants, but don't cover the circus." Charlie and Mrs. Pynchon agree that the newspaper's integrity is at stake and fire Liz.

"Scandal" apparently had its roots in a controversy stemming from the romantic relationship between a *Philadelphia Inquirer* political reporter, Laura Foreman, and a Pennsylvania state senator, Henry Cianfrani. In an August 1977 story about a federal tax probe of Cianfrani published just six months before "Scandal" aired the *Inquirer* reported that Foreman had accepted gifts worth twenty thousand dollars from the senator, who had been both a news source and a subject for her stories on local politics. The *Inquirer* did not learn about Foreman's relationship with Cianfrani until after she had been assigned to another beat. The newspaper took no action against her, and she joined the Washington staff of the *New York Times* in early 1977. After the *Inquirer* story detailed her relationship with the senator, the *Times* forced Foreman to resign because she was an embarrassment to the newspaper.[99]

"Spies" explored the news media's responsibilities to government and their role as an independent institution.[100] The *Tribune* staff is divided over whether to honor a request from the Central Intelligence Agency not to investigate two drug arrests later linked to an espionage scheme. Mrs. Pynchon notes that in the past the *Tribune*, like many other newspapers, routinely provided information to the CIA. Lou does not agree with Charlie that issues of national security are an automatic consideration. "Every time anyone mentions national security," Lou says, "we shut our eyes and turn our heads. Nobody even wants to know the time of day. I say let's open our eyes and keep going."

Later, reporter George Driscoll tells Lou he sees nothing wrong with helping the government. "Why should I have to choose between being a newspaperman and being an American?" Lou responds, "Do you think it's possible to have a relationship with the CIA and still look the public in the eye when everybody knows the CIA used its ties with the media to angle news coverage its way?" As they pursue the story, the staff becomes paranoid that someone at the paper is a CIA operative. Even Charlie and Lou suspect each other at one point. When the CIA releases the drug suspects because it lacks evidence and does not want to make possible espionage public, the *Tribune's* investigation ends. Yet Lou still wonders whether there is a CIA plant in the newsroom.

The series apparently drew inspiration from a landmark privacy case when crafting the episode "Hero."[101] In 1975 a San Francisco man may have saved the life of President Gerald R. Ford by thwarting an assassination attempt. Media coverage later revealed the man's homosexuality, and he sued for invasion of privacy. The case resulted in a United States Supreme Court decision defending the media's right to report news about public figures, even when people unwillingly become public figures.[102] In "Hero" a bystander knocks down a would-be assassin's gun, saving the life of a gubernatorial candidate. When the *Tribune* reveals that the hero is an investment counselor with a criminal record, he loses clients and his girlfriend. Only after the *Tribune* carries a story about the personal damage that the unwanted fame has brought the hero does he gain new clients and the confidence of former ones.

The episode "Sports" examined the nature of sports reporting and how a newspaper's actions can raise the ire of readers.[103] It also revisited the "Cophouse" theme of biased reporting. The *Tribune*'s veteran sportswriter ignores reports of wrongdoing in a popular college sports program, saying a story will hurt the team and anger readers. Charlie agrees with Lou that sports should be covered with the same zeal used for other news. "We can't be against hustling, manipulation, payola, crookedness on the front page and for it on the sports page," Charlie says. A story by the city staff results in hundreds of canceled subscriptions and even a death threat against Lou.

The plot of "Sports" resembled an incident involving the University of Oklahoma football program and the *Oklahoma City Times*. On October 25, 1976, little more than one year before "Sports" aired, the *Times* reported that the National Collegiate Athletic Association was investigating reports of ticket scalping by Oklahoma football players. The *Times* sportswriter received dozens of death threats, hundreds of *Times* readers canceled their subscriptions, and some angry Oklahoma fans called for boycotts of *Times* advertisers. The sportswriter was placed under police protection for four days while tempers cooled.[104]

The issue-oriented episodes dealt with nuclear waste and religious cults. "Poison" mirrored the well-publicized case of Karen Silkwood, a nuclear plant worker in Oklahoma who died in a suspicious car accident in 1974 while delivering documents to a *New York Times* reporter investigating unsafe nuclear plants.[105] In the television story a friend of Rossi's is struck and killed by a car while bringing Rossi documentation of problems at the nuclear plant where he works. Despite circumstantial evidence of the nuclear company's involvement in the fatal incident and unsafe plant practices, Lou refuses to publish a story without support from sources or documents. The story has a more satisfying ending than the Silkwood case; the friend had mailed a copy of the documents to Rossi in case anything happened to him.

"Sect" examined the Hare Krishna faith and the impact on a family when a member joins what they view a religious cult.[106] The episode brought sharp criticism from an anti-Hare Krishna organization. In the story Charlie's son Tommy joins Hare Krishna. Charlie plans to have a "deprogrammer" kidnap Tommy and take him to Lou's home. He calls off the plot, however, when he realizes he must respect his son's decision to make his own choices. The *Lou Grant* producers gave Hare Krishna officials script approval in exchange for permission to film scenes in a Los Angeles temple. But Charlie's acceptance of his son's decision drew a rebuke in a newsletter by the Citizens Freedom Foundation in Los

Angeles. "We believe the program will give Hare Krishna and other cults favorable publicity and be prejudicial to the numerous lawsuits now in progress involving cults," the newsletter stated. "Any program which depicts cult membership as the result of free and independent decision making instead of coercive persuasion, brainwashing, behavior modification, etc. does a disservice to the public."[107] The group urged members to contact the show's sponsors, CBS, and MTM Studios and express their views. The episode also angered a group that supported Hare Krishna. CBS Television President James H. Rosenfield later revealed that the Individual Freedom Foundation of Educational Trust had scared two sponsors into pulling their ads from *Lou Grant*.[108]

Two human-interest stories completed the first twenty-two episodes of *Lou Grant*. In "Renewal" the *Tribune* tries to help an elderly man whose apartment building has been condemned.[109] The final show, "Physical," depicted Lou's reaction to a diagnosis of thyroid cancer and his subsequent surgery. The episode ends warmly with Lou lying in a hospital bed surrounded by his friends from the *Tribune*.[110]

Over twenty-two episodes *Lou Grant* expanded the personalities of its recurring characters. For instance, viewers discovered the egotistical Rossi had a tender side and valued his friends.[111] Animal was not quite the simpleton he appeared; he spoke fluent French from his days at a Paris art school.[112] Mrs. Pynchon, far from the cold matriarch, cared about her staff members and their problems.[113] Art Donovan, the office wisecracker, was sensitive and caring.[114]

Reynolds deliberately broadened the characters from the simple sketches that begot them. "I like to look at the characters as three-dimensional," he said. "I think of it like a statue. Just turn it a little bit and you begin to see a different portion of the character. Human beings and characters are ambiguous. They have great ambiguity and contradictions. Heroes are not all that wonderful, the villains are not all that flawed."[115] Indeed, the heroes of *Lou Grant*—the regular characters—were depicted as flawed personally and professionally. Lou is sexist and dictatorial at times and not above punishing reporters by assigning them stories they do not want.[116] Billie's devotion to her profession inhibits her ability to have a meaningful relationship with a man.[117] Rossi breaks newspaper policy in his zeal to get a story, and Animal trespasses on private property to take a photo (and is praised by Lou for his initiative).[118]

These human qualities probably made the characters more appealing to viewers. That may be part of the reason the series rose steadily in the ratings. The 1977–78 television season ended on April 23, 1978. Of the

109 series that had aired *Lou Grant* had tied for thirty-ninth place with an average rating of 18.7.[119] Failing to break the top thirty shows was not a good omen for a new series. Yet the weak showing of other CBS series, particularly its new programs, boosted the chances that *Lou Grant* would return for the 1978–79 season. Of the forty-two series that CBS aired in 1977–78, *Lou Grant* was the thirteenth highest-rated.[120] It also had gained the aura of a prestigious series, one of the few of the season to be hailed by critics for its intelligence. The season had been rough for CBS, which announced in May that it would renew only three new shows for 1978–79: *Dallas, The Incredible Hulk,* and *Lou Grant.*[121]

Good news for the cast, crew, and production team of *Lou Grant* came throughout the summer of 1978. Reruns of *Lou Grant* became some of the most-watched shows on television. The series reached the second spot in the weekly Nielsen ratings in early June and reached first during a week in July.[122] Industry analysts believed the strong summer showing would help CBS shore up its Monday night schedule when the new season began in September. Still, the competition would be tough. ABC planned to air its popular *Monday Night Football* program, and NBC scheduled movies and special programs. But for now, *Lou Grant* had survived. Reynolds told the *Los Angeles Times:* "The big thing in this business is to get on the air and stay there. The real accomplishment is to stay on the air with something you're proud of. I think we've done that, and it's very gratifying."[123]

The popular new series impressed the television industry. In August 1978 the Academy of Television Arts and Sciences nominated *Lou Grant* for five major Emmy Awards. Academy members nominated the series for best drama series and Asner for best actor in a drama series. Marchand and Kelsey received nominations for their supporting roles. In the category of single performance by an actor in a comedy or drama Barnard Hughes was nominated for his role in the episode "Judge." When the awards were handed out on September 17—almost exactly one year after the series had premiered—*Lou Grant* won three of the golden statues for the work of Asner, Marchand, and Hughes.[124]

The first season of *Lou Grant* was a success, albeit a qualified one. Considering the numerous problems that could have led to its demise, its most obvious accomplishment was gaining renewal from CBS. Yet cancellation would not have diminished the series's overall artistic achievements. Brooks, Burns, and Reynolds had crafted a newspaper drama that breathed new life into a venerable but flawed television genre. By focusing on authentic issues in journalism *Lou Grant* challenged viewers' concept of the profession. They showed that a series could realistically portray journalism and human relations in an intelligent, entertaining way if those in charge were creative and committed to that goal. The first season of *Lou Grant* set an honorable standard, one the producers hoped to surpass as they prepared for their second year of production.

6

Second and Third Seasons,
1978–1980

Meeting entertainment reporters was a routine part of Ed Asner's summer break from filming *Lou Grant*. In interviews he discussed changes in the series, the press, and other topics. Between the second and third seasons in the summer of 1979 Asner enjoyed telling reporters a revealing story that he believed might be apocryphal.[1] In Philadelphia a series of articles by an investigative reporter had exposed the questionable activities of a prosperous businessman and had led to a grand jury indictment. The reporter liked the businessman, and he approached him after the court hearing. "Hey, listen," he said. "I'm sorry. I was just doing my job." The businessman was said to have replied: "Don't worry, I understand. I watch 'Lou Grant'."[2]

Other people who watched *Lou Grant* may have believed they, too, understood how journalists worked and what motivated decisions at a newspaper. Journalism themes, which had dominated the series's first year, continued in many of the episodes aired during its second and third seasons. The show solidified its reputation for offering a realistic depiction of the press, at least in the eyes of many television critics and other journalists. At the same time episodes that revolved around a social issue or a human-interest story grew in number during the 1978–79 and 1979–80 seasons. Moreover, they attracted more attention than the journalism-oriented episodes.

These two years were in many ways the high point of *Lou Grant*. The series won more accolades—including a Peabody Award and consecutive Emmy Awards as Outstanding Drama—than it would in its two remaining seasons. Critics continued to praise *Lou Grant* as an example of the high quality of entertainment that television could achieve. In terms of its audience the series averaged a respectable one-third of television viewers during its time period.[3] Although unable to break into the top twenty-five shows during the regular season, *Lou Grant* remained a spring and summer favorite of audiences.

★   ★   ★

The most obvious change in the second season of *Lou Grant* was in its title sequence.[4] The whimsical opening that traced the evolution of a newspaper from forest to bird cage was replaced with a sequence that firmly established the series's newspaper setting and focused on its characters, who were now more familiar to viewers. As the scene fades in the camera moves in a tracking shot past desks in the *Tribune* newsroom. Three characters—Billie Newman, Joe Rossi, and Adam Wilson (a recurring character played by actor Allen Williams)—are talking on the phones at their desks.

BILLIE

Hello, I'm calling from the *Trib*. I'd like to confirm a quote. . . .

ROSSI

I've been getting the runaround for two hours. . . .

ADAM

Approximately how much money was involved? Was it over a thousand dollars? Was it over ten thousand?

Patrick Williams's theme music rises as the camera stops behind a fourth person working at a typewriter. The scene changes to Lou Grant walking from behind his desk, and the credits begin.

The name of each actor flashes on the screen when he or she appears. A grim-looking Lou Grant apparently returns a story to Rossi, who seems to be complaining. Lou walks over to Billie for a brief conversation. They are joined by Charlie Hume, and all turn to see a smiling Art Donovan. Then, the scene shifts from the newsroom to a darkroom as photographer Dennis "Animal" Price develops a photograph and munches on a sandwich. Another shift takes the scene to the offices of Mrs. Pynchon, who sits behind her desk with her dog. As production credits appear the scene moves to a meeting room where all the characters (except Mrs. Pynchon) are avidly talking, arguing, or eating. The sequence ends with Lou reading the *Tribune*, his feet on his desk in an empty newsroom.

More traditional than the 1977–78 opening, the new title sequence provided an overview of the setting and characters of *Lou Grant*. In just six lines of dialogue the sequence depicted the essential functions of a newspaper reporter: providing accurate information, tenaciously gathering facts, and probing for news. The sequence also presented the basic functions and, to an extent, the personalities of the characters. The title sequence remained almost unchanged for the remainder of the series. Beginning in the third season, the reporters were shown typing on video display terminals rather than typewriters, signaling the *Tribune*'s belated entry into the computer age. Thus, when *Lou Grant* changed title sequences, it traded whimsy for realism. Given the series's focus on journalism, social issues, and human relations, it was a sensible change.

Seven of the second season's twenty-four episodes focused on journalism issues or themes. The first show of the season, "Pills," was one of the series's strongest journalism episodes.[5] In it a young man whose girlfriend dies of a prescription pill overdose breaks into a doctor's office. He turns over stolen files to Rossi, who has been investigating the doctor for unethical and illegal practices. When the story based on the stolen records appears in the *Tribune*, police use a search warrant to raid the newsroom. Rossi refuses to cooperate with the investigation when asked to reveal how he obtained the files, standing on the principle that sources must be protected to allow a newspaper to gather information. Later, he is found in contempt by a judge and jailed. Only when the young man who stole the files turns himself in to police is Rossi freed.

The story line of "Pills" resembled the well-publicized case of *New York Times* reporter Myron Farber. His 1976 stories about the suspicious deaths of several patients at a hospital in New Jersey helped bring murder charges against a physician. In the spring of 1978 Farber refused to turn over his notes to the doctor's defense team and declined to testify at the physician's trial. Despite claims of confidentiality he eventually served forty days in jail for contempt, and the *Times* paid more than five hundred thoudsand dollars in fines and legal fees. Although the Farber case was not resolved until October 1978, one month after "Pills" aired, it apparently served as the model for the episode.[6]

"Pills" dramatized the issue of source confidentiality in a scene in Mrs. Pynchon's office. Although Lou says that he would break the law to get a story, he admits he would not commit murder. "So," Mrs. Pynchon replies, "we newspaper people are only above *some* laws." When Rossi draws a parallel to the Pentagon Papers, which were stolen documents turned over to newspapers in 1971, Mrs. Pynchon notes: "But that was a matter of national importance. I don't think this case is comparable." Lou retorts, "Oh, so stealing's O.K. if the stakes are high enough?" *Tribune* lawyers warn the staff that publication of a story based on the stolen files will result in action by the district attorney and fines against the newspaper. When all agree that the story is important enough to take those risks, Mrs. Pynchon approves publication.[7]

The episode "Conflict" dramatized an important issue in journalism ethics, conflict of interest.[8] The codes of conduct of journalism groups and individual news organizations usually include guidelines regarding memberships, political involvement, the acceptance of gifts, and other behavior that might create a conflict for a journalist.[9] In "Conflict" nearly everyone on the *Tribune* staff has a potential conflict of interest: Lou's friendship with the owner of a sports team; Billie's activism with a group hoping to stop a city project on her block; Mrs. Pynchon's support of a charity under investigation by the paper; Donovan's work for a Senate candidate; and Charlie's wife's work as a paid staff member for a political candidate.

Rossi, ever the loner, has no such ties. He is appointed the *Tribune*'s in-house media critic, but his terse memos criticizing the staff anger everyone. He soon finds what he calls "conflict of interest, self-serving reporting, and enough home-grown stupidity to populate *The Gong Show* for a year." Billie believes Rossi goes too far in his criticism of people's activities. "You think the issue is not having opinions," she tells him. "That's not it. It's not letting opinions screw up your story." Two conflicts have serious consequences. Mrs. Pynchon tells Charlie his wife must resign from the political campaign or he will lose his job. Although Charlie considers quitting, Marion Hume says she loves him too much to see him give up his work.

Mrs. Pynchon's charity work creates bad feelings between her and Lou. He approves a story critical of the fund-raising tactics of the charity's manager, which nearly destroys the charity campaign and denies help for needy people. "All for the sake of twenty-four column inches," an angry Mrs. Pynchon tells Lou. "Did you ever think of them [needy people] when you were chasing after Ronald Ferguson and One For All with your bucket of tar?" Lou responds with a defense of newspaper independence: "How do you expect me as the city editor to go after any story wherever I find it, no holds barred, if I have to worry that my publisher might be involved in that story? . . . I think your way to be of service to the public is to run the best, freest and toughest paper in town. If you're doing that right, that's service enough." The episode ends on a humorous note. Rossi receives several anonymous gifts from *Tribune* staff members—memberships in a variety of organizations.

Expanding the theme of the newspaper process, the episode "Marathon" explored the important and not-so-important events in a busy day at the *Tribune*.[10] A breaking story, the collapse of a tunnel in the foothills of Los Angeles, keeps the staff busy throughout the day. But there are other challenges that test everyone's patience. Donovan is considering taking a job with the governor's staff, worrying Charlie that he will lose a good editor. Billie bristles at having to interview families of the victims, contending that she gets the "grave-digger jobs" because she is a woman. Rossi argues with her about her coverage of the collapse. Reporter George Driscoll covers a "human fly" who scales a downtown building. Lou contends with a local kook who maintains that he has contact with space aliens.

Throughout "Marathon" the time is flashed on the screen, emphasizing the deadlines faced by the *Tribune* staff. The episode begins at nine o'clock in the morning and ends at two o'clock that night when the weary staff finishes the final edition. The finely crafted script by Gene Reynolds, who was nominated for an Emmy Award, expertly depicted the energy and frantic pace of a newspaper dealing with a breaking story as well as routine problems.[11]

The question of what makes news was the focus of the episode "Murder."[12] No one at the *Tribune* except Billie and Animal is interested in the slaying of a young black woman living in the ghetto. Instead, the editors play up Rossi's story about an elderly, affluent white woman who hits an intruder with a golf club. "People fighting back is news," Lou tells Billie when she complains that her story was buried inside the *Tribune*. "People getting murdered isn't. I don't like it any more than you do." When Lou defends *Tribune* coverage of the attack story, he offers a rationale for news selection by the editors at the daily budget meeting. "In L.A. today there were 100 things that needed to be covered," he says. "Out of that hundred I picked fifteen that I thought had to be covered, and I sent the people out there. When those reporters get back they will all be convinced that they've got front-page stuff. They're going to have to sell me first because in order for me to go in there and sell it, I've got to be convinced." Billie works even harder to develop a feature story on the murder and its impact. Eventually, Lou fights for the story, and it appears on page one. "Murder" resulted in an Emmy Award nomination for its director, Mel Damski.[13]

Building readership through sensationalism created a debate at the *Tribune* in the episode "Singles."[14] Mrs. Pynchon hires a media consultant, Michael Barton, to help the newspaper boost its circulation. His efforts rely on a more sensational approach to stories, which concerns Lou and Charlie. Barton contends, "If you've got a great newspaper that doesn't sell, you don't have a newspaper." Charlie responds, "That may be, but when you have a newspaper that's just cotton candy, that isn't a newspaper either." Barton argues that he is only asking that the reporters focus on the sexy angles of stories. Lou disagrees with his approach. "The real stories in this town, the kinds of things that affect people's lives, are happening in very unsexy places, in board rooms, in government offices, in city council chambers," he says. "Pretty dry stuff. Lots of people don't enjoy reading it. But it has to be offered to them." Mrs. Pynchon supports Lou and Charlie. Thanking Barton for his efforts, she tells him: "We may fail with the *Tribune*. But we have a better chance of winning when we play the game we know."

Of all the episodes in the second season, "Samaritan" was the least fulfilling in terms of its journalism content.[15] In it a serial killer called Samaritan had terrorized Los Angeles five years earlier by announcing his slayings in letters to the press. When the *Tribune* receives new letters from Samaritan, it appears that the city is targeted once again. Jim McCrea, a *Tribune* reporter who had made a reputation covering the earlier murders, is assigned the story. Yet, the detective who investigated the murders contends that the letters are not from the same person. Confronted by a suspicious Lou, Jim admits he wrote the letters to bring excitement back into his life and to seal a book contract.

"Samaritan" concluded without offering any discussion or depiction of the impact such a hoax would have on the reputation of a newspaper. Obviously, the incident would be a major scandal at a real newspaper, yet its consequences were ignored. Instead, the episode dealt with the ethical dilemma of whether a newspaper should report the existence of a threat. Although they turn over the letter to authorities, the *Tribune* editors agree that the responsible action is to withhold its existence from the public. An unrealistic plot twist takes place when columnist Jack Towne writes about the letter in his column, forcing the *Tribune* to cover the possible reemergence of Samaritan. It is doubtful that a topic hotly debated by the editors would appear in a column despite their disapproval and, moreover, without their knowledge.

The episode "Convention" featured only a tenuous connection to journalistic issues by depicting a similar theme, the impact of a terrorist threat on a newspaper convention attended by *Tribune* staffers.[16] The fear that the group will carry out a threat to kidnap someone leads to comical incidents involving Lou and others. Lou demands that the *Tribune* not publish anything about terrorist threats unless there is confirmation from other sources. When Billie interviews the leader of the left-wing faction, the woman tells her that the group's tactics have worked—the convention is in turmoil over the mere threat of violence, and the media have helped publicize the group's cause. Played mainly for humor, "Convention" dealt in only minor ways with media coverage of terrorism.

★   ★   ★

Twelve episodes focusing on social issues aired during the second season of *Lou Grant*. The program titled "Home," an examination of problems facing elderly Americans, drew more reaction and controversy than any episode that season.[17] In the story Billie takes a job as an aide at a nursing home suspected of providing poor care to its residents. Indeed, she discovers that the home is understaffed and apparently overmedicates its patients to keep them docile. When Billie complains to the nursing home administrator about poor care for a woman crying out in pain, she is immediately fired. Rossi, meanwhile, explores home-care options and related issues. Lou's friendship with an elderly man further dramatizes the question of how to care for the elderly.

Chicago Tribune television critic Gary Deeb called the episode "a text-book example of how to translate a serious social problem into a provocative and exciting TV program."[18] CBS reported that it received about five hundred letters in response to "Home"; about one of four was critical and came from the nursing home industry.[19] Several groups and organizations, however—including the Gray Panthers, the commissions on aging in California and Ohio, and the National Association of Area Agencies on Aging —praised the program for raising awareness of problems facing the elderly. The American Association of Retired Persons and the National Retired Teachers Association presented Asner and the *Lou Grant* producers with its public-service award. The organizations said "Home" had sensitively portrayed many aspects of the aging process and the success and failure of society in dealing with them.[20]

The nursing home industry's lobbying organization, the American Health Care Association, bitterly criticized "Home" for what it called "distortions and untruths."[21] Association President Don Brewer complained to CBS that repeating the episode would "cause offense to, and unwarranted anxiety among, a significant segment of your viewing audience."[22] The organization contended that problems depicted in "Home" were based on problems from five to fifteen years in the past, most of which no longer existed.[23] Reynolds, the series producer, pointed out that the episode was partly based on series in the *Los Angeles Times* and the *Chicago Tribune*, both of which were published the previous year.[24] He called the episode "a very moderate depiction . . . not nearly as bad as the real situation."[25]

With "Home" scheduled to air again on August 27, 1979, the lobbying organization asked CBS's two hundred affiliates not to carry the program. In addition, the organization contacted sponsors of *Lou Grant* and urged them not to advertise during the broadcast. Two companies, Kellogg's and Oscar Mayer, withdrew their commercials from the program, citing the controversy.[26] CBS, meanwhile, refused to remove "Home" from its broadcast schedule. The president of the network, James H. Rosenfield, sent a statement to station managers of CBS affiliates and released it to the news media. The July 25 statement said, in part:

> We resent the pressure being brought to bear by the AHCA on the network, the producers and the advertisers to prevent the rebroadcast of the dramatic episode, however controversial.
>
> As we pointed out in our earlier responses, LOU GRANT is a fictional series which uses contemporary social topics as dramatic premises. Unlike news and public affairs broadcasts, it does not purport to present a journalistic treatment of any issue—although the AHCA is clearly treating the program as if it did.[27]

Interestingly, the series's creators and television critics had hailed *Lou Grant* for its realism and intelligent treatment of issues. When faced with controversy, CBS felt compelled to point out that *Lou Grant* was only a dramatic program.

"Home" aired as scheduled. No affiliates dropped the program although at least one, KFDA in Amarillo, Texas, carried a disclaimer advising viewers that *Lou Grant* was fictional and not meant to be taken literally.[28] Television critics, apparently unconcerned about the distinction CBS tried to make, applauded CBS for supporting the series. Gerald B. Jordan of the *Kansas City Star* wrote, "CBS, which has been known to knuckle under, stood rigid and . . . had the courage to stick to its plan to rerun the show."[29] An Associated Press writer drew a parallel to the series's fictional setting: "Through the course of the storm, CBS stuck by 'Lou Grant,' just the way *Tribune* publisher Mrs. Pynchon would have stuck by her cityside staffers. And now, the 'Lou Grant' show can be more realistic than ever, having suffered the wrath of an offended subject. Welcome to the news biz, 'Lou Grant'."[30]

Although not drawing controversy, the episodes "Prisoner" and "Vet" brought more praise to the series and several awards as well. "Prisoner" explored the subject of government-sanctioned torture, gaining its dramatic focus by involving a member of the *Tribune* staff.[31] In the story Charlie's nightmares about his five-week ordeal in a cell in the fictional nation of Malagua coincide with a visit by the wife of that nation's dictator. The *Tribune* staff interviews supporters of the government as well as protesters of the regime. "Prisoner" immediately drew a letter of appreciation from Amnesty International, which called the episode both accurate and perceptive.[32] Reynolds later received an Emmy nomination and a Directors Guild of America award for directing it, and writer Seth Freeman won the Writers Guild of America award for the script.[33]

"Vet," written by Leon Tokatyan, explored problems facing Vietnam veterans.[34] The episode juxtaposes Animal, a vet still haunted by his experiences, and Sutton, a black panhandler who cannot find work because of Vietnam-related social problems. Animal, supported by his friends and colleagues, finds the determination to face his demons and get help. Sutton's efforts are spurned by an uncaring society, and he merely disappears among the homeless. Inspired by a friend who had served in the war, actor Daryl Anderson had suggested the topic to the *Lou Grant* writing staff.[35] Allen Williams, who played Adam Wilson, was a veteran himself and had aided in the research.[36] The writing staff also had contacted a specialist in veterans affairs who had researched stress disorders among Vietnam veterans.[37]

Praising "Vet" for its sensitivity and accurate depiction, the United States Labor Department bestowed upon *Lou Grant* its Award of Merit. In a letter to Reynolds, a Labor Department official said Anderson had given "an extra dimension to his role that indeed helped those watching gain an insight into some of the problems our Vietnam-era veterans encounter."[38] In addition to an Emmy Award nomination and a Writers Guild award Tokatyan also received a Humanitas Prize.[39] The prestigious award from the Human Family Educational and Cultural Institute honors writers of nationally broadcast programs that communicate human values.[40]

Other issue-oriented episodes depicted a wide range of social ills and problems. For instance, "Slaughter" examined a health risk from tainted meat and the impact such a discovery could have on a farm community.[41] "Schools" explored problems of violence in inner-city schools, featuring a three-minute inspirational speech by the Reverend Jesse Jackson.[42] (The episode brought *Lou Grant* another Emmy Award nomination, this time for Burt Brinckerhoff's direction.)[43] In "Babies" Billie and Rossi went undercover to expose a black-market adoption ring.[44] Other issues dramatized in the second season included arson, investment fraud, illegal immigrants, the homeless, and nuclear terrorism.[45]

Although the episode "Mob" focused on the influence of organized crime, it essentially was a mystery story in which Lou, Rossi, and Animal vainly tried to expose a Senate candidate's ties to mobsters.[46] A seemingly innocuous entry, "Mob" infuriated a United States congressman running for reelection in the Los Angeles area. Shortly after "Mob" aired on October 23, 1978, viewers contacted the offices of 38th District Representative Jerry Patterson, an Orange County Democrat. They claimed that Patterson had been depicted in the episode as a lawmaker with ties to organized crime. One person asked if Patterson was still a candidate after the "exposé" carried by CBS.[47] Viewers apparently had confused Jerry Patterson with the fictional character, who was named Jack Patterson and described as a California assemblyman, not a congressman. De Forest Research, the firm that checked names in scripts, had approved usage of the name Jack Patterson. The de Forest report had noted that "there are currently no Congressmen with this exact name, nor California Assemblymen. Do not consider usage here to conflict."[48]

With the election two weeks away Jerry Patterson was convinced that the similarity was not accidental. "It was almost like somebody in the *Lou Grant* organization thought, 'Well, here's a way to zing one to Patterson'," he recalled. "I have no idea if that was the case, but that's the way it seemed to me then."[49] Eight days after the show aired, Patterson wrote the CBS affiliate in Los Angeles that he had been libeled by the program. He demanded a correction and a retraction. In a letter to the Federal Communications Commission he asked that the FCC invoke the Personal Attack Rule of the Fairness Doctrine and order CBS to give him time to respond to the attack.[50]

CBS Vice-President Gene P. Mater responded in a letter on November 2. While expressing regret that the episode had caused problems for Patterson, he pointed out that *Lou Grant* was a fictional television show whose purpose was "purely to entertain."[51] Pointing out the differences in the character's name and occupation, Mater said reasonable viewers were expected to treat the program as fictional. After Patterson easily won reelection he dropped the matter. "It may have been totally innocent," he said in retrospect. "I guess I believed them, ultimately."[52] The incident, which occurred before the flap over "Home," suggested that not everyone viewed *Lou Grant* as fiction.

Five episodes of *Lou Grant* explored human-interest stories that had neither a strong journalistic focus nor a pressing social issue. In fact, these dramas could have taken place in almost any setting, such as a police station or a hospital. For instance, the episode titled "Dying" examined Art Donovan's relationship with his mother as well as his inability to accept that she was terminally ill.[53] Art believes at first that she will improve and then vainly tries to find a miracle cure for her, even planning a trip to a clinic in Mexico. Then, he comes to terms with her illness and faces the prospect of life without her. The episode, written by Michele Gallery, was one of the series's most heartfelt. It also provided actor Jack Bannon a showcase for his talents. "Dying" won an Emmy Award for Gallery's script.[54]

Other human-interest episodes included "Hit," which featured a woman's single-minded pursuit of justice.[55] Although her son had been killed by a hit-and-run driver two years earlier, she had continued to search for the killer. Rossi, impressed by her tenacity, helps her. Eventually, they have enough evidence to bring charges against a traffic judge who had struck her son. "Hooker" was a character study about the life of a prostitute.[56] "Denial" examined Lou's efforts to convince his daughter that her son was becoming deaf and needed help.[57] "Romance," the final episode of the season, explored different relationships, from a rock star being sued by a former girlfriend to a teenager who wanted a baby in order to afford a home.[58] At the *Tribune* Lou considers moving in with his girlfriend, police officer Susan Sherman. He proposes marriage instead, but she is not ready for a commitment. Still, they remain together.

Artistically and critically, the second season of *Lou Grant* was a triumph. In addition to the awards already cited the series won Emmy nominations for Asner as best actor, Robert Walden and Mason Adams as best supporting actor, and Linda Kelsey and Nancy Marchand as best supporting actress (none of the cast won the awards). The series was named Oustanding Drama, taking the Emmy Award over rival nominees *The Rockford Files* and *The Paper Chase*.[59] Perhaps the most prestigious accolade came from the Henry W. Grady School of Journalism at the University of Georgia, administrator of the George Foster Peabody Awards. The school's national advisory board called the series "the entertaining yet realistic look at the problems and issues which face those who are involved in the 'Fourth Estate'."[60]

Yet the series's performance in the ratings did not equal those accomplishments. In the first thirteen weeks of the season *Lou Grant* ranked twenty-eighth of seventy-six programs with a 19.8 rating. Its strong competitors, *NBC Monday Night Movie* and *ABC Monday Night Football*, ranked seventeenth and twenty-fourth, respectively.[61] By April 22, 1979, the end of the regular season, *Lou Grant* had averaged a 19.2 rating for thirty-second place among 112 programs. Still, it was the ninth-highest-rated of the thirty-six series CBS had aired that season.[62] It continued to pull larger audiences during the rerun months, often breaking into the top ten programs.[63]

When CBS prepared its 1979–80 schedule, *Lou Grant* remained part of its Monday night lineup, following *The White Shadow*, *M★A★S★H*, and *WKRP in Cincinnati*. B. Donald "Bud" Grant, the network vice-president for programs, called the schedule for that night "a class act all the way, every show an absolute gem."[64] ABC and NBC also retained their Monday night lineups. *Lou Grant*, laden with awards and critical acclaim, was secure. It came as a relief to Asner, who had continued to feel immense pressure even after the second season had begun. He had been in such a hurry to get to the studio for the first day of shooting for the second season that he seriously cut his face with a razor while shaving. A plastic surgeon repaired the damage, and Asner appeared on camera in "Pills" and "Prisoner" wearing a bandage. "There was still angst about doing the show, even then," he recalled. "I don't think we ever breathed securely until maybe the beginning of the third year."[65]

★　　★　　★

After two years of playing a city editor on prime-time television Asner had settled into another role—spokesman for the press and press freedom. Terrence O'Flaherty of the *San Francisco Chronicle* contended, "Most newspapermen probably consider him a very good spokesman for the profession."[66] Indeed, Asner appeared in print and television ads promoting newspaper readership for the Newspaper Readership Council. Through interviews, he told the public that he had learned to value the First Amendment and the freedom of expression it guaranteed. He even chastised the press for not doing a better job of explaining its important and honorable function in American society.[67] "I think the press needs me," Asner told a reporter as he prepared for the third season of the series. "I think there is a great deal of antagonism toward the Fourth Estate, and there always has been."[68]

Within the profession *Lou Grant* was honored for its efforts to present the press in an accurate and favorable light. For example, the Detroit chapter of the Society of Professional Journalists made Asner an honorary member of the national organization and the local press club. The award said that Lou Grant "exemplifies what every editor hopes and likes to think he is: a dedicated and keen newsman, tough in the clinches, compassionate and honest, willing to stand up against all pressures (including his publisher), dedicated to truth, good Scotch and his staff (all two reporters and one photographer)."[69] The Associated Press Managing Editors association also awarded an honorary membership to Asner. In a humorous resolution the organization contended that Asner as Lou Grant "epitomizes us all as the journalistically aggressive, ethically pure, even-tempered, heart-of-gold romantics we always knew we were."[70]

Columnist Walter Saunders of Denver's *Rocky Mountain News* wrote: "Lou Grant is the best damn newspaperman on television. . . . For the most part, Lou Grant as a city editor, and 'Lou Grant' as a weekly TV series, have projected a legitimate view of newspaper life."[71] Greg Moody of the *Milwaukee Sentinel* agreed after he and other journalists met the actor: "To many of the newspaper people in the room, Ed Asner was their hero."[72] The series also may have inspired journalism students. "It's a good role model," Mary Ann Kerzich, a senior at Central Michigan University, said of the series and its star. "There's integrity, equality, and he seems to care."[73] Although he acknowledged that *Lou Grant* had its faults, Asner believed that the press appreciated its efforts to depict the substance of the profession. "I think we do a good job in showing the nuts and bolts of the business," he said.[74]

Ironically, Asner's oft-stated belief, that the press did not always communicate well with the public, fell victim to one of the press's worst mistakes—the misquotation. While speaking to the Detroit chapter of the Society of Professional Journalists on February 26, 1979, Asner noted that a portion of the public perceived reporters as "privileged punks." Some published accounts of the speech reported that Asner had used the words to describe how he viewed reporters. Angry journalists sent letters to Asner, and at least one radio station broadcast an editorial suggesting that reporters need Asner's advice "like he needs a wart on the end of his nose."[75] The actor pointed out the erroneous report in subsequent interviews, and he mailed transcripts of his speech to journalists who complained. *Detroit News* editor Bill Giles wrote that Asner had "gotten a bit of a bum rap."[76]

Robert Walden also enjoyed acclaim from journalists for his role in *Lou Grant*. He visited more than thirty newspaper city rooms during the series. "Journalists were stunned at how many papers I actually set foot in. I would tell them things about other city rooms," he remembered. "Everywhere I went . . . I was their champion in some way, the reporters especially. They all wanted me to meet their Rossi."[77] Many reporters told him that the series had improved their relationship with sources. "They said, 'People finally understand what we're doing. That we're not trying to compromise them, hurt them, expose them . . . that we're trying to help tell the truth'."[78] Walden was invited to speak at journalism schools and professional meetings, and he began writing for newspapers and magazines. For instance, he covered an American Indian demonstration for the *Los Angeles Free Press*, wrote a feature on ticket scalping for a New York magazine, and covered the Democratic National Convention in 1980.[79]

Numerous women journalists complimented Linda Kelsey for her portrayal of Billie Newman. "They were thrilled that there was a Billie," she said. "I had a lot of women journalists say, 'Keep it up, you're doing this for us. You keep on your editor and you keep asking for the good jobs and don't you let Rossi get to you'."[80] She declined requests to speak at journalism schools. "I'm not a journalist. As far as I was concerned, I didn't get it," she said, puzzled as to why an actress playing a reporter would be sought to speak about journalism issues. "I never knew what to say to those people."[81]

Lou Grant was becoming part of American popular culture. For instance, the *Tampa Times* included Mason Adams in its list of "most trusted Americans." The actor who played Charlie Hume was pictured on Mount Rushmore with journalist Walter Cronkite, cowboy star Gene Autry, and baseball player Steve Garvey.[82] A sign that *Lou Grant* had arrived on the American scene came in March 1979 when *MAD* magazine parodied the series in a six-page feature titled "Lou Grouch."[83] (The parody is reproduced in app. E.) The series was roasted in typical *MAD* style, which included jabs at journalism and the series's unrealistic elements. "I don't get it," Lou says. "I'm the boss of 200 people here in the city room, and not one of them ever speaks to me." Charlie responds: "They're extras who are just hired to sit there. See, our producer thinks they make it more believable when you and I and two reporters seem to be putting out the paper all by ourselves!"[84]

★   ★   ★

When *Lou Grant* debuted in the 1979–80 season, it did not feature a strong journalism episode as it had done in the previous two years. Instead, its premiere focused on homosexuality.[85] Titled "Cop," it later became the most-honored drama series episode of the television season, winning Emmy and Directors Guild awards for Roger Young and an Emmy for Seth Freeman's script.[86] In the story a gay police officer, Mike Tynan, is drawn into the investigation of the murder of Lou's neighbor, also a gay man. Lou and Rossi suspect that Tynan is part of the probe because he is gay, which Tynan reluctantly confirms. In off-the-record conversations with the journalists Tynan discusses the difficulties he faces as a gay policeman. He fears that he would be ostracized if he made his sexual preferences known, even to his partner and friend, Robert Dennahy. When Tynan finally admits to Dennahy that he is a homosexual, Dennahy seeks a transfer because he believes a gay man is emotionally unstable and unfit to be a policeman. Before the transfer can take place, the officers track down the murder suspect, a gunfight ensues, and a wounded Tynan saves Dennahy's life. Dennahy realizes he is wrong about his partner and apologizes to him. At the *Tribune* Rossi and Lou agree that Tynan's homosexuality has no bearing on the story and omit it from the article.

An ethical decision carried the episode's secondary story line, which focused on how the *Tribune* would report the news of a fatal fire at a gay bar. Billie discovers that the victims include a lawyer, a minister, an Army captain, and the son of a prominent philanthropist. "I hate it, I hate it, I hate it," Mrs. Pynchon responds when Charlie and Lou consult her. "Print this list and you brand every one of these men as homosexuals." Charlie responds, "All of these men had families and friends that could be hurt by this disclosure. But how can a newspaper not print the truth just because the truth is painful?" Lou agrees that the *Tribune* has a responsibility to its readers. "If the newspaper doesn't print the names this time, how can the public know that we're not withholding other information from them in the future?" Finally, Mrs. Pynchon approves publication of the list. The story line apparently was drawn from the ethical dilemma that the media faced in Washington, D.C., in 1977 when eight people died in a fire at a homosexual film club.[87]

Lou Grant aired twelve other issue-oriented episodes in its third season. Journalism themes dominated seven episodes, and the remaining four programs told human-interest stories. Broadcast one week after "Cop," the episode "Exposé" explored the power of the press and its ability to damage people's lives.[88] Mark Worth, the alcoholic husband of city supervisor Bonita Worth, gains unwanted attention for making a drunken threat against Charlie after the *Tribune* publishes a story about his wife. Asked for comment, Mrs. Worth tells Billie, "Perhaps if a few more husbands threatened to punch a few more reporters, newspapers would be a bit more careful about what they write about people's private lives." When the *Tribune* criticizes him in an editorial, a drunken Worth bursts into a *Tribune* budget meeting and bitterly complains about being subject to press scrutiny. Later, Worth is in a car accident while in the company of a cocktail waitress. Lou assigns Rossi to write an analysis of how Worth's behavior is affecting his wife's reelection campaign.

Coverage of Worth sparks a debate between Lou and Mrs. Pynchon. The publisher believes that the *Tribune* has unfairly brought notoriety to Worth at the expense of his wife. "We turned the spotlight on him because his wife was in a position of power," the publisher contends. Lou argues, "People in our business have an instinct to take on the big guys. That's what makes good reporters. If we didn't, all we'd be printing is the daily horoscope and movie guide." Mrs. Pynchon, in a rare scene in which she has the last word, responds: "Yes, that's all very true. Meanwhile, here is a good public official in a dilemma I don't see any way out of. I think we helped put her there." The episode ends with Mrs. Worth resigning her public office.

The episode "Hazard" depicts the predicament facing a newspaper when the only way to get crucial information is to pay for it.[89] In the story a motorcycle manufactured and marketed for young consumers is suspected of serious design flaws. A company official tells Rossi that the manufacturer determined it would be more expensive to repair the motor-cycles already made than to pay off death and injury claims. (This element of the story mirrored allegations in 1978 that the Ford Motor Company ignored design flaws in its Pinto automobile rather than make costly re-pairs.)[90] The official, however, demands four thousand dollars to supply documentation of the manufacturer's decision.

Lou reluctantly recommends that the *Tribune* pay. "If that's what it takes to get it," he contends, "and we're not doing anything illegal, and for $4,000 we break a national story and save a life or two, then I say we spend it." Mrs. Pynchon adamantly refuses. "The *Tribune* does not pay its sources—ever," she argues. "I will not become subject to charges of checkbook journalism. Once that precedent is set, there's no end to it." Although Lou later points out that the *Tribune* is paying to serialize the memoirs of a former government official, Mrs. Pynchon does not budge. In the course of the series it was one of the few times she did not change her position under pressure from Lou.

The term "checkbook journalism" became well-known in the mid-1970s after highly publicized incidents in which news organizations paid for exclusive stories. For instance, CBS paid Watergate figure H. R. Hal-deman one hundred thousand dollars for two interviews in 1975.[91] The episode of *Lou Grant* took a twist on the ethical question, however. Rossi, without telling his editors, uses his own money to buy the documents. Then, he discovers that the official has sold the documents to other media, ruining his exclusive. Yet, he refuses to reveal his source, preserving his integrity as a journalist. Interestingly, the episode did not show the *Tri-bune* editors' reaction to Rossi's violation of newspaper policy.

Billie fell victim to an elaborate scheme to embarrass the *Tribune* in the episode "Frame-Up."[92] The story line dramatized the criticism a newspaper can face when it reports unpopular news about business and industry. Anacott Industries chief Curtis Folger cites Billie's story about the company's poor environmental record as the reason he has dropped plans to build a factory in Los Angeles. City officials and some readers accuse the *Tribune* of being anti-industry. Even *Tribune* editors question whether the story was fair. "Since when is it our purpose to scare away new business, new jobs?" an editor asks Lou. He replies, "Since when is it our purpose to serve as boosters for new business?" The editor answers, "We've done it plenty of times."

Folger later reverses his decision, but Billie discovers that the company never stopped building its new facilities. A disgruntled employee, Nell Wheeler, gives Billie a memo that shows Anacott used the threat merely to get better tax breaks and other incentives from the city. But when the story appears, Wheeler disappears and Folger files a libel suit against the *Tribune*. Billie contends she was set up, but her colleagues at the *Tribune* are not convinced. Charlie questions whether she has become too close to an environmental group. Billie tells him, "I wouldn't slant a story to sell that point of view." Her reputation is saved when Rossi tracks down Wheeler and exposes the ruse created by Folger. Lou then orders Rossi to turn over his notes to Billie so she can write the story. Considering that the episode touched on the issue of bias in reporting, its ending was flawed. Since Billie had become the focus of the story, she would scarcely be the reporter most capable of writing a fair, objective account. Still, the episode depicted the importance of a reporter's reputation, both to the reporter and to the newspaper.

The series again examined the media's scoop mentality in the humorous episode "Kidnap."[93] This time, Billie and Rossi try to scoop each other as much as their colleagues from other media. The two reporters wage a turf war over who covers the main story when a small town's high school basketball team is kidnapped. Billie outsmarts Rossi by letting him go to a remote crime scene while she waits for a possible break in the case. She ultimately gets the first word that the kids are safe and the kidnappers captured. The episode's secondary story line has a newspaper chain offering to buy the *Tribune* from Mrs. Pynchon. Despite the lucrative offer she decides that local control is best for the paper.

"Kidnap" was written after *News Photographer* magazine published letters from photographers who were unhappy with Animal's appearance. In a humorous acknowledgment of the criticism the story included a photographer who dressed as formally as Animal dressed casually. *Tribune* photographer Cy Wood wears a suit, white shirt, and bow tie. Eying Animal with disdain, Wood tells the other *Tribune* staffers: "I think we ought to get on him about how he looks. I mean, he represents photographers. It's a reflection on all of us. They see a guy like that coming in and they all think we're a bunch of beatniks." When the *Tribune* crew poses for a picture at the end of their assignment, Animal clips a bow tie to his collar. Wood snaps, "That's not funny."

The episode "Lou" won an Emmy nomination for writer Gallery.[94] It deftly mixed character study with newsroom activities by focusing on a day in the life of the *Tribune* city editor.[95] Lou faces numerous problems from reporters who do not like their assignments and an irresponsible columnist to a reporter who plagiarizes the work of a college newspaper (he is fired). He does not always handle the stress, losing his temper at times under the pressure. Charlie orders him to delegate authority more often and to take a vacation as soon as possible. As in the previous season's "Marathon" the time of day appeared throughout the episode. Not only did the show explore Lou's personality, but it depicted the myriad of problems that a city editor may face. Unlike most episodes, "Lou" showed the character's flaws.

"Charlatan" cleverly juxtaposed two First Amendment issues: religion and the press.[96] Rossi and Billie investigate the leader of a religious crusade whose former followers accuse him of fraud. They discover that many people, including other religious leaders, decline to criticize him because they would not want the government to inhibit religious practices. Meanwhile, Lou reluctantly agrees to testify on behalf of a pornographer ordered by a judge not to publish the names of undercover drug agents. Although unhappy to side with "a cruddy magazine like that," Lou contends that prior restraint should be resisted at all times.

In the final journalism episode of the season the series once again showed how a newspaper covers a breaking news story. In "Blackout" the city sustains a power outage after a minor earthquake.[97] Although thrown in the dark, the *Tribune* still covers looting, riots, and other events stemming from the blackout. Working by candlelight, the staff puts together the next day's issue and sends it to a nearby Long Beach newspaper for printing. As it had with "Airliner" in the first season and "Marathon" in the second the series depicted the dedication of the *Tribune* staff in getting the news to its readers.

★   ★   ★.

The series's only two-part episode, "Andrew," was a hybrid of social issue and journalism.[98] The plight of the mentally ill, misunderstood by society and rejected by the system until a tragedy occurs, was the focus of both segments. The second part also explored the problem Andrew's case presented the *Tribune* staff. "Andrew, Part 1: Premonition," introduced Art's mentally ill cousin Andrew Raines. Despite a history of mental and emotional problems Andrew is released from a hospital. After listening to Art and to Andrew's mother talk about Andrew, Billie decides to explore the problems of the mentally ill. A furious Art later complains: "Don't you think that's going a little far, Billie? Using my private life to get your ideas for stories? So what do I do now? Start worrying about censoring myself with my own reporters?" The family's fears that Andrew will do something terrible are realized when he is arrested for killing a young woman who had been a friend of his mother's.

The second segment, "Andrew, Part 2: Trial," followed the case through the legal system. At the *Tribune* Art fears that publicity will hurt Andrew's chances for a plea bargain. Lou contends that the murder is not special enough to warrant coverage, but Mrs. Pynchon and Charlie argue that they cannot ignore the story because it will appear that they are protecting one of their editors. When Rossi and Billie write news and feature stories about Andrew's case, including his brief escape from custody, Art complains bitterly that his connection with the *Tribune* is hurting Andrew. "Aren't you going all out to prove how unbiased you can be?" he asks Charlie. "And Andrew's getting shafted because he has the bad grace to have a cousin who works for the Trib." Instead of receiving a plea bargain, Andrew is tried, convicted of second-degree murder, and sentenced to fifteen years in prison.

The "Andrew" episodes were a good example of the series's ability to base a compelling drama on a social issue. In that vein "Inheritance" dramatized the problem of diethylstilbestrol, or DES, an artificial hormone prescribed to pregnant women with a history of miscarriages.[99] Twenty years later, scientists discovered that female children of women who took DES were suffering cancer related to the drug. In the episode Billie discovers she, too, is a so-called DES daughter while writing about a young woman's lawsuit against the drug companies that manufactured the hormone. She then grapples with the fear that she might develop cancer and with mixed feelings toward her mother. The series's reliance on topical issues most likely led writers to DES. In early 1979, several months before "Inheritance" aired, a federal lawsuit filed by a young woman against drug manufacturers went to trial.[100]

Although the DES controversy had been reported in the news media during the 1970s, "Inheritance" motivated many viewers to determine whether they might be the offspring of DES users. Reaction by viewers surprised actress Linda Kelsey. "The letters, my God," she remembered. "Women in the hospital recovering from their cancer surgery saying they didn't know why they got cancer and they watched TV and called their mother and learned then."[101] Larry McMullen, a columnist for the *Philadelphia Daily News*, told readers that the DES episode had frightened his family because his wife had taken a drug while pregnant but had not bothered to check with her doctor to see whether it was DES. Spurred by the television show, she contacted her doctor and was relieved to learn that he had not prescribed the hormone. "It took a television show to make my wife want to know for sure," McMullen wrote. "My family owes Lou Grant."[102]

Other issues dramatized during the third season of *Lou Grant* included inmate rights, urban American Indians, dog fighting, censorship, gun smuggling, children and stress, gambling, and medical research.[103] The episode "Influence" depicted alcoholism by examining financial editor Adam Wilson's drinking and its impact on his life.[104] Not only did it win an Emmy nomination for Reynolds's direction, but it was the first episode that focused on the character played by actor Allen Williams, who appeared in the series's credit sequence.[105] Williams, a native of Lebanon, Pennsylvania, who studied acting at Syracuse University, had appeared in three episodes in the first season and in most episodes in subsequent seasons.[106] Until "Influence," however, his role had been limited to a few lines in each episode.

Adam Wilson served an interesting function as a minor character on *Lou Grant*. While Lou and the other major characters had to remain likable to appeal to audiences, Adam could be flawed. Hence, when the writers wanted to place a problem such as alcoholism in the *Tribune* newsroom, they chose Adam or created a new character. "They couldn't put that burden on someone like Rossi, and certainly not on Lou or Donovan or any of those guys," Williams recalled. "They gave me the most cynical jokes, the jokes that Donovan couldn't say."[107] In addition to being in the cast of a highly praised drama series, Williams later directed four episodes of *Lou Grant*.

"Hollywood," one of the human-interest episodes that aired during 1979–80, broke from the established tone of the series in favor of a different style.[108] Beginning with Lou's narration ("it was one of those Sundays when you don't want to heat up the kitchen, and making a sandwich reminds you you're only cooking for one.") the episode played like a film noir mystery from the 1940s. A feature about a reclusive woman who lives above an abandoned restaurant leads the *Tribune* staff to investigate an old murder case tied to faded movie stars and other personalities. Although several leads are followed, the case remains an enigma. The episode, which brought an Emmy nomination to director Brinckerhoff, was essentially a stylish, entertaining character study.[109]

While the episode "Brushfire" showed the *Tribune* covering a breaking news story, it focused on the impact a fire could have on people.[110] Charlie and his wife, Marion, decide to separate, but after saving their home from the flames (and realizing how much they shared and needed each other) they reconcile. The script by Reynolds and Allan Burns earned *Lou Grant* yet another Emmy nomination.[111] In "Witness" police place Billie in protective custody after a key figure in an assault case is murdered after an interview with her.[112] "Cover-Up" featured two incidents that never appeared in the *Tribune* because Rossi and Billie could not get those involved to cooperate.[113] Rossi follows a false charge of child molestation that cost a teacher his job while Billie uncovers a film studio executive's kickback scheme. (The latter story line probably was influenced by the highly publicized case of David Begelman, a film producer charged with embezzlement after forging a check in 1977.)[114] In both incidents all the people involved preferred to avoid publicity and to keep the matters private.

Lou Grant ended the season much as it had the year before: enjoying critical acclaim, numerous awards, and stable if not spectacular ratings. The series placed in a four-way tie for thirty-third place among the 105 series that had aired in the 1979–80 season, ranking as the fourteenth-highest-rated of CBS's 36 series.[115] Its share of the audience during its time period remained at one-third.[116] When the Emmy nominations were announced in August 1980, *Lou Grant* led all series with fifteen nominations. Another CBS series, *M*★*A*★*S*★*H*, garnered eleven. "If you're not on 'Lou Grant' or "M*A*S*H," you don't get nominated," actor Judd Hirsch joked.[117] In addition to three writing nominations and four directing nominations the series won acting nominations for Asner, Walden, Adams, Kelsey, Marchand, and "Hollywood" guest star Nina Foch. Emmys went to Asner, Marchand, "Cop" director Young, "Cop" writer Freeman, "Hollywood" composer Patrick Williams, and Reynolds and Freeman for producing the year's outstanding drama.[118]

The formula for *Lou Grant* did not significantly change during the first three years it aired. It remained a drama set at a newspaper, and it explored contemporary issues and human relations in a journalism context. Although only one-third of the episodes in the second and third seasons focused on journalism, most of its issue- and human-interest episodes included scenes and dialogue that touched on newspaper practices and ethics. For example, brief debates over the use of deception to gain news appeared in several episodes. Charlie and Lou argue about how to get information on a black-market baby ring in "Babies." Charlie contends: "I don't want our reporters lying about their identities in order to cover a story. It's not ethical." Lou retorts: "What these guys do hurts a lot of people, innocent babies and desperate parents. And anything she [Billie] has to do to expose them is justified." Charlie reluctantly agrees to allow Rossi and Billie to pose as a couple seeking a child. Deception, however, was not always discussed before it took place. In different episodes Rossi lies about losing his wallet to board a bus filled with protesters, does not correct a woman's belief that he is a police detective before interviewing her, and misidentifies himself to get a phone number.

Several episodes showed Lou's concern that biased reporting should not appear in the *Tribune*. In "Mob" Lou orders Rossi to rewrite his story because it obviously is biased. Rossi then admits that his father was shaken down by mobsters when he ran a barber shop. In "Murder" Lou complains that Billie has lost her objectivity in writing about a woman's murder. Yet in "Hooker" Lou tells Billie it is all right for her feature story on a prostitute to show that she likes the woman. Lou also criticizes a reporter for giving his own opinion instead of facts in the episode "Exposé." In "Romance" Billie is tempted to give advice to a teenager contemplating having a baby, but Charlie tells her that is not her job.

Bits of dialogue also gave episodes the flavor of a newspaper even when journalism was not the focus. In "Slaughter" small-town editor Chip Murphy says, "I'm not the most popular guy in town. I wouldn't be doing my job right if I were." A lawyer tells Billie in the episode "Fire," "I've been doing this long enough to know the press always manages to distort what you say." At one point in "Sweep" Charlie explains to Mrs. Pynchon's niece what a newspaper means to him: "A newspaper is special. Every day we have to fight six deadlines, and we never know what the product will look like from one day to the next. But it's still the best job in the world. Today you might interview a president, tomorrow cover the birth of a baby gorilla. It's fun, that's what it is." In "Witness" Rossi tells a source: "I'm a reporter. A lot of times I have to creatively agitate people. Part of my job." Charlie comments on obituaries appearing in the trade journal *Editor & Publisher* in "Fire," and an old-fashioned *Tribune* reporter tells Lou he prefers a typewriter to a computer in "Blackout."

In creative terms the second and third seasons expanded the personalities of the series's characters by playing off the traits established in the opening year. For instance, viewers learned that Animal was a Vietnam veteran and that Charlie had been tortured as a foreign correspondent. Billie often grappled with her desire to act professionally and her concern for the people she interviewed. Wisecracking Art Donovan showed an emotional side when dealing with his mother's death and his cousin's mental illness. Rossi and Billie grew closer when they talked about the breakup of her marriage and his relationship with a woman and her two children. Lou's relationship with his children and girlfriends explored the private life of a middle-aged man. Mrs. Pynchon may have changed the least; she remained the stern *Tribune* matriarch although she obviously cared about her staff.

No wonder journalists still enjoyed *Lou Grant* after three years. It depicted their profession with unusual accuracy for television from the ringing phones and chattering teletypes of the *Tribune* newsroom to the complaints of reporters unhappy with their assignments. Moreover, the series showed reporters as caring professionals who took their work seriously and attempted to perform a public service by covering important events and digging for information. In producing an excellent television series the creative forces behind *Lou Grant* depicted journalists at their best.

7

Fourth and Fifth Seasons, 1980–1982

Ed Asner called September 7, 1980, a "red-letter day" for *Lou Grant*.[1] That night in Pasadena, California, the Academy of Television Arts and Sciences presented its Emmy awards. Asner's series had earned fifteen nominations, the most for any television program that year. By the time the ceremonies ended, the newspaper drama had won six awards, including those for Outstanding Drama and Outstanding Lead Actor in a Drama. Yet Asner was not present at the Pasadena Civic Auditorium to accept his seventh Emmy, a record for a male performer. "I'd give anything to be there," he had told reporters.[2] Nearly every television actor had boycotted the event in support of a seven-week-old strike against the television networks by the Screen Actors Guild and the American Federation of Television and Radio Artists. On any other night the triumph of *Lou Grant* would have headlined news reports. Instead, the boycott was the big news. The *Los Angeles Herald Examiner* termed the festivities "The Night the Stars Didn't Shine."[3]

The turmoil caused by the strike had a ripple effect that was felt less than two years later when CBS abruptly canceled *Lou Grant*. Asner, a longtime crusader for many humanitarian and political causes, became a public spokesman for the striking actors. Guild officials had asked him to participate in the first news conference about the strike. He later told a reporter, "Somehow that day, with the TV cameras, with the battery of microphones in front of me and with the constant barrage of questions, it just mobilized the best in me."[4] As the leader of union members unhappy with the settlement of the strike, Asner was elected its president on November 3, 1981. The position had groomed Ronald Reagan for a political career, but Asner's outspoken criticism of the Reagan administration later would fuel a conservative-led backlash that many observers believed prompted CBS to cancel the series.

Lou Grant began its fourth season on September 22, 1980. With Emmy victories and continued support from critics the series appeared headed for a long run. Forces outside the MTM studios, however, eventually would take a damaging toll on *Lou Grant*. The public perception of Asner would change as he became embroiled in political disputes. Although critics generally remained loyal to *Lou Grant*, they found a new cause in another drama with weak ratings, a police show produced by MTM called *Hill Street Blues*. In time MTM's newest drama replaced *Lou Grant* as the most critically acclaimed series on television. It also provided Asner's series stiff competition for Emmys and other awards. Thus, the factors that had helped *Lou Grant* overcome tepid ratings—Asner's participation, critical acclaim, and prestigious awards—gradually diminished and left the series vulnerable to the network ax.

★   ★   ★

Lou Grant began its fourth season with the episode "Nightside," a humorous character study of the people who finished the *Tribune* after the dayside staff had left.[5] When Lou is forced to fill in for an ailing night editor, he discovers that evening staffers are laid-back and quirky with a routine of their own. The crash of a small plane and a suspicious explosion aboard a yacht turn a quiet night into a scramble for news. Billie and Donovan help cover the yacht explosion, which is linked to drugs and organized crime. "Nightside" mirrored two earlier episodes, "Airliner" and "Marathon," by depicting the coverage of unexpected news events.

A stronger journalism story came with the episode "Pack," which aired just eight days before election day in 1980.[6] The episode dramatized flaws in news coverage of political campaigns, reflecting several issues raised in *The Boys on the Bus*, a classic study of political reporting used by the series's researchers.[7] In the episode Billie is assigned to the campaign of Senate candidate Jim Carlisle when Charlie and Lou replace the *Tribune*'s veteran political reporter for a fresh perspective. Almost immediately, the new beat frustrates Billie. Her editors criticize her for clichéd reporting, the candidate delivers the same speech from rally to rally, she is criticized for not reporting what other journalists are reporting, and her colleagues in the "pack" resent her for replacing their friend.[8]

When Billie reports Carlisle's quick temper, Lou wonders why the other reporters do not have the story. An angry Billie tells him, "First you complain that I write like everybody else and now you're mad because I don't." Lou responds, "I just hope this is nailed down. I don't like being alone on this." Billie, even more frustrated, answers: "Perfect. The first exclusive I get and you're nervous because everybody else doesn't have it." The story further alienates Billie on the campaign trail. Carlisle's press secretary is unhappy with the negative coverage, and her colleagues are angry because her story puts them on the spot with their editors.

Having had enough of the reporters' snubs, Billie finally lashes out at them. "You're all so smug," she says. "You all sit around here and you talk only to yourselves and you all file the same story. What about the people you're writing for, huh? They have a right to know what's going on, and you're all so impressed with yourselves that you've forgotten that." Chastened, the reporters later join Billie in unusually tough questioning of Carlisle about gun control. Surprisingly, he admits that he favors gun control (depicted as an unpopular stand in California) because of the shooting death of a friend. The revelation becomes a major story and, because of positive reaction to his honesty, a turning point for Carlisle's campaign. Billie wins the respect of her colleagues and her editors. Both entertaining and incisive, "Pack" earned director Burt Brinckerhoff an Emmy nomination.[9]

The consequences of using deception to gather news were examined in the episode "Goop."[10] An investigation of illegally dumped hazardous waste leads Billie and Rossi to the Dillard chemical plant. Suspecting that company officials are lying when they claim that all waste is stored at the plant, Billie proposes that she get a job at the plant. Charlie, however, bridles at the notion of misrepresentation to obtain information, even if it is the only way. He argues, "Maybe there are some stories that we just don't get if we don't like the way we have to get them." Lou and Billie suggest that she use her real name and list the *Tribune* as a former employer. "If Billie went to work for Dillard, she wouldn't be committing a crime," Lou says. "And if they're really dumping hazardous materials on the sly, that's despicable." Charlie reluctantly agrees to the plan.

A short time after Billie is hired as a clerical worker, Mrs. Pynchon raises her misgivings about the way the *Tribune* is getting its information. She points out that a journalism awards committee on which she served refused to honor a reporter who gained a story through misrepresentation. (In a well-publicized ethics case, the *Chicago Sun-Times* lost its bid for a Pulitzer Prize in 1979 because it used deception to uncover corruption in government.)[11] Mrs. Pynchon argues: "The press has a profound responsibility to be totally honest about the way it gets a story. If we are to feel in any way justified in decrying dishonesty in government and in business, by using deception we lower ourselves to the level of those we object to."

Charlie, only a recent convert to the other side of the issue, points out that the *Tribune* is committed to the story and has a duty to find the information.

> I don't like it very much, but I don't want to get so self-righteous about our methods that we deny ourselves and the public important stories. We have to take it a case at a time. . . . Would you rather wrestle with your conscience over our tactics in getting a story, which really hurt no one, or over our not telling people that they may be getting cancer from the water they drink because someone is callously and calculatingly polluting it?

Mrs. Pynchon allows the investigation to continue. Soon, Billie finds that leading a double life is personally unsettling. She becomes friends with Teri, a young woman on a work-study program from school. Billie's co-workers at Dillard even throw a surprise birthday party for her. Meanwhile, she looks through company records for evidence of waste dumping.

Billie discovers a record of payments to truck drivers for unclear assignments, another of which is scheduled for that night. Rossi and Animal follow the truck, which dumps waste into a stream. Rossi contacts the company the next day for comment. When he leaves the Dillard office, Teri remarks to Billie: "Typical reporter. Reporters are the lowest. My dad told me. Everybody knows it. They're all pushy and grubby. All they care about is getting their story."

Having returned to the *Tribune*, Billie writes her story and includes her undercover role at Charlie's insistence. Feeling guilty over her deceit, she arranges to meet Teri at a restaurant to explain why she had to misrepresent herself. Teri rejects Billie's explanation; both her uncle and her boyfriend are in trouble because of the *Tribune* story. "I think what you did stinks," Teri says. She calls their friendship a lie and orders Billie to leave. Ending on a bitter note, "Goop" showed the personal cost to a reporter who deceives people for a news story as well as the justification for deceit.

"Libel" explored the difficulty of suing a publication for libel and how the threat of a libel suit can discourage a newspaper from investigative reporting.[12] Tennis star Eddie Daniels blames all journalists when his wife, upset by a *National Spectator* story on the couple, wrecks her car and suffers a miscarriage. "You did this, you reporters!" Daniels shouts at Billie when she approaches him at the hospital. "You made us lose our baby. You lie, you distort things, just to make your news." Billie later tells Lou, "They're confusing the public about who's a legitimate reporter and who's a creep." Lou assigns Billie and Rossi to write a story about the *Spectator* and the people it profiles. Some are suing, but others admit the publication is too big and a suit too expensive, to pursue.

The *Tribune*'s lawyer points out that the *Spectator* story may not be worth publishing if it results in a libel action, even if it is accurate. He warns, "Being right may be just as expensive as being wrong." Indeed, the *Spectator* sues the *Tribune* for sixty million dollars. The *Tribune* staff finds itself buried in paperwork to meet the demands of the lawsuit. Depositions of the journalists inquire about their states of mind, a line of questioning that angers Lou. "If editors are forced to testify about their doubts, bare their thought processes to the root, do you realize what a chilling effect that's going to have?" he asks. "Every time an editor has to make a decision or is faced with a hard choice, he's going to wonder if he's going to get hauled into a nuisance suit like this one, maybe incriminating himself or one of his reporters." At the *Tribune* financial editor Adam Wilson admits he is dropping a corruption probe because it could result in a libel suit. Charlie orders him to pursue it anyway. Lou decides to refuse to answer questions about his state of mind, incurring a $100-per-day fine. Mrs. Pynchon and Charlie urge him to cooperate, saying they must get on with fighting the suit. Lou reluctantly agrees.

"Strike" dramatized labor relations at a newspaper by showing the economic forces that can lead to a strike and the divisive feelings a walkout can create.[13] In the episode Charlie and union representative Jim Bronsky disagree over the *Tribune*'s use of computers to eliminate jobs in the composing room and save money. Editorial and other divisions of the newspaper vote to support a strike by the printers' union. Although a strike appears likely if computerization takes place, Mrs. Pynchon agrees that the millions of dollars the *Tribune* will save will keep the newspaper from losing money.

The possibility of a strike worries the staff. Animal says he does not want to choose sides, but a prounion Rossi points out that sides will choose him. Meanwhile, Charlie and Lou learn how to paste up the newspaper in preparation for a walkout. With a strike authorized by the union talks continue well into the night. When a strike is called, Billie and others reluctantly leave the newsroom, and Rossi angers Lou by purging the computer of notes on an important story. Adam, who needs his job to pay for a new house, remains on the job. Lou participates half-heartedly in strategy sessions with Mrs. Pynchon and Charlie.

As pickets protest outside the *Tribune* building one of the printers suffers a fatal heart attack. The strike continues for three weeks. When Billie is injured by a wrench thrown from a *Tribune* truck, Lou tells Charlie he can no longer oppose his friends; he joins the picket line.

Against the advice of her business manager, Mrs. Pynchon comes to terms with the union. At the conclusion of the episode Lou visits Billie in an effort to reach an understanding about their differences. One flaw in "Strike" was its failure—and that of subsequent episodes—to show how the strike had affected the relationships of management and other non-striking employees and those who picketed. The otherwise perceptive episode earned Emmy nominations for April Smith's script and Gene Reynolds's direction.[14]

The sometimes-strained relationship between a business and a newspaper was depicted in the episode "Business."[15] Rossi and Billie cover a suspicious fire at Cal Electronics, a major employer and a frequent advertiser in the *Tribune*. They discover that the company had been cited for safety violations in the past. As the reporters write about the fire and subsequent investigation company officials offer little comment and cooperation. Adam objects to a follow-up story by Billie, calling it slanted and misleading. The next day, the fire marshal's report attributes the blaze to ruptured gas pipes caused by city road maintenance.

Cal Electronics chief Russell Davidson complains to Mrs. Pynchon that the *Tribune* has a reputation for being unfair to big business. He contends that the suggestion that the fire was the company's fault has cost them an important loan. Later, the company prepares a full-page ad complaining of the *Tribune*'s coverage. When Davidson complains to Lou and Charlie about coverage of the fire, the men debate the responsibilities of business and the press. At one point Charlie argues: "You guys try to blame everything on the media. Imports are threatening, the quality of goods and services deteriorates, you have national recalls, and somehow it's our fault. Well, I don't buy that." Davidson responds: "I want a little more consideration. We're tired of constantly reading that American business is second-rate, that we're riddled with inefficiency. You print that often enough and you make it come true."

Despite their best efforts Rossi and Billie fail to find any evidence that Cal Electronics had done anything wrong. The meeting between company officials and the *Tribune* editors apparently benefits both. Charlie decides to publish guest columns by people in business and industry for a different perspective on issues. Davidson, in announcing a restructuring of the company, gives plenty of information to the press. Adam points out that the company appears to be honest and straightforward with reporters. Rossi, ever the skeptic, says: "Yeah, I know. That's what worries me."

Nearly two-thirds of the episodes aired in the 1980–81 season focused on social issues or human-interest stories. The social issues the series examined included sexual harassment, "sting" operations by authorities, tension between police and inner-city blacks, poor products sold overseas that had an impact on American consumers, the survivalist movement, and America's violent society.[16] Perhaps the most dramatic of the issue episodes was "Rape," which depicted a sexual assault and its aftermath by following a *Tribune* reporter through her ordeal.[17] At one point Mrs. Pynchon criticizes the *Tribune*'s coverage of rape and the legal system. Lou's comment that "everyone is vulnerable to attack" angers her. "Not this kind of attack," she answers sharply. "You can't help but wonder if men were the ones being raped, then would the problem get solved?" Seth Freeman's script earned the series another Emmy nomination.[18]

As they had in previous seasons the human-interest stories told during the fourth year of *Lou Grant* often spotlighted the *Tribune* staff—and the series's performers. For instance, Mrs. Pynchon suffered a stroke in one episode; Nancy Marchand expertly portrayed a woman's struggle to regain her health and dignity.[19] In "Venice" Animal (Daryl Anderson) became obsessed with the suicide of an attractive young woman, trying to understand why she would kill herself.[20] Billie fell in love with a baseball player in "Catch."[21] The different way in which Charlie and veteran reporter George Driscoll handle disappointment and frustration in their lives was explored in "Depression."[22] The problems between elderly, middle-aged and young people was dramatized in "Generations," and a *Tribune* staffer tried to find her birth mother in "Search."[23]

By the end of the television season ratings for *Lou Grant* had changed little. The series finished the season with an average rating of 19.5, the same score it had earned for the 1979–80 season. With a season-average 32 share, the series had again drawn nearly one-third of the television audience for its time period. Its strongest competitor, ABC's *Monday Night Football*, remained strong with an average rating of 20.1. On NBC the *Monday Night Movie* drew a rating of 18.[24] Backed by respectable ratings, CBS executives once again included *Lou Grant* in the fall lineup.

Industry accolades were another matter. After two years of dominating television awards, the newspaper drama suddenly found itself overwhelmed by the phenomenon of *Hill Street Blues*. The NBC police drama had weaker ratings than *Lou Grant* ever experienced, ranking eighty-seventh among the ninety-six series aired in prime time.[25] Critics, however, rallied around the series and helped it win an unlikely renewal. The tide of acclaim continued when both the Directors Guild of America and the Writers Guild of America awarded its television honors to *Hill Street Blues*. No one was prepared for its sweep of the Emmy nominations. *Hill Street Blues* earned a record twenty-one nominations. *Lou Grant* remained a strong contender, receiving thirteen nominations.[26] But when the awards were announced, *Hill Street Blues* defeated *Lou Grant* in every category except supporting actress; the venerable Marchand won her third award.[27] There was no question that *Lou Grant* remained a series of high quality. Yet *Hill Street Blues*, with its low ratings and tremendous acclaim, had become the most-talked-about show on television.

★　　★　　★

To the majority of the public Ed Asner probably seemed as tough, lovable, and trustworthy as Lou Grant, the character he had played for more than one decade on television. In the aftermath of the actors strike his off-camera activities became better known to the public. They also began to draw public criticism. When *TV Guide*, the nation's second-largest magazine, profiled Asner on April 11, 1981, it described him as a "charismatic and controversial leader in Hollywood."[28] The article, published in a magazine with a circulation of 17.6 million, presented a side of the popular actor many Americans may not have known.[29]

Asner, the profile reported, was an unabashed liberal, unreformed by Ronald Reagan's landslide victory in the previous fall. He had worked for the American Civil Liberties Union, the National Committee for an Effective Congress, Common Cause, and other liberal groups. Moreover, his political activities had alienated some of his Hollywood colleagues. Producer David Gerber told *TV Guide:* "Ed Asner has gone too far. He thinks he's Lou Grant and he is rubbing people the wrong way."[30] Grant Tinker, the president of MTM Productions and soon to be the president of NBC, added: "I love him dearly, but what's troubling me is that Ed Asner is doing his talking with Lou Grant's credibility and he's thinking with Ed Asner's judgment. It's too bad."[31] Asner was not convinced that his off-screen activities conflicted with his acting career. "Bull," he told the magazine. "If they think my usefulness as a performer has ended, let them prove it."[32] After he was elected president of the Screen Actors Guild in November scrutiny of Asner by the industry, the news media, and the public became more intense.

SAG elections were held the week *Lou Grant* began its fifth year on CBS. That season Billie Newman married her ex-ballplayer boyfriend. In the episode "Wedding," which began the new season, the demands of a career have clearly taken their toll on the personal lives of Billie and Lou. She hesitates to accept Ted McCovey's proposal of marriage, fearing that her career will be a constant burden. Lou's career already has strained his relationship with daughter Janie. Both finally decide to put their careers second. Billie accepts Ted's proposal, and Lou plans a reunion with all three of his daughters in Chicago. A computer problem at the *Tribune* forces Lou to cancel, however, and makes the entire staff—including Billie—work through the night. The next day, a tired but happy staff witnesses Billie's marriage. Later, Lou is surprised by his daughters, who have traveled to Los Angeles to be with him.

The marriage did not result in changes in Billie's personality or her work as a journalist. Rather, it opened new situations for the character. Actress Linda Kelsey, who was married and planning a family, had asked the producers to develop a relationship for the character in case she became pregnant. She recalled that there was talk at one point of Billie and Ted having a child and later divorcing, which would make Billie a working single mother.[33] In the fifth season, however, Billie's marriage was seldom a factor in story lines. In one episode she and Ted disagreed about the merits of having a halfway house for disturbed youth on their block. In another, she sought a transfer to Sacramento to be closer to Ted, who spent much of his time traveling as a baseball scout. Had the producers prepared scripts for a sixth season, Billie's marriage may have had a more significant impact.

The fifth season also introduced a new *Tribune* reporter, Lance Reinecke, played by actor Lance Guest. A native of California, Guest had studied acting at the University of California at Los Angeles before dropping out to seek film and television roles.[34] His first professional appearance as an actor was in the episode "Survival," which aired during the fourth season. He played a minor character, a *Tribune* copyboy named Mark. "I was this sort of young, real eager, not very together, scatterbrained kind of guy," Guest remembered. "It was very exciting to me because it was the first time I'd seen a movie set."[35] Nearly one year later the producers contacted Guest's agent about casting him as a young reporter at the newspaper. The script that was sent to Guest, the actor recalled, referred to the character as "a reporter, Lance, possibly the Lance from last year's show." The name of the actor had become the name of the character. "What's weird is that they remembered me as Lance, they didn't remember me as Mark," Guest said. "They remembered me by my name, which indicated to me they thought, 'Hey, I like that guy.' "[36]

Guest appeared in six episodes during the final year of *Lou Grant*. At first Lance Reinecke was a slightly comical character, a likable eager-beaver who made mistakes. "They wanted to have a lot of fun with him," Guest said. "Their idea was to make him sort of a comic character, a high-energy guy who was always doing all this physical stuff, more action-oriented things. It was very important for him to be green and learn as he went along."[37] With his long curly hair and casual dress, Lance Reinecke brought youth and naîveté to the *Tribune* city room. (Guest was twenty or twenty-one when he worked on the series.) The producers asked him to join the cast as a regular for the sixth season. His character then became the focus of "Suspect," which aired late in the fifth season.

Guest had no journalism experience and little time for research. His main sources of information about reporters and newspapers were the scripts and his fellow actors. Yet in the year he worked on *Lou Grant* he changed his generally negative view of the news media. "When I was younger, it sort of seemed like journalists were always out to break people down and find out dirt on somebody," Guest said. "That always kind of annoyed me personally. Then I realized a lot of it was for a greater good. I pretty much got my mind changed around about that. People I had thought were not idealistic were revealed as being idealistic."[38]

The fifth season of *Lou Grant* featured several strong journalism episodes. The episode "Reckless" examined whether a newspaper should act as an arm of the police.[39] Charlie, fuming over the vandalism of his car, proposes that the *Tribune* establish a hotline that offers rewards for information about crime. Mrs. Pynchon does not like the idea, saying, "I'm just not sure that the function of the *Tribune* is to turn its readers into stool pigeons and snitches." Despite her misgivings she agrees to work with the police department on establishing the "Private Eye" hotline. At first, the hotline seems a success when a caller tips police to a murder suspect. The suspect's lawyer, however, blames the *Tribune* for encouraging anonymous accusations and sensationalizing its own importance. The editors later agree that a citizens' group would be better-suited to operate the hotline, allowing the *Tribune* to remain independent. Lou says, "The way I see it, you can be Dick Tracy or Clark Kent, but you can't be both."

The consequences of promising confidentiality to a source were studied in "Risk."[40] *Tribune* reporter Sharon McNeil's story about a nine-year-old girl allowed by her mother to appear in pornographic films raises the ire of public officials and readers. Having promised the mother anonymity, Sharon refuses to reveal the girl's identity. Lou and Mrs. Pynchon are unhappy that she made the promise, yet they support her decision to stand by it. Police Lieutenant McPhee tries to convince her that the promise is not valid because it was given to a woman who is harming a child. Sharon contends: "Next time it might be a drug addict, it might be a counterfeiter. Who's going to believe me if I say I only betrayed a confidence once?" McPhee answers: "To me, one human life is worth more than all of the principles you can come up with. You're sacrificing the life of a child to protect your reputation."

Police later determine where the girl and her mother live. By the time they arrive the two are gone, probably having moved to another town. Sharon feels guilty, believing that her silence has allowed the mother to continue to abuse the child. She tells Rossi that she will not give a promise of confidentiality so easily again. "Maybe next time I can be shrewder," she says. "Maybe I'll be able to find a way to get the story without playing that card." The subject was a natural for *Lou Grant*. The ethics of confidentiality, including whether a reporter should gain permission from an editor before promising it, had been debated in the profession for several years.[41] Writer Michele Gallery recalled that "Risk" had been inspired by the case of Janet Cooke, a *Washington Post* writer who won a Pulitzer Prize for a feature story about an eight-year-old drug addict.[42] "Risk" took a decidedly different spin on the Cooke incident. The *Post* story was revealed to be a hoax, and the award was rescinded.

The episode "Friends" explored the dilemma a reporter faces when a friend is the subject of a news story.[43] Rossi's jogging partner Burt Cary is a candidate for the board of supervisors. He resists Lou's suggestion that he cover the board, arguing that his friendship with Cary would be seen by others as a conflict of interest. Later, Rossi is shocked to learn that Cary has participated in a plot to link his opponent to a cocaine purchase. When Rossi confronts him, Cary says, "You've got a problem, don't you? Whether to be a reporter or a friend." After struggling with his conscience, Rossi tells the *Tribune* reporter covering the campaign about Cary's shenanigans. Then he searches for a new jogging partner.

Several issues in journalism were depicted in "Cameras": the impact of television on news coverage, the competition between newspapers and television, the use of television cameras in courtrooms, and the role of editing in news writing.[44] When two gunmen take children hostage at a restaurant, the *Tribune* cannot compete with the immediate coverage provided by television crews at the scene. "The whole city is having breakfast and watching this," Rossi comments as the *Tribune* staff gathers around a television set. Lou wryly asks, "You mean they're not sitting there glued to their newspapers, waiting for further developments?"

The children are freed unharmed within hours. Later, Mrs. Pynchon questions whether the *Tribune* and other news media are exploiting the children with follow-up stories of the hostage event. Charlie and Lou argue that the *Tribune* is providing human interest and matching the stories of other news media as well. The editors then assign Billie to write about whether the children are being exploited by their parents for possible monetary gain. When a judge seeking reelection allows cameras in the courtroom during the hostage-takers' trial, Rossi wonders whether the

decision was aimed at gaining the judge publicity. At the *Tribune* the staff
debates the value of cameras in courts.

CHARLIE

Trial coverage has always been the one place that newspapers
have had all to themselves. I know cameras in the courtroom are
going to hurt us. Even so, the cameras belong there. It's another
form of freedom of the press.

LOU

Good for you, Charlie. I haven't heard that phrase 'freedom of
the press' raised in an argument all day.

ROSSI

It's a bad ruling. First of all, TV doesn't explain what's going on.
The average guy sitting in front of his TV set doesn't understand
what he's watching. In the second place, TV is show biz. They
just go over the fastest, most sensational stuff. I don't trust anybody in TV.

When Lou and Art edit Billie's story, they decide her description of
one of the mothers does not go far enough. They change the phrase
"under his mother's watchful eye" to "under his mother's manipulation."
Deciding that the word "manipulation" is too strong, they change the
word to "coaching." Billie, livid after reading the change in the newspaper, tells Lou: "That story was deliberately slanted. I didn't write it that
way." Although the mother accuses Billie of doing a "hatchet job," she
later admits that she had coached the child. Finally, an angry Billie confronts Lou. "I may not be the best writer in the world, but one thing I've
got going for me is my integrity," she says. "So when something I write
gets changed around to satisfy someone else's notion about what makes
good copy, I get furious." Lou admits he should have called her to alert
her to the change. Yet he stops short of an apology, saying only, "I
hear you."

How and whether the news media should regulate themselves was
dramatized in the episode "Review."[45] The story also touched on the
question of whether a public official's private remarks should remain private, even if overheard by a journalist. In the episode Charlie is appointed
to the Western States News Council, a panel of journalists and other
community members who listen to complaints about news coverage. Lou
is unimpressed, saying: "What do we need it for? If we're wrong, we print

a retraction." The *Tribune*'s decision to publish the fact that a councilman often makes racial jokes draws the council's scrutiny. Lou represents the *Tribune* at the council meeting, contending that the newspaper has acted fairly in the matter. Still, the council determines that the councilman's complaint about an unfair report is warranted. Although Rossi favors ignoring the council's decision, Lou suggests that the *Tribune* publish a news story about it and an editorial stating the paper's position as well. Charlie and Mrs. Pynchon agree, believing that the *Tribune* can withstand the criticism.

The episode "Fireworks" revisited the problem of conflict of interest by exploring Billie's efforts to cover her ex-husband's activities and debating the place of awards in journalism.[46] When Billie goes to Sacramento to write about lobbying and legislation that would end fireworks regulations, she meets ex-husband and lobbyist Greg Serantino. Although pleasant at first, Greg angers Billie by breaking a dinner meeting and declining to cooperate. At the *Tribune*, meanwhile, Mrs. Pynchon is pleased that the paper's medical series has been nominated for a prestigious Greenwood Foundation award. Rossi, however, does not want to accept the award because the foundation was started by a company with a poor environmental record and a history of selling unsafe products overseas.

Billie discovers that Greg, a fireworks-industry lobbyist, wrote the legislation. He accuses her of pursuing the story only because her ex-husband is involved, a charge she denies. Even without his help, Billie writes her story. Meanwhile, Charlie is angry that Lou wants to pull out of the Greenwood Foundation contest. He claims the award would boost the *Tribune*'s prestige. "It's going to make a big difference in influence," Charlie argues. "Maybe we won't have to fight so hard to convince the best students that this is a first-class place to work." Lou leaves the decision up to the staff, which decides to shun the contest. Lance, the *Tribune*'s newest reporter, asks Billie, "The work is kind of its own reward, don't you think?" She answers, "Depends on where they put your story."

"Suspect" mocked the untold number of motion pictures and television shows in which an intrepid reporter solved a murder.[47] In the episode Lance Reinecke suspects a man killed by a hit-and-run driver may not have been an accident victim after Lance uncovers a link to prostitution. Lou tells him to take his information to police, but he continues to investigate on his own. He gets more than he bargained for when an angry pimp catches him talking to one of his women, but the police arrive in time to save Lance from a certain beating. Later, the young reporter learns that his theory of murder is wrong and that the death was indeed an accident.

Lou eases up on Lance, assuring him that his instincts to find the truth were sound even if his methods were not.

The episode "Beachhead" depicted the negative impact a newspaper story can have on a tense situation.[48] Charlie pushes to place Rossi's story on surfer gangs at the beach on page one. After the story appears a rival gang shows up at the beach, and a fight breaks out among the surfers. Charlie dismisses Lou's suggestion that the story was a factor in the fight. Even though he opposed the story, Lou represents the *Tribune* before the city council of the beach community. One official tells him, "We had the situation under control until you printed that article." Despite the criticism Lou stands by the *Tribune*. At the newspaper, however, he lashes out at Charlie: "We gave a handful of beach bums more coverage in one day than they should get in a lifetime. We provoked trouble in a town where they are trying very hard to maintain peace. We hurt them, Charlie." The managing editor responds: "Don't tell me after the fact that I made a mistake. Tell me how the reader is going to respond tomorrow to what we're writing today."

The editorial and advertising departments clashed once again in "Blacklist," which also examined the blacklisting of Communists during the 1950s.[49] The *Tribune* draws reader ire when it begins to carry "Dr. Valentine," a syndicated sex column aimed at teenagers. Protesters call for a boycott of the paper and demonstrate outside the *Tribune* while advertisers begin to drop their accounts, angering the advertising staff. Charlie, supported by Mrs. Pynchon, refuses to drop the column. "Stop trying to solve advertising problems by changing editorial policy," he tells the paper's chief advertising executive. "We decide what to write. You decide how to market it." Writer Seth Freeman earned an Emmy nomination for his script.[50]

The episode "Charlie" echoed the third-season show "Lou" by depicting a typical day in the life of the *Tribune*'s managing editor.[51] In doing so the episode showed the myriad of problems that face a newspaper executive. He counsels Art when he fears that his girlfriend is pregnant (and again later after she has an abortion). He incurs Billie's wrath by not transferring her to Sacramento, which she requested as a way of spending more time with her husband. He clashes with Mrs. Pynchon when she overrides his decision to fire a staffer over a conflict of interest and force another into retirement because of his drinking problem. (Mrs. Pynchon later relents.) Charlie, fatherly at one moment and thoroughly professional at another, handles everything thrown at him.

Eight episodes, including "Wedding," reflected the series's penchant for human-interest stories, often told by focusing on a member of the

Tribune staff. In "Hometown," which earned director Gene Reynolds an Emmy nomination, Lou made a sentimental trip to the Michigan town where he grew up.[52] "Double-Cross" was a complicated mystery story about a gold cross and a feuding family.[53] "Drifters" featured Charlie's nephew Scott, a young man with emotional problems.[54] In "Jazz" Rossi helped reunite a legendary jazz group.[55] Billie explored a haunted house in "Ghosts."[56] The episode "Victims" examined the aftermath of two shootings; one of the victims was Lou, robbed and shot outside the *Tribune* at night.[57]

"Obituary," written by April Smith, was one of the series's most heartfelt episodes, expressing in an understated way the frailty and value of life.[58] Billie is to join other journalists on a small plane headed to cover a prison riot. At the last moment she is pulled off the assignment to cover another story. The plane crashes, killing the three journalists on board. Unsatisfied with the obituaries that appeared in the *Tribune*, Mrs. Pynchon asks for profiles of the three who died. Lou, Rossi, and Billie discover that each of the journalists had a complex life and faults that were not apparent to their colleagues. Juxtaposed with their work is Animal's effort to find and photograph a rare moth. He gives up the assignment after realizing that if the photos run in the paper, collectors will find the field in which the moths live and further endanger the species.

Among the social issues the series dramatized during the year were capital punishment, the problems of Vietnamese refugees, the litigious society, and guilt by association.[59] The episode "Hunger" examined the complex issues that caused hunger in the United States and abroad and the problem facing a reporter involved in a complicated story.[60] At first, Rossi cannot convince his editors to publish the story. They believe it has no central point and is too complicated to interest readers. Through perseverance, Rossi finally produces a story the editors deem good enough for the front page. "Think it will interest anybody?" one editor asks. "Not many of our readers are starving," Lou says, "but maybe they should know why millions of people are." Reynolds won a Humanitas Award for the script of "Hunger," which the Human Family Institute said "courageously probed the taboo issue of the world's half-billion people who live on the edge of starvation."[61]

Many episodes during the course of *Lou Grant* had open endings in which issues and problems were not neatly resolved. No ending was more open-ended than that of "Unthinkable," the series's most provocative entry.[62] Media historian and critic Todd Gitlin called "Unthinkable" the first realistic-style television-series episode to dramatize the possibility of nuclear war.[63] The episode depicted the first days of a nuclear crisis, displaying the day and time to heighten the tension. The United States and the Middle East nation of Kulari already are at odds when a Kulari jet is shot down. The conflict quickly leads to an oil shortage. Officials and others suggest that the United States may use nuclear weapons to preserve access to oil fields. In Los Angeles *Tribune* reporters cover civil-defense preparations, public reaction to the nuclear threat, and the growing panic.

Billie, however, is covering a different story. A school bus crash has severely burned a young girl. As the girl struggles to survive in a hospital burn unit, Billie learns how much care is required for a single burn victim. The international crisis grows when the Kulari parliament is taken over by leftists after an explosion. Later, a U.S. oil tanker is destroyed. The episode ends with the girl's doctor expressing guarded optimism that she will recover. Unlike other dramatizations of nuclear war in which war is averted, however, "Unthinkable" did not resolve the crisis. Instead of being reassured that war somehow would be stopped, viewers were left to ponder such a fate. In addition, the episode offered disturbing statistics about the potential death toll and other horrors. Finally, the burned child's experience showed how futile medical efforts would be in the aftermath of a nuclear explosion.

When it aired on May 3, 1982, "Unthinkable" drew a rating of only 10.9 and a 19 share, the lowest audience marks in the history of the series.[64] Perhaps that was not surprising, given its heavy subject matter. Another factor, however, may have been a political controversy that swirled around Ed Asner, whose outspoken views on United States relations with El Salvador had caused considerable debate. With CBS deciding its fall slate of programs in the same week that "Unthinkable" aired the poor rating could not have come at a worse time. Three days later on May 6, 1982, CBS announced it had canceled *Lou Grant*, one of television's most honored programs. Network officials contended the cancellation stemmed from weak ratings, not Asner's activities.[65]

Ratings notwithstanding, CBS angered fans and numerous television critics. The network's action probably cheered those who believed Asner was using his high profile to promote a liberal agenda that they thought was dangerous for the nation. The cast and crew of *Lou Grant* had been well aware of the controversy. Although some ignored it as best they could and planned for another season of work, others thought it might hurt the show. Still, the news that their work on the award-winning series was finished was a shock for many of them. "I was devastated," Linda Kelsey recalled. "I never thought they'd really do it."[66]

8

Controversy and Cancellation

People tuning into the *CBS Evening News* on February 15, 1982, saw a familiar face in a report from Washington, D.C. It belonged to an actor rather than a politician. The setting that President's Day was a news conference in the nation's capital. In his report anchor Dan Rather left no doubt that viewers were watching the star of a popular television series. "Television's Lou Grant, actor Ed Asner, was in Washington today," Rather reported. "He led a group of show-business personalities opposed to President Reagan's policy in El Salvador. And they announced a campaign to raise one million dollars as a donation to Salvadoran rebels. Asner handed over a check for twenty-five thousand dollars to a Mexican doctor who was supposed to use it for the health-care system of rebel forces."[1]

Rather's report came six minutes into the newscast and lasted only twenty seconds. Significantly, it failed to explain fully the purpose of the fund-raising campaign. Thus, Asner may have appeared to be sending money to Marxist rebels fighting the pro-American junta government supported by the Reagan administration. In fact, the effort was humanitarian rather than political.

Asner told reporters in Washington that the money, raised by donations from eight thousand people, was meant to help rural citizens of a nation racked by a bloody civil war. Medical supplies purchased in Mexico —not money—would be given to the rebels, who were the only people with a health-care system that reached rural areas. He noted that the Salvadoran government was not providing such care for its citizens. "If we want to deliver medical aid assistance, frankly, we must do it through the rebel forces," he stated.[2] In the months ahead Asner's critics and the news media would blur the distinction between providing humanitarian aid to a suffering people and funding a communist rebellion.

A report that night on *ABC Evening News* was no more clear than the CBS story (NBC did not carry a report). First, ABC reporter Sam Donaldson told viewers that President Ronald Reagan was preparing a speech criticizing Cuban adventurism in the Caribbean Basin and likening it to foreign intervention in El Salvador. Then, Donaldson noted that some Americans opposed Reagan's policy in Central America. "Earlier today in a Washington hotel, a group of television actors was taking the other side of the El Salvador argument," Donaldson reported. "Led by Ed Asner, the group announced it has raised $25,000 for medical assistance to the leftist rebels there." Film of the news conference showed Asner saying, "Today we want to say clearly to President Reagan in the White House and Secretary Haig in the State Department that their enemies in El Salvador are not our enemies." Donaldson then added: "Such anti-administration rhetoric, so reminiscent of the Vietnam era, is still quite faint over El Salvador."[3]

Tens of millions of Americans saw the CBS and ABC reports. Producer Gene Reynolds was among Asner's *Lou Grant* colleagues who watched news reports about the speech and followed the ensuing controversy. "I was very surprised," he recalled. "I don't know what role he was playing, but he was Broderick Crawford suddenly, very truculent, kind of tough and cocky."[4] Despite five years of awards and acclaim for *Lou Grant* the producer became concerned that the Emmy-winning show could be canceled in the wake of controversy over Asner's actions. He also believed that Asner's public pronouncements of his political beliefs hurt the series dramatically because Lou Grant stopped being a dispassionate newsman. "The American [public] was so aware of Ed Asner's position politically, and that's one thing that you shouldn't have," Reynolds said. "You shouldn't really know where he is. He should be a kind of guy that says, 'Is this what happened? Is that what worked out? O.K., then you print it'."[5]

Writer Michele Gallery also recalled the Washington announcement as a turning point. She, too, believed that people who had thought of Asner as Lou Grant, a character she described as a "heartland America conservative," began to distinguish the actor from his role. "People were looking at the character of Lou Grant and seeing Ed Asner," Gallery said. "I felt on that President's Day that the show was running out of good will."[6] Reaction to the donation disturbed Robert Walden. "It was set up as him being pro-communist," the actor remembered. "That was what was in all the papers about it. What was basically initiated as an act of humanity became a political situation."[7] To writer Steve Kline it was obvious that viewers who disliked Asner because of his politics would register their disapproval by not watching the series. "Once Ed started going on television, I knew it right away," Kline said. "I never once decried his right to say what he felt, but the way he said it was almost guaranteed to get the show thrown off."[8]

Ironically, Asner had told *Playboy* magazine in 1980, "I can never divorce a person from his or her politics."[9] Yet the cancellation of *Lou Grant* cannot be blamed on a single news conference by its star. By the time CBS decided not to renew the series Asner had been publicly criticized for months, fairly or unfairly, for his actions as Screen Actors Guild president and as a private citizen. Numerous people, from his fellow actors to conservative national leaders, had attacked him relentlessly. Some had called for boycotts of the sponsors of *Lou Grant* in retaliation for his beliefs. Meanwhile, the ratings for the series had dropped steadily, perhaps because of negative public reaction to the ongoing controversy.

Lou Grant, however, was not without flaws. Several television critics contended that its ability to present social issues and other relevant stories in an entertaining way had diminished in the 1981–82 season. Conceived in the 1970s with a liberal point of view, the series may have seemed out of step with the Reagan revolution and the conservative mood of the nation. By many accounts the cast and crew were exhausted after five years of production. Thus, many factors contributed to the demise of *Lou Grant.*

★   ★   ★

When ballots were counted on November 2, 1981, Asner was elected president of the Screen Actors Guild by a vote of 9,689 to 7,188. Although nearly 50,000 SAG members were eligible to vote in the mail election, the relatively small number of ballots returned was larger than usual for an election.[10] He had defeated incumbent William Schallert, contending that the guild under Schallert had settled for a poor contract in order to end the strike the previous year. Schallert questioned whether Asner had the experience or the time to be SAG president. "It's very difficult to go from the picket line to the presidency," he said.[11]

After the election Asner told reporters he hoped to fight the tide against unionism in the United States, which he blamed in part on Reagan.[12] Such talk probably confirmed the fears of those in SAG who thought Asner would turn the guild into a more political organization that leaned toward liberal causes. Traditionally, SAG remained neutral in most national political issues. The labor writer for the *Los Angeles Times,* Harry Bernstein, noted after the election, "Asner will have the dual platform of speaking as a famous actor in the role of conscientious newspaper editor and as president of a politically influential union."[13]

When Asner was elected, politics inside the guild centered on whether SAG should merge with the Screen Extras Guild and the American Federation of Television and Radio Artists. Asner and others favored the mergers as a way of strengthening the guild's bargaining power with producers. Some SAG members, however, such as Charlton Heston and Robert Conrad, opposed the merger with SEG. The antimerger forces contended, among other things, that a merger would merely add more unemployed people to the SAG's rolls and diminish the status of professional actors by grouping them with extras, who generally appear in non-speaking roles.[14] Heston, who would emerge as Asner's most vocal critic, charged that Asner favored merger because it would increase his power and that of other guild officials.[15]

The merger question was of little interest to those outside the acting community in Los Angeles. Guild politics, however, gained national attention just one month after Asner's election when the SAG board of directors declined to present Reagan with its top award. The unnamed award was presented each year to a person who had done the most for the guild on behalf of actors or the acting industry. Although the award for Reagan had been recommended by a committee, the ninety-nine-member board voted four-to-one not to present the honor to its former president and lifetime member. Guild spokeswoman Kim Fellner told reporters that the action reflected the guild's disapproval of Reagan's handling of an air traffic controllers strike and a variety of social concerns.[16] The 1981 strike by the air traffic controllers, which Reagan ended by firing those who refused to return to work, had prompted the guild to donate five thousand dollars to the union the previous summer in what was termed a show of solidarity.[17]

Both actions by the guild infuriated guild members such as Heston, a Reagan supporter and a former SAG president. The war of words that had brewed between Asner and Heston received increasing attention from the news media. A dispute between two well-known actors probably interested the general public even if the issues over which they clashed did not. The *Los Angeles Times* was only one newspaper that played on the fact that television's Lou Grant and the movies' Moses were at odds. To Heston, the guild had slighted the president of the United States and proved it was becoming increasingly political. He told the *Los Angeles Times:* "We can, as individuals, speak out on issues, as we frequently do. But it would be wrong for Ed Asner, as president of the guild, to advocate or oppose public issues or candidates because that would be taking an unfair advantage of our position."[18]

Asner was critical of American involvement in El Salvador well before his election as SAG president. In the summer of 1980 he told *Playboy* magazine that he was trying to "get the word out" on El Salvador by working on a documentary and raising money for refugees.[19] He was among two hundred people who signed a *New York Times* advertisement in February 1981 that criticized the government's policy. At the time he told reporters that Americans should know more about El Salvador before their government became too deeply involved in supporting a wealthy elite against the demands of the poor.[20] In early 1982 the Reagan administration contended that torture, indiscriminate killing, and other human-rights abuses by the Salvadoran government were diminishing. Yet reports of a mass slaughter of peasants by government forces in January 1982 threatened administration efforts to send more aid to El Salvador.[21]

When Asner traveled to Washington to join other activists supporting medical aid for El Salvador, he was not appearing on behalf of the guild. Neither CBS nor ABC referred to the actors union in their reports, nor did a United Press International story that appeared in the *Los Angeles Times*.[22] More important to the controversy was what Asner did not say and what journalists did not report,—namely, that he was *not* speaking on behalf of the guild. "That's what so many people, particularly Mr. Heston, pilloried me for and so many people thought to be a major crime," he recalled.[23] To make matters worse, he added, the news media during the controversy "misconstrued, misreported, [and] falsely reported" the group's intent to help the people of El Salvador receive medical supplies. "[The press] created a groundswell of antipathy against me as having been revealed as a commie, or a president of a union who was using his union's funds illegally or incorrectly, all of which, of course, turned out to be totally false," he said.[24]

Criticism for not distancing himself from SAG was not on Asner's mind after his Washington news conference. He feared that his candid statements opposing American policy in El Salvador would end his career. When asked by reporters how he would react if free elections produced a communist government in El Salvador, Asner had given a weak, noncommittal answer to avoid creating a controversy. Within moments he regretted his feeble answer and asked to respond again to the question. He then stated that if the people of El Salvador chose a communist government, they should have it. "At that point," Asner recalled, "in my mind I said, 'I am dead. I am literally dead in show biz for having given that answer.' This is in 1982 . . . the height of Reaganism, and I thought I was a dead fish. When I came back to L.A. I was actually prepared to find myself [unable] to be an actor, at least in film and television."[25]

Two days after the news conference in Washington, Asner received a telephone death threat. A caller to SAG headquarters claimed that a group of antiblack, anticommunist former Marines had targeted Asner and his wife because of his support of Salvadoran rebels. Bodyguards were assigned to the actor, and security was increased on the set of *Lou Grant*.[26] On the same day, a guild member angry with Asner began a petition to recall him as SAG president. Although Heston said he did not support the recall effort, he criticized Asner for being "carelessly derelict" in not making it clear that the guild was not involved in the medical aid donation.[27] In a guest column for the *New York Times* Asner defended his right to criticize the government. He wrote, "I think that it's not only a right but an obligation for every responsible citizen to speak out when our government is acting in ways we believe are wrong." Then, he outlined his reasons for believing that the United States was on the wrong side of the Salvadoran war, comparing it to American involvement in Vietnam.[28]

Criticism of Asner did not abate. SAG headquarters was plastered with leaflets that read, "Ed Asner is a Communist swine." Signed "Voice for an Independent Poland," the leaflets were thought to be in response to guild support for Solidarity, the suspended Polish trade union.[29] On February 25, ten days after the Washington statement, Asner and his bodyguards met the press. After a meeting of the guild board he admitted he had made "a slight goof, an honest mistake" in not stressing that he was speaking in Washington as a private citizen.[30] While promising to be more careful of what he said and how it might affect the guild, he insisted he would not surrender his right to speak about issues as an individual. The guild board passed a resolution supporting his right to speak and concluded that he had not done anything improper.[31] The statements by the guild and Asner ended the recall drive, but Heston and other opponents continued to criticize him and the direction they contended he was taking SAG.[32]

Unlike the political issues within the guild Asner's position on El Salvador brought responses from around the nation. In an editorial titled "Lou Grant, Demagogue" the *Virginian-Pilot* in Norfolk, Virginia, criticized Asner for "vague half-truths [and] some outright lies" about the political situation in the Central American nation.[33] The *Greensburg Tribune-Review* in Pennsylvania published an editorial titled "Asner, the Traitor?" It stated: "What can we do about 'celebrities' who aid the enemy? In lieu of the firing squad, we should soundly reject them as actors and actresses."[34] Conservative columnist Patrick Buchanan chided Asner for believing that people in any nation had ever "chosen" a communist government. He also criticized what he said was favorable treatment of Asner by the Washington press: "Asner's local reviews could not have been more syrupy had they been produced on assignment by Rossi."[35]

Editorial cartoonists of all political persuasions also commented on the flap. Ed Gamble of the *Florida Times-Union* pictured Asner and other actors giving money to grinning guerrillas as a stagehand held a movie clapboard that read "Pinks."[36] In the *Los Angeles Herald Examiner*, Bill Schorr offered readers a quiz: "Name the Screen Actors Guild president who keeps making rash statements about El Salvador." The answer was a caricature of Reagan.[37] Steve Sack of the *Minneapolis Tribune* showed Reagan and Asner reading newspapers featuring stories on their statements about El Salvador. Both say, "All right—Let's see what mess that radical, two-bit actor has made of my Latin American policy this time."[38] *Los Angeles Times* political cartoonist Paul Conrad took a swipe at Asner, Heston, and Reagan, drawing a cartoon that showed the smiling trio in tuxedos. The caption read, "Three reasons why actors shouldn't get into politics."[39]

Letters to both the *Los Angeles Times* and the *Los Angeles Herald Examiner* echoed the issues raised by the celebrities. Contending that Asner had drawn on his Lou Grant persona in his public speeches, Luis H. Aguilar of Los Angeles wrote: "I agree with Charlton Heston that show business should have no place in national politics. . . . If Asner and company truly believed in democratic fairness, they would not abuse the inherent political power of a medium for entertainment."[40] Two other writers supported Asner. "Thank God for the Ed Asners of the world," wrote Elinor Ashkenazy of Pasadena. "We ought to be feeding hungry children and not supporting reactionary and repressive regimes."[41] Sylvie Strauss of Las Vegas contended: "As an American citizen, Asner has the inalienable right to freedom of speech. That's not treason—it's a two-way street. To disagree with Reagan is to be branded un-American?"[42]

Two letters showed how closely some people linked the actor with his role on television. "Is this the Lou Grant who defends the rights of the little guy who speaks out?" asked Sonya Jason of Woodland Hills. "Hardly. His iron-fisted grab for political power is running roughshod over those in his organization who cannot speak up."[43] H. F. Hardy of Morro Bay wrote: "Asner has a right to his perceptions. I have a right to mine. It is my perception that Asner is a traitor. I will never again watch any program or support any cause in which he is involved in any fashion whatsoever."[44]

Even the impact the controversy was having on the series was a source of contention. Gary Deeb, syndicated television critic for the *Chicago Sun-Times*, blamed Asner for the declining ratings of *Lou Grant*. Although agreeing that Asner had the right to speak, he said Asner was earning a bad reputation with the public. "It isn't so much that folks disagree strongly with Asner's championing of the Salvadoran rebels," the critic wrote. "What bugs people is Asner's status as a professional dilettante."[45] *Los Angeles Times* critic Howard Rosenberg questioned whether Asner was the cause for the ratings decline. He suggested that the series may not have been as interesting as it had been or that viewers were simply tired of the five-year-old series. He concluded, "Ed Asner speaking his own mind on El Salvador as a private citizen has nothing to do with 'Lou Grant'."[46]

★   ★   ★

Lou Grant finished filming episodes for its fifth season during what *Newsweek* called "the biggest political controversy in Hollywood since Jane Fonda's visit to North Vietnam in 1972."[47] The pressure was evident on the set at MTM Studios. After the death threat Daryl Anderson bought Asner a bullet-resistant vest.[48] The cast and crew were issued identification badges to gain access to the sound stage.[49] One crew member stopped wearing his satin *Lou Grant* jacket in public because people harassed him, Michele Gallery recalled. "He got sick of people saying, 'You tell Ed Asner to cut that out.' And, 'Oh, you work on that show? I wouldn't watch that show'," she said.[50] Linda Kelsey also remembered how "bizarre" the atmosphere became on the set. "I'm sure in that fifth year it looked pretty weird," she said.[51]

Jack Bannon was among those who believed the series was in trouble after Heston claimed Asner was abusing his guild position. "I thought Ed was speaking as a private citizen," he said. "I never saw him dragging in the guild."[52] Walden said: "Ed was everybody's favorite uncle up till then. He brought a spotlight to a politically embarrassing situation without realizing the extent of what was going on and became a spokesman for women and children in a civil war."[53]

Although he thought Asner had been treated unfairly by his critics, Reynolds believed the future of the series was threatened by the controversy. He urged Asner to maintain a lower profile. "I went to Ed and I said, 'If I were you, I'd be cool for a while and just kind of lay back and don't make yourself so damn available'," Reynolds remembered. "And he went right to the press and said, 'My producer is trying to throttle me, trying to suppress me.' And, of course, I thought that was very foolish, very unfair, very unfair. But he loved the idea that somebody was trying to stop him from speaking, I guess."[54]

Asner thought such advice had come too late, well after the damage had been done. He could not allow Heston and his other critics to go unanswered. "They [the producers] would have wanted me to shut up totally, no further provocations," the actor recalled. "And if the lies would have continued for months afterwards, and if I refused to see the press, if I had refused to make a comment after I had seen the press, then I would have credited those lies with the truth." [55]

Within one week of Reynolds' meeting with Asner, a conservative group called for a boycott of *Lou Grant*. The New York-based Congress of Conservative Contributors criticized Asner for interfering with and attempting to subvert American foreign policy. "Mr. Asner is free to say what he pleases," said the group's executive director, Donald Pemberton. "But he is actually giving one million dollars to communist-backed guerrillas. The boycott is the only way we can reach him." [56] On March 10 the president of Vidal Sassoon complained in a letter to CBS Chairman William S. Paley that thirteen letters had been written by viewers "who have taken exception with Ed Asner using his position for political purposes." [57] Sassoon President Joseph Solomon said the hair products firm did not want to be pressured into dropping its sponsorship but added that it did not want to have its products suffer "because of an unfortunate association with a political issue." [58] In a response dated April 5 CBS President Thomas H. Wyman contended that the network did not involve itself in its performers' activities. "We may not agree with Mr. Asner's opinions and politics," he stated, "but he is entitled to hold those views." [59] Another *Lou Grant* sponsor, Kimberly-Clark, also received letters in March complaining about its sponsorship of the series. The form reply by the manufacturer of Kleenex tissues assured those who wrote that it had withdrawn its advertising from the series. In at least one instance Kimberly-Clark sent the letter to a viewer who actually complimented the firm for its sponsorship of *Lou Grant*. [60]

The assault on *Lou Grant* continued in April. A conservative Republican, Representative John Le Boutillier of New York, endorsed a four-page letter calling for a boycott of *Lou Grant* sponsors and requesting donations for a little-known organization called the Council for Inter-American Security. "If you liked Jane Fonda," the letter began, "you'll love Ed Asner. . . . If Ed Asner won't stop aiding the Marxist enemy, then we Americans can retaliate by boycotting those who sponsor his TV show." [61] The mailing, which the congressman told reporters was sent to fifty thousand homes, included a list of eight *Lou Grant* sponsors and postcards to Paley promising support of a boycott. [62] During the same month the Reverend Jerry Falwell, head of the conservative group Moral Majority, published an advertisement in the *Los Angeles Times* headlined, "Where Do You Stand on This Vital Issue?" Falwell accused Asner, whom he identified as "Lou Grant on television," of defying American policy and lending aid and comfort to the nation's enemies. "Are we supposed to stand idly by and allow Hollywood radicals to dictate America's foreign policy?" he asked.[63]

By the time the episode "Unthinkable" aired on May 3 (resulting in the series' record-low audience) *Lou Grant* had been rocked by charges that its star was derelict in his duties as an actor, union president, and loyal American. As CBS would later point out when defending its decision to cancel the series ratings for *Lou Grant* had fallen slightly from November to February compared with the previous season, averaging 17.5 with a 28.3 share. Other CBS programming had dipped in the ratings as well, but the audience for the newspaper drama had plunged since February 15, the day of the Washington news conference. When CBS officials gathered that first week in May to determine the fall schedule, the average rating for *Lou Grant* was only 14; it drew a mere 23.8 percent of viewers.[64]

Matters may have been aggravated further by Asner's appearance on the popular talk show *Donahue*, which was taped May 3 for broadcast the next day. Before answering host Phil Donahue's questions Asner pinned a button to his shirt that read, "Ed Asner, Private Citizen." He recapitulated the months of controversy, maintaining that the intense scrutiny and criticism since the Washington news conference had shocked and surprised him. "All I was doing in my participation with medical aid to El Salvador was helping to purchase medical supplies for people that had no access to them, and I would do that even for Communists if they needed it that badly, and to call attention to the terrible conditions in El Salvador where we were involved," he told the audience. "I wanted to participate in getting the American people to know what was going on down there."[65]

Asner also criticized Kimberly-Clark, which he called "our little Kleenex makers," for withdrawing sponsorship from the series. At a time when officials with CBS or MTM may have hoped the controversy would quiet down the *Donahue* appearance further stirred up the issues of contention.

Reynolds later heard that the *Donahue* show aired as Paley and other CBS officials laid out the fall schedule. "And he's taking shots at Kimberly-Clark that day," the producer said. "I heard that Paley came in and said, 'No, no, you don't want that show,' and they took it down."[66] For his 1983 book *Inside Prime Time* author Todd Gitlin interviewed a CBS programming executive who asked not to be identified. The executive, who had attended the scheduling meeting, said no one was enthusiastic for renewing *Lou Grant* for the 1982–83 season. The series was criticized by the executives for having become preachy, self-congratulatory, and dull even though it was well-made, well-acted, and well-written. The executive told Gitlin: "Finally, Paley said, 'If you have so little enthusiasm, why are you pushing it?' We figured, let's put a new show on."[67]

When asked in 1992 if he thought Paley would have ordered the cancellation of *Lou Grant*, former MTM president and former NBC president Grant Tinker said Asner's political activities and criticism of CBS sponsors probably would have irritated the CBS chairman and founder. Part of the reason the show was canceled, he guessed, was that Paley did not think the series was worth the aggravation. Tinker also noted that *Lou Grant* was weak in the ratings, which would have made programmers favor a replacement. "When you look at your pilots, each one is lustrous in your anticipation," he said. "You tend to want to go with pilots which you lovingly created and brought to fruition. So putting a promising pilot in for a marginal incumbent show is something that happens a lot."[68]

CBS officials announced on May 6 that the network had canceled *Lou Grant*, contending that the Asner controversy and the boycotts it spawned were not factors in the decision. Instead, ratings were cited as the culprit.[69] In retrospect Arnold Becker, CBS vice-president for television research, noted that the *Lou Grant* audience had diminished considerably during the 1981–82 season. Its season-average 16.6 rating was three points lower than the previous season, and its 27 share was down from 32. Moreover, the decline in the audience since the 1978–79 season was the greatest among viewers below age fifty. Ratings had fallen 20 percent among men under fifty and 17 percent among women under fifty. "Adults below the age of fifty are a prime marketing target for many advertisers," Becker noted. "In the fifth season, the program's ratings plunged."[70] Still, the audience for *Lou Grant* was estimated at nearly twenty million people.[71]

Although no one could have known in 1982, *Lou Grant* may have been a victim of what was to become a fifteen-year decline in the size of the network television audience. In the 1978–79 season 91 percent of the television viewing audience watched CBS, NBC, and ABC.[72] As cable television grew rapidly and offered viewers alternatives to the three traditional broadcast networks the size of the networks' audience diminished steadily to just 61 percent by the 1993–94 season.[73] The share for CBS fell from about 30 in 1982 to just 20 in 1988.[74] "We were canceled with a 27 share," Asner noted in 1991, "which you'd kill for now."[75]

At the time CBS canceled *Lou Grant* Asner contended that lower ratings were expected because of specials aired by the other networks and an above-average season of professional football aired by ABC. He charged that CBS had canceled the series "without lifting a little finger."[76] When the cancellation was announced, executive consultant and cocreator Allan

Burns said, "They stuck with us when our ratings were safe, but once they became marginal, I think they showed a shocking lack of respect for what we've done."[77] Although he believed the Asner controversy was a factor, Reynolds told reporters at the time that the low numbers justified CBS's action. "I don't think it's justified in what's good for television," he said. "But I think when you're marginal all those things come into play, and we were definitely marginal."[78] In retrospect Walden believed that *Lou Grant* would have survived with stronger ratings. "If the show had been in the top twenty," the actor said, "he could have driven drunk through the Salvation Army window on Christmas Day and that show would have been on the air."[79]

In the ensuing years Reynolds changed his mind about the impact of the ratings. "The ratings were good," he said in 1991. "The ratings were healthy. The ratings were not overpowering, but it never was one of those top 10 shows."[80] But he also recognized that the liberal bent of *Lou Grant* was out of step with the times. "Reagan was in. The country was moving to the right," he said. "I tried to deal with issues even-handedly. . . . It was a forum for ideas, but liberal ideas certainly got the sympathy."[81] Although he thought at the time that Asner was responsible for the cancellation, Reynolds later believed that the liberal tone of the series was a factor. "I think that the show itself belonged to the sixties and the seventies," he said, "and the eighties had arrived."[82]

Having finished filming for the season weeks earlier, the cast and crew of *Lou Grant* were not on hand when CBS called to say the show was canceled. Reynolds and Burns contacted their colleagues to break the news that they would not return for a sixth season. "Gene and Allan called me on the phone and told me," Nancy Marchand remembered. "I wasn't surprised. As I say, I think there was too much going on. They were tired. And I think Mr. Paley had had it up to here. It was too much for everybody."[83] When Burns called Mason Adams at his home in Connecticut, Adams remembered, "we commiserated with each other because we hated to see the show go off. But I expected it. You expect it each year. It's a weird business we're in."[84] Linda Kelsey was on the set of a television movie when Reynolds reached her. "That was so classy, by the way, so classy," she said. "Believe me, I've been in series that have been canceled since and producers don't even call."[85] Daryl Anderson met other *Lou Grant* colleagues for lunch. "There were six or seven of us who huddled together that day . . . and sort of toasted it. It really didn't hit me for a long, long time."[86] April Smith, who was to become a producer for the sixth season, was devastated. "I was totally taken by surprise," she remembered.[87] Ironically, she became a producer for *Cagney and Lacey,* the series that replaced *Lou Grant* on CBS. When Reynolds told Gallery, she burst into tears upon realizing that "I wasn't going to be working with these people again."[88]

★　★　★

Fans of a canceled series often write networks to complain that their favorite show will no longer air. In the case of *Lou Grant* protesters took to the streets in an unusual show of support for Asner and his newspaper drama. Chanting "Asner Yes, CBS No, Censorship Must Go," an estimated one thousand people demonstrated at the CBS Television City studios in Los Angeles on May 10. The protesters marched from 10:00 P.M. to 11:00 P.M., the hour that *Lou Grant* aired. Demonstrators included members of labor unions, a group favoring nuclear disarmament, a group critical of American involvement in El Salvador, the National Organization for Women, and the American Civil Liberties Union (ACLU).[89] Ramona Ripston, executive director of the ACLU of Southern California, told reporters: "This is a clear issue of free speech. Ed Asner, like any other public figure, has a right to political beliefs and should not be threatened with economic reprisals for saying what he believes."[90] A leaflet handed out at the rally declared: "Ed Asner stuck his neck out and got his head cut off. If CBS and a few corporate sponsors can silence Ed Asner from speaking out, who's next?"[91] Another demonstration the next Monday, May 17, drew a crowd of similar size and makeup.[92]

Numerous television critics, columnists, and *Lou Grant* fans did not believe CBS when it claimed that Asner's politics and the controversy they stirred were not behind the cancellation. Despite the drop in the ratings many thought CBS had caved in to pressure brought by a relatively small number of people and had failed to support Asner's right to free speech. "CBS's cancellation of 'Lou Grant' is a stupid, cowardly act that only makes sense if CBS was under extreme pressure," wrote *Chicago Tribune* syndicated columnist Marilyn Peterson.[93] "Does anybody really believe that 'Lou Grant' is being dropped because of low ratings, rather than Ed Asner's political activities," asked Herb Caen of the *San Francisco Chronicle*. "Joe McCarthy died a long time ago but he's far from dead."[94] In an editorial the *Oakland Tribune* stated, "A network that prides itself on having stood up to Sen. Joseph McCarthy might have tried harder to protect its reputation for courage."[95] Other journalists, such as Eric Mink of the *St. Louis Post-Dispatch*, believed that both the ratings and the controversy were responsible. "Add all that together," he wrote. "If you had been CBS, what would you have done?"[96]

Not everyone thought the cancellation was akin to blacklisting. For instance, the Nashua, New Hampshire, *Telegraph* editorialized that Asner had been a victim of public opinion, which was what had made him a star in the first place. "It's too bad that Mr. Asner declines to accept the fact that he is a product of the public which he serves," the newspaper stated. "What the public can give, the public can take away. And so it is with Mr. Asner's 'Lou Grant Show'."[97] The *Los Angeles Herald Examiner* wrote that it was wrong for someone to be threatened because of his politics but added: "That doesn't mean political action is—or should be—without consequence or that viewers are obligated to watch 'Lou Grant' despite its star's politics. To argue the opposite devalues bold political action."[98]

To some observers, the series itself was at fault for the decline in ratings. While praising the show as one of television's best, Michael Dougan of the *San Francisco Examiner* also lamented that *Lou Grant* was dramatically uneven. "It's sometimes contrived, heavy-handed and over-acted," he contended. "The writers can stretch too far for relevance, turning the show into a kind of self-parody."[99] Striking a similar note, Mike Duffy of the *Detroit Free Press* stated: "The series also had become so issue-oriented that it sometimes came off like a bleeding hearts lecture series. Tedious, though well intentioned."[100] Ed Bark of the *Dallas Morning News* said *Lou Grant* was not as good as it used to be. "No, it wasn't up to its glorious past, and that's another reason why some viewers rejected it."[101] Mike Drew of the *Milwaukee Journal* suggested another reason for the lower ratings: "Maybe Americans have had enough newspaper stories for a while."[102]

Judging from letters to newspaper editors, viewers also were divided over the cancellation. Dougan of the *San Francisco Examiner* said he received more than two hundred letters in response to his column about the cancellation, and fewer than ten supported CBS. "I cannot understand how the people at CBS could take this show off the air," Mary Victorine of San Jose wrote. "Whatever Ed Asner's personal political views, his acting skills on the program are what counts."[103] Carlyle P. Johnson of San Francisco disagreed. "I am one of those former viewers who celebrate the cancellation. . . . We will not stand for the world views that Mr. Asner and his ilk wish to promote."[104] A *Cincinnati Enquirer* reader said she was dismayed at the cancellation, noting the series was "totally engrossing, invariably enlightening, superbly written, directed and acted."[105] Two readers of the *Philadelphia Inquirer* disagreed about the merits of Asner's views. "The only thing Ed Asner is guilty of is putting forth his political principles with courage and dignity," wrote James M. Cory of Philadelphia.[106] John Silvero of Devon stated: "It is so refreshing to see Ed Asner's 'Lou Grant' taken off the air. It's about time this country came to its senses and began defending its friends and attacking its enemies."[107]

Four days after the cancellation the Screen Actors Guild announced that its members had narrowly rejected the proposal to merge with the Screen Extras Guild. The results of mail balloting showed 11,394, or 56.7 percent, in favor of the merger and 8,670, or 43.3 percent against it. The measure fell short of the 60 percent needed for passage. Although Heston called the results "a shattering defeat" for Asner and other pro-merger officials, Asner said "the only winner in this situation is management."[108] In a speech in New York Asner charged that Heston, whom he described as "President Reagan's stooge," and his supporters had used lies to defeat the measure. An Associated Press story about the speech misquoted the actor by saying he suspected that the White House as well as his SAG opponents may have worked to have the series canceled.[109] The story was corrected by the wire service the next day, but *TV Guide* missed the correction and chastised Asner for "suffering delusions of grandeur" for thinking that the president cared about the "foundering series of an egotistical star."[110] More than one month passed before the magazine published a letter from Asner pointing out the AP correction.[111]

In the days, weeks, and months after the cancellation Asner spoke to numerous journalists about the end of *Lou Grant,* the reasons for its demise, and his political views. Some commentators had had enough of the affair. "Ed Asner is beginning to get on my nerves," wrote Bob Wisehart, television editor of the New Orleans *Times-Picayune.* "This 'smacks of McCarthyism' business is bona fide, 100 percent baloney. Such a crock is it that I'm surprised so many people are buying Asner's line."[112] "In a very short time," Gary Deeb of the *Chicago Sun-Times* wrote, "Ed Asner has become a tiresome, pompous bore."[113] In the *New York Post* Roger Simon stated: "If I had three wishes, two of them would be for Ed Asner to shut up. I have become even more tired of his whining these last few days than I am of his TV show."[114]

Fans of *Lou Grant* viewed the cancellation as an abrupt end to a favorite television program. But for the people who worked on the show the cancellation cost them their jobs. "There were a lot of people put out of work when that show went off the air," writer Steve Kline said, adding that it was "so impolitic in the way he [Asner] chose to make his feelings known that it's a case of personal conscience over the welfare of the many."[115] Kline and other writers, directors, and actors interviewed for this study stressed that they did not resent Asner. "I felt resentment toward Jerry Falwell and John Le Boutillier," Daryl Anderson said. "I see Ed as the victim."[116] April Smith said: "I thought he had the right to his political opinions. I thought the sponsors were the ones who showed great cowardice, and the networks."[117] Although director Roger Young did not feel resentment toward Asner, he knew people who did. "You know, that's understandable," he said. "We're talking about something that was pretty precious to a lot of people."[118] Allen Williams, who played financial editor Adam Wilson, said some people remained resentful that Asner's actions had hurt the series. "When I'd talk to them and they'd bring that subject up, they'd say, 'That fucking Ed, if he'd just kept his mouth shut we'd still be on the air,' " according to Williams. "I know that they'd say those things to me because they know that I know how much they love Ed. It's only people that you love that you get that angry at and that resentful of."[119] Gallery also said she did not resent Asner after the show had ended. "I don't resent the fact that Ed kept going because I don't think Ed is just a casually political person. I think he's deeply committed," she said. "It might have been hardest of all for Gene because Gene was the protector of that show."[120]

Reynolds admitted that at the time he felt "some" resentment toward Asner. He and several others also acknowledged that they had worked on the series long enough. "After five years you develop certain kinds of ambivalence toward the show," he said. "You're a little unhappy with the people you're working with and so forth. So, I wasn't altogether depressed."[121] Marchand recalled: "I was ready to move on. I certainly hated the thought of not seeing the guys anymore. . . . Saying goodbye to that was very sad, and I even miss it now."[122] Williams felt ambivalent about losing his role. "I was very disappointed when the show was canceled because I didn't have a job anymore," he said. "Part of me was relieved not to have to go back and do it again because I was so exhausted."[123] Producer Seth Freeman also looked forward to new creative challenges. "But I was disappointed because I felt whether I continued with *Lou Grant* or not, or any of us did, *Lou Grant* should have continued for some more years," he said.[124]

Asner knew at the time that some people who worked on *Lou Grant* resented him because they lost their jobs. "And I carry guilt on that," he admitted. "A fine show which provided livelihood for a number of people was stopped. I don't know that it wouldn't have been stopped anyway."[125] He later spent "a small fortune" having lawyers research whether he could file suit over the cancellation but eventually decided the potential damage to himself and his family was not worth it.

Looking back on the controversy after nine years, Asner said working on *Lou Grant* had reminded him of why he liked and respected the journalism profession. "It's what made me love the press," he said of the series, "but it's unreal. And that reality was brought home in my own personal experience."[126] Indeed, the ordeal of the cancellation ultimately changed his view of the news media in the United States.

> Those five years of *Lou Grant*, I was like a sacred cow. Nobody ever touched me. The [*National*] *Enquirer* did a couple of double-dealing things on me, stuff like that. Mainstream press, no. And then when the controversy arose over me and Central America, El Salvador, it was like . . . out of the woodwork came maybe a third of the body that had been quiet up 'til then, couldn't wait to level off at me, react to my accusations as poppycock and this and that and so forth and so on, CBS's justification in canceling the series and this and that.
>
> I realized that as long as things were kosher, I was the greatest p.r. implement known to journalism. They dared not bite the hand that feeds them. But once I showed some warts and was no longer the great p.r. vehicle for journalism, then they pulled out all the stops. . . .
>
> A few years ago I finally arrived at a thought that made me think the average Russian under the former U.S.S.R. probably had a better awareness of the truth—perhaps I'm fantasizing too much—but I think he had a better awareness of the truth, certain truth anyway, than did your average American. Because the average Russian knew he lived in a dictatorship subject to controlling the press . . . and knew what he was hearing on official state radio could not possibly be the total truth, far more than the average American who thinks he lives in the world of the free press and reads it or sees it on the tube and says, well, it's a free press and this is what I'm seeing and hearing, it's got to be the truth. And never realizing that for the most part the news channels are copying each other, taking it off the wire, not reflecting any individual research on their own at all, taking the gospel as delivered from Washington or New York. . . .
>
> Because he's told that he lives in the land of the free press, he never exercises that scrutiny and judgment that he should and probably is lied to. Or lies succeed more often with him than succeeded with the average Russian in a controlled press.[127]

The years after *Lou Grant* were lean for Asner as an actor. He was offered few roles and was turned down for many of those he sought, a situation he attributed to industry blacklisting after the El Salvador controversy. "I wouldn't say I starved," he recalled, "but we constantly beat the bushes."[128] The seven-time Emmy winner did not return to series television until the short-lived series *Off the Rack* (1985) aired on ABC.[129] Then, he worked steadily in the medium that made him a star. Asner the union leader fared better, winning reelection as SAG president in 1983.

The candidate he favored to succeed him in 1985, Patty Duke, was elected in balloting viewed by some as a referendum against Reagan, Heston, and other conservatives within the guild.[130]

Reruns of *Lou Grant* were broadcast through the summer of 1982. Two episodes filmed in the spring of 1982, "Victims" and "Charlie," were aired for the first time in late August and early September instead of in the serie's sixth season as planned. The cancellation did not allow the writers or producers to create a special final episode, which bitterly disappointed April Smith.

> The cruelest blow of all was just to pull the plug on the characters and the situation as if they didn't matter. I think that was the hardest part. I think if you're going to end the show, O.K., but give us a chance to end it. Give us a chance to write that last episode. And they never did.
>
> And that betrayed such calculating, cold-hearted, inhuman strategy on the part of the network. It just made you think that they never got it in the first place, which they didn't. These characters were real to millions of people, but in the end to them it was just patterns of light on the screen that didn't matter.[131]

Home Box Office (HBO), the national pay-television channel, proposed a two-hour *Lou Grant* finale in which the *Tribune* would close. Reynolds rejected the HBO proposal and decided not to pursue a series finale. "The idea of a newspaper folding is an unhappy project," he said. "It's just too much of a downer."[132]

Anyone hoping *Lou Grant* would be vindicated at the Emmy awards in August must have been disappointed. Despite eight nominations, including those for dramatic series and dramatic actor, it won only one award. For the fourth time in five years, Marchand was honored for her work in a supporting role. As it had in the previous year *Hill Street Blues* dominated the awards with twenty-one nominations and six Emmys.[133]

After the Emmys all that was left was the final broadcast. When "Charlie" aired on September 13, 1982, Burns served as host of a farewell party for his colleagues. Bannon remembered it as a bittersweet night. "It was the pride of having had five wonderful years with a terrific group of people who put out a really nice product," he recalled, "and the sadness that it was done."[134] Before the episode began Bannon told his friends: "No matter what has happened to the show or anything, the one thing that can never be taken away from anybody who worked on this show is that you are part of television history at its best."[135]

9

The Legacies of *Lou Grant*

As fans mourned the loss of *Lou Grant* from prime-time television in 1982 journalists across the nation delivered eulogies for the series. Several focused on its realistic portrayal of their profession. "The biggest and possibly the best newspaper in America went out of business the other day," columnist Tom Brazaitis of the *Cleveland Plain Dealer* wrote. "Its editors and reporters pursued the tough stories, no matter whose toes they stepped on."[1] In an editorial the *Detroit Free Press* called Lou Grant "the editor we wished we had, the editor every editor wanted to be."[2] To columnist David Israel of the *Los Angeles Herald Examiner* the series was "the best thing television—which has killed more newspapers than inept publishers or apathetic readers—ever did for our business."[3]

Journalists also commended *Lou Grant* for dealing with important issues and raising the quality of television entertainment. Syndicated columnist and *60 Minutes* commentator Andy Rooney called the series one of the best ever. "It was dramatic, funny and often thoughtful," he wrote. "An adult could spend an hour watching it without being ashamed of himself for wasting time."[4] *Dallas Times Herald* writer Steven Reddicliffe concluded: " 'Lou Grant' operated on the assumption that viewers were smart, not stupid; that intelligent adults deserved intelligent programs. This fall, there will be no 'Lou Grant.' What are we going to do?"[5] In the years after the series left the air, this latter perspective—that *Lou Grant* was an entertaining and thoughtful television series surrounded by mediocrity—dominated assessments of the program in popular surveys of the entertainment medium.[6]

In scholarly studies of television researchers found evidence in *Lou Grant* to support various theories. For example, one study cited the series as an early hybrid of styles (comedy and drama, episodic and serial, relevance and melodrama) that matured with *Hill Street Blues* and *St. Else-*

where.[7] An ethnographic study explored *Lou Grant* from an anthropological perspective, treating its production offices as a "village" in the television world.[8] One scholar viewed its cancellation as evidence of economics and politics combining to silence views that disrupt commercial television's conservatism.[9] Other studies included *Lou Grant* in discussions of television's different uses and gratifications for various audiences, the ties between family culture and workplace settings in television, and the medium's depiction of American society.[10]

The series's portrayal of journalism, however, has not been examined in detail until now. In addition to exploring the history of a landmark television series this study sought answers to a pair of broad questions related to journalism. First, how did the medium's most-acclaimed newspaper drama portray the profession? Second, what were viewers told about journalism? The answers are intertwined and rooted in the major forces that shaped the series.

The series creators and original production team—Gene Reynolds, Allan Burns, and James L. Brooks—obviously had the greatest influence on *Lou Grant*. Their conviction that journalism should be depicted as realistically as possible and that human issues should be explored set the tone for the series. "I've never seen a show that so exhausted the resources at hand, trying to find out what newspapers were and how they worked," Ed Asner recalled. "If we ever made a departure from reality, it was never unknowingly. It was always for a purpose."[11]

Indeed, it was the producers' decision to carefully research modern journalism, to base story lines on real incidents, to make stories relevant by closely following current events, and to employ technical advisers to ensure realism. Their belief that viewers would respond to issues and ideas presented through a realistic context remained unmoved even when network pressures and lackluster ratings tempted them to follow a more popular formula. The producers gave *Lou Grant* its world view that journalism could be a positive force in society.

Journalists contributed to the series in three important ways. First, they helped the producers discover the practices, ethics, and personal stories of modern journalism through interviews and through the articles and books journalists had written about their profession. "It wasn't some desire to set the record straight," *Los Angeles Times* journalist David Shaw said while explaining why he spoke to the *Lou Grant* staff. "Here were some people who were serious, who seemed to want to do this thing accurately, and I ought to cooperate and help."[12] The realistic flavor of episodes owed a great deal to the reporters and editors who made their views known to the producers.

Second, journalists served as technical advisers. By reading scripts and answering questions from writers, actors, and directors the technical advisers promoted a realistic depiction of their profession. Third, television critics aided the series by acknowledging its realistic flavor, which set it apart from other newspaper dramas, and by encouraging people to watch. As *Lou Grant* approached cancellation in its first thirteen weeks, favorable reviews gave the series an aura of quality and helped it earn time to develop an audience.

Network censors played a key role by determining the boundaries of realism in *Lou Grant*. It did not matter that in real life people used obscene words and racial slurs, that all prostitutes in certain areas of Los Angeles were black, or that torture and rape were brutal and violent acts. Nor did it matter that people were surrounded by consumer goods whose brand names were recognizable and part of the language. To avoid complaints from advertisers and viewers the censors set limits on how accurately *Lou Grant* could present the real world. Their work contributed to the homogeneity of television entertainment.

Finally, the medium had a strong influence in shaping *Lou Grant*. Al Martinez, both a *Los Angeles Times* journalist and a writer for television, noted: "Television is a medium of drama. Gene's [Reynolds] main point was accuracy and reality within the framework of how drama could portray it."[13] The conventions of dramatic television in the late 1970s and early 1980s demanded a setting and characters that appealed to audiences. The central character, played by the series star, must be the voice of reason and wisdom no matter where he is in the chain of command. Story lines must involve the audience emotionally; intellectual involvement was a goal of the producers but not a requirement of the medium. Conflict, the essence of drama, must be central to every episode, if not every scene. Thus, the medium's conventions provided the framework for a series that sought to explore journalism and ideas in new ways while meeting the demands of the television drama.

All four forces that shaped *Lou Grant* affected the depiction of journalism and what viewers were told about the profession. Interestingly, the tension created by these forces ultimately made *Lou Grant* both entertaining and relevant. Producers and journalists strove for realism, but the conventions of the medium (and the censors) diminished those efforts. Conversely, the medium's conventions required the drama and emotional appeal that an accurate depiction of journalism and social problems might have lacked.

An example of this tension was the action in *Lou Grant* that journalists often cited as being inaccurate—that no city editor would have left the city room as often as Lou Grant. The implication was that episodes did not consistently show Lou doing the real work of a city editor. Yet Lou Grant could not have been the central character had he not become involved in story lines outside the *Tribune* city room. "If they obeyed reality," Asner said, "I'd have to be chained behind that desk, which is too boring—too boring for me, and certainly too boring for the show."[14] Thus, the producers sacrificed accuracy for drama. Journalists also noted that the *Tribune* seemed to have only two reporters and one photographer. Although the drama could focus on only a limited number of regular characters, the result was a distortion of reality.

Another example was the way story lines often were tied to *Lou Grant* characters. To make a journalism or social issue more dramatic, scripts often involved the characters in the issue in personal ways. Assuming that viewers developed an interest in or emotional attachment to the characters, placing the characters in a dramatic situation would heighten the viewers' involvement in the story. Thus, Billie discovered her mother had taken a dangerous drug during pregnancy as she investigated the drug's consequences, Rossi's father's alcoholism colored the reporter's view of derelicts, Lou found an old friend on skid row while the newspaper investigated a series of murders, Art Donovan's mentally ill cousin was the subject of news coverage, memories of Vietnam troubled Dennis "Animal" Price, and Mrs. Pynchon discovered her husband profited from Japanese-American relocation during a probe of war profiteers.

Grouping story lines involving Charlie Hume provided an extreme example of how *Lou Grant* played off characters to heighten dramatic impact. During the series Charlie's daughter was aboard an airplane in peril, his son joined a religious cult, nightmares of torture haunted him, his nephew became an aimless drifter, federal agents used his home for a "sting" operation, fire threatened his home, and swindlers bilked him of his life savings. Although it is possible that one family could have had such a variety of experiences, it is unlikely. Yet, critics and audiences probably accepted these distortions because they recognized them as inherent to the dramatic form. Every other television drama departed from reality in these ways; the fact that *Lou Grant* did too was scarcely worth noting.

Critics and many other journalists did find worthy of comment that *Lou Grant* stayed as close as it did to reality, particularly when dealing with journalism. "I saw a lot of faults in it, but my general impression is a positive one," recalled former *Los Angeles Times* journalist Mark Murphy, who was interviewed during the research phase of the show's creation.[15] Narda Zacchino, another *Times* journalist who had aided the

producers, contended: "They did a fabulous job of being really true to
life. I thought they did a superlative job of actually creating in dramatic
form what happens in real life."[16]

Thus, it can be said that *Lou Grant* portrayed journalism realistically
but not accurately. By definition, to be accurate is to be free of error.
Without question, *Lou Grant* erred at times in its presentation of life at a
daily newspaper. Neither its creators nor its most ardent supporters in the
profession claimed otherwise. Instead, they chose the more qualified
praise of calling *Lou Grant* realistic; its portrayal of journalism and people
had the ring of truth that had eluded other newspaper dramas on television. Journalists' praise of *Lou Grant* cannot be noted, however, without
pointing out that the series depicted their profession in a favorable light.
Had the *Tribune* staff been mediocre journalists uncommitted to truth and
the public good (and surely there are such journalists), perhaps critics
would have been less likely to praise the series.

An idealized depiction of journalism may have been unavoidable
given the medium's demand for appealing characters whom audiences
would want to see week after week. "TV naturally tends to glamorize its
institution," according to Steve Kline, a *Lou Grant* writer and former
journalist. "It's a glorified look at journalism. It's journalism the way
journalists like to think of it."[17] On the surface nothing appears deceitful
about portraying any profession as it should be practiced. Yet, as Asner
noted, the idealized journalism practiced at the fictional *Los Angeles Tribune* may have given some viewers unrealistic expectations. "My one regret is the prestige of the show and the effectiveness of the show convinced
a lot of young people to enter the field," he said. "They saw *Lou Grant*,
were influenced by it and then discovered life."[18]

Critics told viewers that *Lou Grant* was television's most realistic portrayal of life at a daily newspaper. What, then, did the series tell viewers
about journalism? First, it showed viewers that journalism is a process.
By following stories from conception to publication, viewers learned how
reporters gathered information, how editors refined it, and how photographers produced the pictures. They also learned about the hierarchy at a
newspaper and how editors decided what to publish and where to place it
in the paper. Actor Lance Guest, who appeared in several episodes in the
final season, noted, "The clearest example of something I learned from
that show was the process of journalism and who gets involved and why
they get involved."[19] Depicting the mechanics of journalism in a dramatic
medium while remaining realistic was a major triumph of *Lou Grant*. For
regular viewers the journalism process was not a mystery.

Second, *Lou Grant* showed viewers the ethical concerns of the profession. "[Reynolds] was very big on that," *New York Daily News* journalist Bill Brink remembered from his discussions with the producer. "He liked the ethical issue, which was beginning to emerge, and he was very prescient about that because the ethical issue has become larger since then."[20] In turn, viewers learned about conflict of interest, a fair trial versus a free press, source confidentiality, libel, and other issues. Episodes frequently depicted the importance of independence from government and other institutions and the necessity of integrity. Phrases such as "freedom of the press" and "right to know" took on deeper meanings when presented in the form of a drama. Journalists considered the consequences of their actions, and those who broke the standards of the profession were punished. Another triumph of *Lou Grant* was its ability to present in a compelling form opposing points of view regarding journalistic issues as well as problems facing society.

Indeed, *Lou Grant* showed that journalists disagreed over how best to practice their profession. Instead of always acting in concert, the *Tribune* staff often was at odds over ethical issues and other challenges facing the press. Conflict existed between reporters, between reporters and editors, and between journalists and publishers. Moreover, journalists often clashed with the advertising staff and other business-related personnel on the newspaper. Viewers who believed that journalists thought and acted alike instead saw a variety of personalities and opinions shaping the daily newspaper.

The impact of *Lou Grant* on viewers' perceptions of journalists and their profession cannot be measured, only surmised. Collectively, its 114 episodes over five seasons represented many of television's finest hours, evidence that episodic television can have value and meaning. On another level the series chronicled the problems that faced American journalism and society in the late 1970s and early 1980s. Many of those problems remained years after the series faded from prime time. Yet with its humanitarian point of view that people could find common ground and understanding through communication *Lou Grant* offered hope for the future.

1. The cast of *Lou Grant (left to right)*: Mason Adams (Charlie Hume), Nancy Marchand (Margaret Pynchon), Daryl Anderson (Dennis "The Animal" Price), Robert Walden (Joe Rossi), Linda Kelsey (Billie Newman), Allen Williams (Adam Wilson), and Jack Bannon (Art Donovan). *Seated*: Edward Asner (Lou Grant). *Courtesy of the author*.

2. Lou and Billie. *Courtesy of the author*.

3. Billie and Rossi at a meeting. *Courtesy of the author.*

4. Donovan, a *Tribune* printer, and Animal on strike. *Courtesy of the author.*

5. Reagan and Asner. (Copyright 1982 by Steve Sack and the *Minneapolis Tribune*. Used with permission.)

6. Asner and Salvadorans. (Copyright 1982 by Ed Gamble and the *Florida Times-Union*. Used with permission.)

7. Asner aid coupon. (Copyright 1982 by Henry Payne and the *Nassau Weekly* of Princeton University. Used with permission.)

8. Asner/Grant reads the classified ads. (Copyright 1982 by Steve Greenberg and the *Los Angeles Daily News*. Used with permission.)

9. Asner as copyboy at *Pravda*. (Copyright 1982 by Mike Smith and Copley News Service. Reprinted with special permission of North America Syndicate.)

10. *Lou Grant* cancelled. (Copyright 1982 by Bill DeOre and the *Dallas Morning News*. Used with permission.)

Appendixes
Notes
Bibliography
Index

APPENDIX A
Newspaper Dramas on Television

The following twenty-three newspaper dramas aired in prime time before the debut of *Lou Grant* in 1977. The list was compiled from Tim Brooks and Earle Marsh, *The Complete Directory to Prime Time Network TV Shows, 1946-Present*, 5th ed. (New York: Ballantine Books, 1992) and Alex McNeil, *Total Television: A Comprehensive Guide to Programming from 1948 to the Present*, 3d ed. (New York: Penguin Books, 1991).

Big Story. 1949–57, NBC.
The Front Page. 1949–50, CBS.
Big Town. 1950–56, CBS, Dumont, NBC.
Crime Photographer. 1951–52, CBS.
Foreign Intrigue. 1951–55, syndicated.
Front Page Detective. 1951–53, Dumont.
Not for Publication. 1951–52, Dumont.
Night Editor. 1954, Dumont.
Wire Service. 1956–59, ABC.
Jefferson Drum. 1958–59, NBC.
Deadline. 1959, syndicated.
Man without a Gun. 1959, syndicated.
New York Confidential. 1959, syndicated.
Exclusive. 1960, syndicated.
Hong Kong. 1960–61, ABC.
The Roaring Twenties. 1960–62, ABC.
Target: The Corruptors. 1961–62, ABC.
Saints and Sinners. 1962–63, NBC.
The Reporter. 1964, CBS.
Night Stalker. 1974–75, ABC.
Gibbsville. 1976, NBC.
The Andros Targets. 1977, CBS.
Kingston: Confidential. 1977, NBC.

APPENDIX B
Character Sketches

Actors were given a twelve-page description of the six supporting characters in *Lou Grant* during the early production of the series. Neither producer Gene Reynolds nor writer Leon Tokatyan recalls who wrote the character sketches.

Backgrounds, traits, and some names of the characters changed by the time the first episode aired. (Bill Hume became Charlie Hume; Carla Madigian became Carla Mardigian.) Yet the sketches provide an interesting look at the early makeup of the *Los Angeles Tribune* newsroom.

Actor Daryl Anderson retained his copy of the sketches. It is reproduced here with his permission.

Margaret Pynchon—Publisher/owner

A woman of great charm and power, somewhat eccentric. She can be capricious, arbitrary, maddening. But it is her paper and she has the right to run it any way she sees fit. (She refused to print LBJ's famous "scar picture".) Her father founded THE TRIB and she roamed the building from the time she was a toddler, knows every crack and brick. But she is not a newspaperwoman, and indeed, since his death, she has lost touch with the reality of life today. The paper—once great —is foundering. That is, the circulation has been steadily decreasing. She has tried many different ways of stemming this attrition in revenue: Market Research people with cockamamie ideas that didn't work; an expanded astrology page one week, taken out the next; a change in type styles, logo, headline size . . . But given the place of newspapers in today's society, what is happening to the TRIB is not endemic to it alone. All-News radio stations, the hype of TV news (she will not watch television, doesn't own a set), the proliferation of news magazines, all these have lessened the power of the daily paper; there are very few people who will take the time to sit and read a paper when they can learn "what's happening" or what they think is happening from other, more succinct sources.

She is conversent [*sic*] with the city's social life, though her eccentricities keep her from being welcomed with a whole heart by the Chandlers and the other shakers and movers in the community. (I'm no good at raising money for the ballet, so I do what I can do. I run this paper.) Her constant companion is a mean little son of a bitch (literally), a Yorky, who hangs out in her lap and snarls or yaps most of the time Lou or anyone else is facing her. (The one positive side of this little beast is that he is an excellent ambulatory alarm system for the City Room staff, his approaching yaps warning everyone that "the Missus" is on the prowl.)

Like Dolly Schiff, she has a penchant for trivia and an affection for gossip, especially personal details involving medical histories of the famous. Despite these shortcomings—if indeed they are that—and great pressures upon her (including the pressure from her nephews and their wives to sell the TRIB) she can and does rise to situations that call for insight, fairness, and decisiveness. Although she concerns herself with trivia, she is not petty (most of the time). And if she is capricious and at times arbitrary, there remains always an underlying strength of purpose. She believes in this newspaper her father founded and her dearest wish is to have it return to the days when it was synonymous with reason, objectivity, truth.

Her clothes are expensive but somehow don't always seem to complement each other. Like Abercrombie and Saks.

She is an avid sports fan, especially LaCrosse and Hockey, and her Sports Department is hardpressed to feature stories pertaining to either of these events.

Because of her reputation for capriciousness and because she is a power, she has been shamelessly catered to by her Editorial staff. No one had the temerity to contradict or disregard the memos in the form of odd scraps of envelopes, torn paper napkins or restaurant checks that would at times almost rain from "The Tower" where she has her offices. (Everyone calls it "The Tower," has for decades, even though the building has no tower and never had. It was a feeling she generated.) To quote Nora Ephron about New York's Dolly Schiff: ". . . her editors, who operated under the delusion that their balls were in escrow, would dispatch reporters" . . . in dutiful answer to these memos.

Until Lou Grant.

Bill Hume—Managing Editor

A careful man with a surface ease belied by two very sweaty palms. A good man, with a very nervous stomach.

He runs the paper with a most sensitive ear cocked in the direction of The Tower. He is painfully aware that he, his family, and all the trappings of success that surrounds them are at the mercy of the publisher, Louise [*sic*] Pynchon.

He is married to a patient woman who is active in the community where they live (Palos Verde Estates). His daughter is at Stanford and somehow confused his income with the Pentagon's budget. His son thinks of himself as Evil [*sic*] Knievel's successor and the insurance premiums that Hume must pay out attests [*sic*] to this. They are counting on his living long enough to finish High School.

He has known Lou for twenty years, though they did not keep in close touch. But Lou made enough of an impression so that when the City Editor slot opened (for the third time in six months) he offered it to him. Now that he sees Lou operate the Desk, crack the whip in the City Room, and lock horns with Mrs. Pynchon, he is not so sure he made the right decision. For some unaccountable reason, he thought he could control Lou. But nobody controls Lou. Not even Lou.

Some Hume-isms:

I'm getting a little offensive—I don't mean to.

When in doubt, we play it safe.

Why don't we table it? (Meaning: I want to see what The Tower—Mrs. Pynchon—feels about it.)

He got his B.A. from Dartmouth, worked briefly for Random House, then began as a cub reporter with the Philadelphia Inquirer, moving slowly from paper to paper in the East and as far west as Detroit. He was a hungry reporter for too long. Whatever it is that makes a newspaperman eluded him. He feels he landed in his present job through a series of lucky mishaps and moves, and he does not want to lose it. As always with insecure men, he feels he is somehow there under false pretenses and that at any moment he will be found out, his incompetences bared and that will be it. Were you to tell him that he is *not* incompetent, that, in fact, he does his job well and would do it better were he not so shakey [*sic*], he would not believe you. At one time he was a crackerjack reporter. Somewhere he had lost his nerve.

Arthur Donovan, Jr.—Assistant City Editor

Donovan is happy.

Donovan has it made.

Donovan is that rarity—a man who is completely satisfied with who he is and where he is. At 42, no small achievement.

A most capable newspaperman, he could have been the desk man on the Metropolitan Desk, but angled it so that they never even asked him. When the job went to Lou, he breathed a cosmic sigh of relief.

Educated in Catholic primary and secondary schools, he enlisted in the Navy at 17, saw some off shore action in Korea, and managed to spend a credible number of hours in Seoul, Tokyo, and San Francisco learning his craft: coition. He graduated *cum laude* one windy Presidio afternoon with a Brigadier General's wife of some maturity, subsequently earned his Master's Degree in Foreplay. He became a newspaperman with single minded devotion after seeing some pornographic pictures of a movie queen taken by a staff photographer for the Los Angeles Times who had actually been on assignment and had overstayed his allotted hour with satisfactory results. (He had also charged the paper with time and a half for that dalliance and of course, had developed and printed the pictures in the TIMES' photo lab.) Obviously, this was a milieu made for Donovan.

He dresses much better than he should, fancies himself a fair expert in food and wine, both domestic and foreign, and is constantly juggling calls from his agents in the field. (If he can put together the condominium deal in Tahiti, he'll make the downpayment on the 54 foot sloop he adores [the only picture in his drawer]; then, by selling the land he optioned near Palm Desert, he could promote the loan of the developer's Lear jet, have it ferried to Tahiti—and on and on.)

He would be the last to admit that he loves being a newspaperman, insists he is there only because it gives him a swinging base and the freedom to operate from it.

He is forever disappearing for "coffee" returning an hour later smelling of expensive perfume, smiling his Errol Flynn smile, and picking long silken hair of varying shades from between his Errol Flynn teeth.

But when Lou must leave the desk, Donovan takes over the Desk with a verve and competence that gives him away. (He could be brilliant, but that might blow his scene. They just might give him a more responsible, better paying, higher ranking job. God forbid.)

He and Lou get along well, though Lou's style of dress makes him wince. (Once he insisted on buying Lou a shirt but after seeing how it looked on him, never mentioned it again.)

Donovan—full of stories and that great Irish charm—is a hell of a lot of fun.

Joseph Rossi—General Assignment Reporter, Metro Desk

To most of the old timers on the TRIB and for that matter, to most of the newer employees, he is and will forever be, "that arrogant, little creep". Their assessment of him won't change, even after the Pulitzer Prizes he is sure he will win. And Rossi couldn't care less.

It's not easy to be 27 years old and know with a monumental certainty that you are destined for greatness. Fortunately for him, his great and unbounded affection for his own talents are matched by these self-same talents. It is obvious he could be the best reporter in the city, if he isn't already.

He is abrasive, rude and obnoxious. He is argumentative, temperamental, a manic-depressive of treatable proportions, and when he is feeling good, just plain belligerent.

But behind his brashness, there is a dark and sparkling charm; and above everything else, he is one hell of a newspaperman. Wherever there is a free press, he would be at home. Wherever there is a balloon filled with hot and pompous air, you'll find him sharpening a needle. He was born cynical, and nothing he has encountered since has mellowed that cynicism. (Tell him it's raining out and he'll not only check with the Weather Bureau, but then go out and look for himself, just in case you and the Weather Bureau have some vested interest in spreading reports of precipitation.)

This giant ambulatory sneer, however, is one of his most effective weapons as a reporter. Let him walk into an office and the object of his visit will immediately think of all the skeletons in all the closets of his life. This master con man's first words convince them that it is futile to deny their existence, since it is obvious he not only holds the key to each closet but has been inside, poking around. Level with him, and maybe, just maybe, it won't hurt too much when you bleed.

A city boy in every sense of the word, you have the feeling that he has played one on one in ghetto concrete courts, that he is familiar with alleys and night crawlers and all the rest that goes into making up the ulcerated underbelly of our society.

And yet, when he wants to be, that is, when he feels it is to his advantage, he can be as silken and charming and caring as any mother's son should be. And there are times, some people say, when his guard comes down for a fleeting moment, and if you're quick about it, you can see the young and vulnerable humanity, the child who was hurt once too often, the youngster who believed in someone too much.

And then it's gone, the deflecting shield up once more, the flip wisecrack that says "Keep away. I will bite the hand that tries to pet me."

Rossi is an enigma. But there are not many people who return to be bitten a second time. They accept him the way he wants them to: an arrogant, little creep with a stupendous ego who lives and breathes for himself and his work. (He began keeping a diary from his first day on the job, notes of conversations, meetings, assignments. When he writes *his* book, it's going to be on the button.)

He is neither liked nor understood, which is—he insists—fine with him. But he is respected, and after the editions have been locked up and the men bury their noses in boozy cameraderie [sic] at the saloon they frequent, if someone gets drunk enough, he will admit that to him, yes, Rossi is an arrogant, little creep—but an admirable one.

Carla Madigian—General Assignment Reporter

Carla Madigian is a woman to become involved with if you are very secure. Make that very, *very* secure. This stunning and talented 28 year old reporter is that rarity among us, a totally honest person. Honest about her own feelings, yet aware of others' sensibilities. While she can be as outspoken as her fellow reporter, Rossi, the difference is that she, unlike him, is sensitive to her fellow human beings. This sensitivity, however, does not interfere with her hates and loves, likes and dislikes. (Example: she cannot stand Rossi and makes no bones about that.)

A tough competitor in what is still basically a man's field, there is no one who has ever called her that stock male business put-down: a ballsy chick. Because Carla is, first and last, that fantasy figure in the very curvaceous flesh: a totally feminine woman not above using her femininity when going after a story or a man she wants, yet who knows her own real worth and is quite comfortable with it.

She is as frank about acknowledging her sexual appetites as the most outspoken male. She is as impatient with the New Feminism as she is with the old masculine chauvinism. She is a graduate of USC, with a major in comparative literature. When she was a child, her father and mother both assured her that she could be anything she wanted to be. It is the Trib's good fortune that she got hooked on journalism.

She resists any effort (unless she's after a story) to cast her in the role of something other than she is. Lou, for example, has a hard time trying to adopt a fatherly attitude with her. She won't have it, though not unappreciative of the motives behind his concern.

Her contacts are varied and broad, and each one of them—mostly male—sees her in a different way. Only once did she find someone she thought she'd like to spend more than a week with, and buried deep within her is the wound that relationship caused. The marriage ended after eight months. No one has touched that secret place since. Nor will she talk about it. Yet, whatever the residual pain, she does not use her maiden name.

Lou would like to ask her about that. She is an enigma to many, a paradox to all. Just when you think you've got her nailed, you discover that the hammer is in her hand. And somehow, though mascochism [sic] is as far from your makeup as it can be, you delight in that fact. Son of a bitch, you might say. Admiringly.

Dennis Price (The Animal)—Staff Photographer

No one ever calls him by his name. To everyone he is The Animal. Twenty six years old, with very long blonde hair pulled back in a pony tail, he is a consummate slob in everything except his work and anything related to his work. At home, for example, there are times when he can't find his bed because of the chaos of books, clothes, old orange peels and magazines. But one could perform brain surgery in his darkroom without risk of infection.

His photographs are Pulitzer prize quality, and in fact, he has won a number of awards. (The plaques are somewhere in his bedroom, and if he ever gets his laundry done, he may find them.)

In the trunk of his car, in addition to the zippered bags of lenses and related photo equipment and the fireman's helmet and heavy clasped coat, is an assortment of props that helped earn him his sobriquet: A pair of baby shoes, worn and scuffed; a child's doll, sad and broken; a blind man's white cane, splintered. He is not above tossing them in the foreground of a freeway accident he is photographing, according to the station of the victims involved. When looking through the viewfinder of his motorized Nikon, he becomes both robot and artist. He is totally without nerves or emotion and some of the pictures, "art" in newspaper parlance, that he brings back make the most hardened editor wince. (Like the murdered woman, lying in her bloody bathtub, with the protruding knife's handle wrapped in a rosary, but the detectives on the scene know better. It's not that he wouldn't have done it; just that someone did it before he thought of it.)

The Animal doesn't talk much. He changes his clothes when the people he's speaking to take an involuntary step backwards. The jeans and workshirt, both unpressed, that he dons is [sic] undistinguishable from the ones he took off. He lives, breathes, is consumed by photography. That is his madness. It matters little to him The Trib is his employer. If any of his latitude were curtailed and Gelson's Markets would promise him the same freedom, he would work for them. He neither drinks, nor smokes nor uses drugs, despite his "dealer" appearance. He drives a Trib car, an unmarked white Buick with the equivelent [*sic*] of fourteen radios. He has the latest scanners and all radios are hooked into five separate speakers. Cruising, waiting for a call from The Desk, or picking up a CHP broadcast or Fire Department call, LAPB broadcast, Rangers, Sheriff's, etc. he often—in a moment of stress—reaches on the seat next to him and touches his camera. It calms him. He is hooked to the Desk at the Trib by direct radio and can also call through the mobile phone operator. His car is Unit Charlie/one eighty eight and he uses this when calling the Desk.

He is unique and only his press card saves him at times from being hauled off for questioning.

Major Awards

Directors Guild of America Awards

The Directors Guild of America honors directors of motion pictures, television programs, and television commercials. *Lou Grant* received five nominations and three awards for best direction in a dramatic series. The (w) denotes winners among the nominees.

1978

Gene Reynolds, "Prisoner" (w).

1979

Gene Reynolds, "Bomb."
Roger Young, "Cop" (w).

1980

Gene Reynolds, "Nightside."
Roger Young, "Lou" (w).

Emmy Awards

The Academy of Television Arts and Sciences bestows the awards. *Lou Grant* received fifty-six nominations and thirteen Emmys. The (w) denotes winners among the nominees.

1977–78 (six nominations; three awards)

Drama Series:

James L. Brooks, Allan Burns, Gene Reynolds, executive producers; Gene Reynolds, producer.

Actor, Drama Series:
Edward Asner (w).
Actor, Single Performance, Drama or Comedy Series:
Barnard Hughes, "Judge" (w).
Supporting Actress, Drama Series:
Linda Kelsey.
Supporting Actress, Drama Series:
Nancy Marchand (w).
Film Sound Editing, Series:
Tony Garber, Dale Johnston, Ron Clark, "Nazi."

1978–79 (fourteen nominations; two awards)

Drama Series:
Gene Reynolds, executive producer; Seth Freeman, Gary David Goldberg, producers (w).
Actor, Drama Series:
Edward Asner.
Supporting Actress, Drama Series:
Linda Kelsey.
Supporting Actress, Drama Series:
Nancy Marchand.
Supporting Actor, Drama Series:
Mason Adams.
Supporting Actor, Drama Series:
Robert Walden.
Director, Drama Series:
Burt Brinckerhoff, "Schools."
Director, Drama Series:
Mel Damski, "Murder."
Director, Drama Series:
Gene Reynolds, "Prisoner."
Writing, Drama Series:
Michele Gallery, "Dying" (w).
Writing, Drama Series:
Gene Reynolds, "Marathon."
Writing, Drama Series:
Leon Tokatyan, "Vet."
Film Editing, Series:
James Galloway, "Hooker."
Music Composition, Series:
Patrick Williams, "Prisoner."

1979–80 (fifteen nominations; six awards)

Drama Series:
Gene Reynolds, executive producer; Seth Freeman, producer (w).

Actor, Drama Series:
  Edward Asner (w).
Supporting Actress, Drama Series:
  Nina Foch, "Hollywood."
Supporting Actress, Drama Series:
  Linda Kelsey.
Supporting Actress, Drama Series:
  Nancy Marchand (w).
Supporting Actor, Drama Series:
  Mason Adams.
Supporting Actor, Drama Series:
  Robert Walden.
Director, Drama Series:
  Burt Brinckerhoff, "Hollywood."
Director, Drama Series:
  Peter Levin, "Andrew Part II: Trial."
Director, Drama Series:
  Gene Reynolds, "Influence."
Director, Drama Series:
  Roger Young, "Cop" (w).
Writing, Drama Series:
  Allan Burns, Gene Reynolds, "Brushfire."
Writing, Drama Series:
  Seth Freeman, "Cop" (w).
Writing, Drama Series:
  Michele Gallery, "Lou."
Music Composition, Series (Dramatic Underscore):
  Patrick Williams, "Hollywood" (w).

1980–81 (thirteen nominations; one award)

Drama Series:
  Gene Reynolds, executive producer; Seth Freeman, producer.
Actor, Drama Series:
  Edward Asner.
Supporting Actress, Drama Series:
  Linda Kelsey.
Supporting Actress, Drama Series:
  Nancy Marchand (w).
Supporting Actor, Drama Series:
  Mason Adams.
Supporting Actor, Drama Series:
  Robert Walden.
Director, Drama Series:
  Burt Brinckerhoff, "Pack."

Director, Drama Series:
Gene Reynolds, "Strike."
Writing, Drama Series:
Seth Freeman, "Rape."
Writing, Drama Series:
April Smith, "Strike."
Music Composition, Series (Dramatic Underscore):
Patrick Williams, "Stroke."
Hairstyling:
Jean Austin, "Stroke."
Film Editing, Series:
James Galloway, "Strike."

1981–82 (eight nominations; one award)

Drama Series:
Gene Reynolds, executive producer; Seth Freeman, producer.
Actor, Drama Series:
Edward Asner.
Supporting Actress, Drama Series:
Linda Kelsey.
Supporting Actress, Drama Series:
Nancy Marchand (w).
Director, Drama Series:
Gene Reynolds, "Hometown."
Writing, Drama Series:
Seth Freeman, "Blacklist."
Cinematography, Series:
Robert F. Liu, "Ghosts."
Music Composition, Series (Dramatic Underscore):
Patrick Williams, "Hometown."

Humanitas Prize

The Human Family Educational and Cultural Institute honors writers of television programs that its directors believe best communicate human values and enrich the medium. *Lou Grant* received four nominations and two prizes. The (w) denotes winners among the nominees.

1979

Michele Gallery, "Dying."
Leon Tokatyan, "Vet" (w).

1981

Bud Freeman, "Streets."

1982

Gene Reynolds, "Hunger" (w).

Peabody Award

The Henry W. Grady School of Journalism at the University of Georgia administers the George Foster Peabody Awards. They honor people, programs, and institutions in broadcasting.

Lou Grant received a Peabody Award in 1978. The citation honored "MTM Productions, Hollywood, and CBS for 'Lou Grant,' the entertaining yet realistic look at the problems and issues which face those who are involved in the 'Fourth Estate'."

Writers Guild of America Awards

The Writers Guild of America honors writers of motion pictures and television programs. *Lou Grant* received fourteen nominations and two awards for best dramatic episode. The (w) denotes winners among the nominees.

1977

David Lloyd, "Christmas."
Leonora Thuna, "Housewarming."

1978

Seth Freeman, "Prisoner" (w).
Gary David Goldberg, "Murder."

1979

Johnny Dawkins, "Slammer."
Gary David Goldberg, "Home."
David Lloyd, "Exposé."
Leon Tokatyan, "Vet" (w).

1980

Steve Kline, "Blackout."
Allan Burns and Gene Reynolds, "Brushfire."
April Smith, "Inheritance."

1981

April Smith, "Strike."
Michael Vittes, "Campesinos."

1982

Jeffrey Lane, "Review."

APPENDIX D
Episode Synopses

The author's summaries are based on episodes as broadcasted.

First Season, 1977–1978

Created by James L. Brooks, Allan Burns, and Gene Reynolds. Developed by Leon Tokatyan.

Executive producers:
James L. Brooks, Allan Burns, and Gene Reynolds.

Producer:
Gene Reynolds.

Regular cast:
Edward Asner (Lou Grant), Robert Walden (Joe Rossi), Rebecca Balding (Carla Mardigian), Linda Kelsey (Billie Newman), Mason Adams (Charlie Hume), Jack Bannon (Art Donovan), Daryl Anderson (Dennis "Animal" Price), and Nancy Marchand (Mrs. Margaret Pynchon).

Episode 1: "Cophouse"
Air date: September 20, 1977
Director: Gene Reynolds
Writer: Leon Tokatyan
Guest cast: Peter Hobbs (George Driscoll), Norman Bartold (Commander Phillips), George Cooper (deputy chief), Paul Larson (watch commander), and Wallace Rooney (Tim).

Fifty years old and with only $280 in the bank, Lou Grant is hired as city editor of the *Los Angeles Tribune*. His first dilemma involves Driscoll, a veteran police reporter who has been sitting on a brewing scandal. Rossi discovers through other sources that officers have had sex with teenage girls on a youth soccer league sponsored by the department. Driscoll resists reporting the scandal, contending that the police are handling it internally and that his sources will dry up if the story is printed. Lou convinces him that his job is to report the news, not hide it. Driscoll not only writes about the scandal, but he reports his involvement in keeping it quiet.

Episode 2: "Hostages"
Air date: September 27, 1977
Director: Charles Dubin
Writer: Seth Freeman
Guest cast: John Rubinstein (Andrew Martin), Patrick Tovatt (Sgt. Pierce), Joyce Jillson (Cathy Anne Wills), Robert Phalen (Agee), and Rachel Bard (Miss Apthorp).

Rossi's story about a fatal shooting of a robber by a store clerk angers Andrew Martin, the victim's brother. He takes *Tribune* staffers hostage in the newsroom, ordering Rossi to write another story about the shooting. Martin contends the store owner owed his brother money and killed him rather than pay. The *Tribune* publishes Rossi's story, but live television reports of the hostage incident reveal that the edition is a phony. Only when Mrs. Pynchon promises to publish the facts of the shooting does Martin surrender. Later, she asks that all news about the incident be published on inside pages of the *Tribune* as a way to avoid encouraging others to demand coverage at gunpoint.

Episode 3: "Hoax"
Air date: October 4, 1977
Director: Jay Sandrich
Writer: Gordon Dawson
Guest cast: Eugene Roche (Jack Riley), Booth Colman (Mr. Curtis), Diana Douglas (Mrs. Cardell), Rod McCary (Ron Allen), and Fred Stuthman (photo editor).

Lou's old friend Jack Riley claims to know the whereabouts of Luther Cardell, a missing industrialist believed kidnapped. Riley convinces the *Tribune* editors to send him, Lou, and Rossi to Jamaica for an exclusive interview with Cardell. While Riley urges a reluctant Lou and Rossi to enjoy themselves on their island trip, Cardell's body turns up in a canyon car wreck in Los Angeles. Riley admits he was having fun at the *Tribune*'s expense. After prodding from Lou the *Tribune* publishes a story about the hoax.

Episode 4: "Henhouse"
Air date: October 11, 1977
Director: Richard Crenna
Writer: Leonora Thuna
Guest cast: Claudette Nevins (Irene Mott), Geoffrey Lewis (sheriff), Patty Mattick (Cecile), David Starwalt (Mark), and Ivy Bethune (waitress).

The attractive woman Lou meets one morning is Irene Mott, the editor of the *Tribune*'s "Today" section. Lou considers it the women's section and not as demanding as hard news. Although "Today" feature writer Billie Newman is in New Mexico on an assignment, Lou sends Rossi there to cover the murder of a prominent playwright. Billie and Rossi clash, which is a mirror of Lou's and Irene's disagreements over the place of women in the newsroom. But when Billie's theory that the murder was actually a suicide is confirmed by police, both Lou and Rossi admit she is a fine reporter. Lou invites her to join the city staff.

Episode 5: "Nazi"
Air date: October 18, 1977
Director: Alexander Singer
Writer: Robert Schlitt
Guest cast: Peter Weller (Donald Stryker), Brian Dennehy (Wilson), Janet Brandt (Mrs. Sturner), Jack A. Lukes (Sgt. Parisi), and Lee Wallace (Kelso).

Publicizing routine protests staged by American Nazis concerns Lou and Charlie after a demonstration becomes violent. Lou assigns Billie to write an in-depth story about the American Nazi movement in Los Angeles, and she discovers that local Nazi leader Donald Stryker is Jewish. After talking to his relatives and former friends Billie confronts Stryker. He threatens her at first and then begs her not to publish the story. On the day the story appears Lou tells a shaken Billie that Stryker has killed himself.

Episode 6: "Aftershock"
Air date: October 25, 1977
Director: Jud Taylor
Writer: Del Reisman
Guest cast: Joyce Van Patten (Gloria), Clyde Kusatsu (Ralph Tumora), Betty Anne Rees (Laurette), Gary Pagett (Harding), and Noble Willingham (hotel manager).

Lou is rattled by the first earthquake tremors to hit Los Angeles since he joined the *Tribune* staff. In the wake of the rumbling Rossi and Animal investigate a researcher's claim that his cockroaches can signal impending earthquakes. But a major earthquake the researcher predicts fails to materialize. More distressing for Lou is the attention he receives from the widow of a recently deceased *Tribune* staffer. She relies on him more and more for advice and comfort until an exasperated Lou bluntly tells her he is not interested in a relationship. They remain friends.

Episode 7: "Barrio"
Air date: November 1, 1977
Director: Mel Damski
Writer: Seth Freeman
Guest cast: Guillermo San Juan (Henry), Phillip Antora (pool guard), Joe Santos (George Delgado), Kiki Quiralta (Amanda), and Edward Gallardo (Claudio).

After a woman is shot and wounded in east Los Angeles Billie pushes for an assignment on Latino gangs. Lou joins her and George Delgado, a man who works with barrio youth, on a tour of the district. They meet Henry, the teenage son of the wounded woman, who explains how gangs protect their neighborhood. Billie visits Henry's home for dinner, which is disrupted by a drive-by shooting. Henry later tricks Billie into revealing which gang has told her they were responsible for recent attacks. George convinces Henry not to join the never-ending cycle of revenge.

Episode 8: "Scoop"
Air date: November 8, 1977
Director: Harry Falk
Writer: Gene Kearney
Guest cast: Bill Beck (photo editor), Laurence Haddon (foreign editor), Michael Irving (Jayson), Vivian Brown (waitress), and Reni Santoni (Jim Keenan).

Attempts to be first with the news while remaining accurate yield mixed results for the *Tribune* staff. Billie's careful coverage of a kidnapping draws Lou's wrath when she misses her deadline. Rossi's exclusive about a politician's impending candidacy for office turns out to be wrong. In a rush to beat the competition Rossi reports a fatal motorcycle accident without waiting for confirmation that the rider is dead (he survived). Billie and Rossi make up for their errors by getting a scoop that the kidnapping was concocted by the victim and his girlfriend.

Episode 9: "Judge"
Air date: November 15, 1977
Director: Irving Moore
Writer: Leon Tokatyan
Guest cast: Barnard Hughes (Felix Ruthman), Phillip E. Pine (Lindsay), Joe Mantell (Simmons), Timothy Jerome (Murray), and Guy Raymond (bailiff).

A woman complains to the *Tribune* that her boyfriend did not receive a fair trial in Superior Court because of a crazy judge. Lou attends a session of Judge Felix Ruthman's court and is jailed briefly for contempt when he tries to leave. Billie and Rossi investigate the judge's bizarre behavior and the difficulties of removing a judge from the bench. Ruthman warns Mrs. Pynchon and Lou that they are asking for trouble if they write about him and promises to fight any attempt to remove him. Their plea that Ruthman leave the court for the good of the system, however, apparently works. The judge orders a new trial for the boyfriend and announces he will retire.

Episode 10: "Psych-Out"
Air date: November 22, 1977
Director: Alexander Singer
Writer: Seth Freeman

Guest cast: Phillip R. Allen (Sackler), Michael Irving (Jayson), Harry Townes (James Heiler), Michael Zslow (Doug), and Ann Sweeny (Dorothy).

When Lou criticizes Rossi for not having more information about patient abuses at a state mental hospital, Rossi checks in as a patient without telling anyone. Meanwhile, the leader of an antiobscenity drive threatens the paper with legal action over Billie's coverage of the issue. When the paper's lawyer heavily edits the story, Lou fears the threat of a lawsuit is chilling the *Tribune*'s effort to report the news. Mrs. Pynchon agrees they must be wary of lawsuits that could ruin the paper. Later, Rossi's plan backfires when he is unable to leave the mental hospital and is heavily medicated. Lou realizes why Rossi has disappeared and has him released from the hospital. Rossi then writes an exposé, and Lou works into the evening with the *Tribune* lawyer to make sure it is legally sound.

Episode 11: "Housewarming"
Air date: November 29, 1977
Director: Mel Damski
Writer: Leonora Thuna
Guest cast: Julie Kavner (Alice), Fredi Olster (Dorothy), Janice Kent (Louise), Robert Rothwell (Sid Arby), and Edward D. Winter (Roger).

Billie meets a battered wife, Alice, as she reports about the problem of spouse abuse. Although her husband beats her regularly, Alice refuses to leave him. Not until a party at Lou's new home does Billie discover that *Tribune* staffer Roger has beaten his wife. In the driveway she confronts Roger, and he almost hits her. Billie refuses to call the police, and the experience gives her more insight into Alice's dilemma. Alice is beaten again and seeks refuge at Billie's home. When her husband shows up to apologize, she refuses to return and endure more suffering. At work Lou suggests that Roger write about wife beating from a husband's point of view and include therapy as part of his research. Roger agrees.

Episode 12: "Takeover"
Air date: December 6, 1977
Director: Gene Reynolds
Writer: Leon Tokatyan
Guest cast: John Anderson (Russell Grainger), Jerry Fogel (Freddie), Paul Kent (Matthews), Allen Williams (Wilson), and William Bogert (Colin).

A *Tribune* board meeting reveals that Mrs. Pynchon controls 49 percent of the newspaper's stock, her two nephews 49 percent, and her attorney 2 percent. The nephews believe the newspaper is a bad investment; the attorney is unhappy that his ideas for changes at the paper are ignored. Later, they promise to support a takeover bid by media mogul Russell Grainger, a charming man who seems smitten with Mrs. Pynchon. Having enjoyed his attention, she refuses to believe that Rossi has uncovered evidence of the bid. When Grainger invites her to become his business partner, she refuses. Before the *Tribune* board votes on a merger with Grainger, Mrs. Pynchon and Lou speak forcefully to maintain the *Tribune*'s reputation as an independent newspaper. Swayed, the paper's attorney votes in Mrs. Pynchon's favor, and the takeover is averted.

Episode 13: "Christmas"
Air date: December 13, 1977
Director: Jim Burrows
Writer: David Lloyd
Guest cast: Verna Bloom (Emily); Tim O'Connor (Malcolm Findlay), Ben Hayes (Walter Harper) and Carol O'Leary (Kay Findlay).

Two Christmas assignments take unlikely turns. Lou assigns Billie a feature about a poor family camping in the woods beside a city highway. To punish Rossi for breaking the *Tribune*'s rule against surreptitous tape recording Lou assigns him a profile on a low-level state official. Billie's story results in a wave of sympathy and donations for the family. Rossi discovers that the state official is a bigamist with two families. The official pleads with him not to publish the story. Later, Billie finds out that the needy family has been moving from city to city getting publicity, sympathy, and money. Rossi, apparently in the Christmas spirit, decides not to publish the story about the state official's bigamy and tells no one about it.

Episode 14: "Airliner"
Air date: January 3, 1978
Director: Mel Damski
Writer: Charles Einstein
Guest cast: Jack Grapes (Mel Brunner), Allan Miller (Hal Pearson), Lou Cutell (Haskins), and Penny Santon (Aunt Rose).

A breaking news story disrupts the lives of *Tribune* staffers. A jetliner carrying 340 people, including Charlie's daughter, cannot lower its landing gear as it approaches Los Angeles. The staff swings into action, dividing up coverage duties as they wait for the plane to make a belly landing. The plane lands safely, and Charlie is reunited with his daughter. Hours later, a tired *Tribune* staff returns to their private lives.

Episode 15: "Sports"
Air date: January 10, 1978
Director: Harvey Laidman
Writer: Bud Freeman
Guest cast: Vaughn Armstrong (Rick Waterhouse), Michael D. Henry (Frank), David Ackroyd (Mike Kessler), Elizabeth Herbert (Ruth Eisle), Michael Morgan (Tom), and John A. Randolph (Sid Locke).

Lou clashes with veteran sportswriter Sid Locke when he refuses to investigate reports of problems within a local college sports program. Lou takes the story for the city side, but Locke warns him that the *Tribune* will anger readers if it runs a negative story about the program. Indeed, the *Tribune* is swamped with protests and subscription cancellations when the story appears, and Lou even gets a death threat. Undeterred, Billie and Rossi interview coaches and players until they have enough to publish an exposé. Sid and Lou agree to disagree about the goals of sports coverage by the *Tribune*.

Episode 16: "Hero"
Air date: January 17, 1978
Director: Mel Damski
Writer: Seth Freeman
Guest cast: Marlene Warfield (Joanne Bartlett), Hazel Medina (Janey), Lola Mason (Ellen), Jim McMullan (William Danvers), and Kerry Sherman (Barbara).

A bystander saves a gubernatorial candidate from a would-be assassin by knocking down his handgun. Animal captures the heroic act on film, but the bystander vanishes before Rossi can interview him. Rossi discovers the hero is William Danvers, a successful San Francisco financial consultant who was once convicted of armed robbery. Rossi's story runs near Billie's feature on a halfway house for female felons. Moved by her story, Mrs. Pynchon donates money to keep the financially troubled house open. When the *Tribune* story includes details of Danvers' criminal past, he loses clients and his girlfriend. After the *Tribune* publishes follow-up stories about Danvers's plight, he gains new clients and old ones return.

Episode 17: "Renewal"
Air date: January 30, 1978
Director: Gene Reynolds
Writer: Ken Trevey
Guest cast: Robert Earl Jones (Earl Humphrey), Phillip R. Allen (Sackler), and James Karen (Tyler Armitage).

A feature on the razing of landmark buildings in Los Angeles leads Lou to Earl, an elderly black man served with an eviction notice. Earl refuses to vacate his room in a condemned building because its walls are covered with intricate murals that he has drawn depicting his life. Lou enlists Mrs. Pynchon in an effort to save the building and the murals from Tyler Armitage, an art patron and developer. Despite a court injunction Earl is forced out and the building demolished. Earl appears at an art show and threatens to slash a priceless painting owned by Armitage. Lou appeals to his love of art, and Earl lowers his knife. Later, Earl begins painting again in a new apartment rented with settlement money from Armitage.

Episode 18: "Sect"
Air date: February 6, 1978

Director: Alexander Singer
Writer: Michele Gallery
Guest cast: James Beach (Orrin Houston), Peggy McCay (Marion Hume), William Boyett (Bill), Richard Erdman (Mal Cavanaugh), and Melissa Newman (Kim).

Charlie and his wife Marion are shocked and worried when their son Tommy joins Hare Krishna. Lou accompanies them on a visit to the Krishna temple, but Tommy will not be dissuaded from his decision. While Rossi and Billie research religious cults for a story, Charlie hires a "deprogrammer" to kidnap Tommy and take him to Lou's house. Before the plan is carried out, though, Charlie has second thoughts about forcing his son to change. Meeting Tommy again, Charlie comes to an uneasy acceptance of his decision.

Episode 19: "Scandal"
Air date: February 13, 1978
Director: Mel Damski
Writer: Seth Freeman
Guest cast: Gail Strickland (Liz Harrison), James Olson (Corwin), Brian Farrell (Larry Kean), Paul Jenkins (Jack Efros), and Virginia Binham (Marsha).

Rossi is pulled from covering the reelection campaign of a city supervisor, Corwin, because they have a poor relationship. A new reporter, Liz Harrison, replaces him and quickly comes up with scoops about the campaign. Rossi suspects Liz and Corwin are having a relationship. When Corwin announces a probe into nursing home abuse after Rossi discovers his financial interests in such a home, Rossi follows Corwin to Liz's home. Liz admits to Lou that she and Corwin are lovers, but she contends it has not compromised her as a reporter. Reluctantly, Charlie and Lou fire her to protect the *Tribune*'s reputation.

Episode 20: "Spies"
Air date: February 27, 1978
Director: Charles Dubin
Writer: Leon Tokatyan
Guest cast: Peter Hobbs (Driscoll), Laurette Spang (Joanie Hume), Michael Strong (Sohner), and Jean Allison (Mrs. Morrison).

The Central Intelligence Agency asks the *Tribune* to stop investigating the drug arrests of two young men, later claiming they are part of a CIA probe into espionage. Mrs. Pynchon recalls that the *Tribune* and many other papers routinely cooperated with the CIA in the past. Lou convinces her to let Rossi and Billie look into the arrests. Paranoia grows at the *Tribune* as rumors spread that a CIA spy is on the payroll. At one point Lou and Charlie suspect each other. The reporters determine that the drug charges are dropped because the government cannot prove espionage charges against the suspects. Lacking confirmation of the facts of the story, the *Tribune* prints nothing. Lou still wonders who in the newsroom might be working for the CIA.

Episode 21: "Poison"
Air date: March 6, 1978
Director: Gene Reynolds
Writer: Michele Gallery
Guest cast: Guy Boyd (Sam Beecher), Belinda J. Montgomery (Carol), and Jenni-
fer Rhodes (Dr. Roberta Giani).

Rossi's friend Sam Beecher claims there are serious safety problems at the
nuclear power plant where he works. After setting an appointment to bring Rossi
photos and other evidence Sam is struck and killed by a car. Billie discovers that
a congressman heading a secret investigation of the plant has to back off because
of sexual blackmail. She also links the car that struck Sam to the nuclear plant.
Rossi is thwarted in his investigation by townspeople unwilling to criticize the
plant that brought jobs and tax revenue to the community. Despite circumstantial
evidence of wrongdoing Lou refuses to publish any stories without verification. In
the mail Rossi finds an envelope from Sam. He had sent a back-up set of photos
and documents that provide the paper the evidence it needs to publish a story.

Episode 22: "Physical"
Air date: March 20, 1978
Director: Charles Dubin
Writer: David Lloyd
Guest cast: Fred Sadoff (surgeon) and Leonard Ross (Bill).

A tired Lou tries to help a copyboy who wants to be a reporter. Then, he
must fire a promising college correspondent who, as a joke, places a phony award
at the bottom of a list of awards. As if Lou does not have enough stress, a routine
physical shows he has thyroid cancer. The *Tribune* staff rallies around Lou after
he is operated on successfully.

Second Season, 1978–1979

Executive producer:
  Gene Reynolds.
Producers:
  Seth Freeman, Gary David Goldberg.
Executive consultants:
  Allan Burns and James L. Brooks.
Creative consultant:
  Leon Tokatyan.
Additional regular cast:
  Allen Williams (Adam Wilson).

Episode 23: "Pills"
Air date: September 25, 1978
Director: Jay Sandrich

Writer: Michele Gallery
Guest cast: Steve Nevil (Peter Tomasso), Richard Bull (Dr. Bonham), Jean Rasey (Gerry), Dean Santoro (Walt Krasner), and Joey Aresco (Arthur Locatelli).

The death of a young girl spurs the *Tribune* to investigate unethical and illegal prescription practices by physicians. The dead girl's boyfriend, Peter, breaks into her doctor's office and steals his files. He turns them over to Rossi, sparking a newsroom debate over how the *Tribune* should act. Mrs. Pynchon agrees with her staff that the story is important enough to risk legal action. Publication leads to a newsroom search by the police and Rossi's incarceration for failing to cooperate with the investigation by revealing his source. After several days Peter turns himself in to police, and Rossi is released from jail. The *Tribune*'s investigation links doctors with pharmacies that run a prescription scam aimed at young people.

Episode 24: "Prisoner"
Air date: October 2, 1978
Director: Gene Reynolds
Writer: Seth Freeman
Guest cast: Silvana Gallardo (Amanda Baroja), Peggy McCay (Marian Hume), Frank Ramirez (Bazan), Jorge Cervera Jr. (Blanco), and Enrique Novi (Flores).

Charlie still has nightmares of being tortured fifteen years earlier by General Baroja, the dictator of the [fictional] nation of Malagua. The *Tribune* staff interviews people supporting and denouncing the Malaguan government when the general's wife visits Los Angeles. Mrs. Pynchon hosts a reception for Mrs. Baroja, but Charlie's tirade against the woman embarrasses the publisher. Encouraged by Lou, Charlie writes a story about his experience. Mrs. Pynchon arranges a meeting with Mrs. Baroja and four protesters to allow her to hear their allegations. The general's wife is shocked to learn that one of the protesters is her nephew. She leaves the United States with a veiled acknowledgment of problems in her country.

Episode 25: "Hooker"
Air date: October 16, 1978
Director: Alexander Singer
Writer: Seth Freeman
Guest cast: Dee Wallace (Patti), Paul Lambert (Congressman Phelps), Gail Edwards (Karen), Michael Alldredge (Sgt. Roche), and Mary-Robin Redd (Ellen).

Covering the murder of a prostitute leads Billie to Patti, a bright young hooker. Her goal is to earn enough money to study real estate and obtain a license. When another body is found and Patti fails to show up for an interview, Billie fears her friend is the victim. When she finds out that Patti is fine, a relieved Billie realizes she has become emotionally involved in her story. She befriends the woman, helping her study for her license test. But the night before the test Patti is arrested for prostitution. Billie bails her out of jail and is shocked when Patti blithely drops her chance to take the test. She returns to a massage parlor, leaving Billie crushed and disappointed.

Episode 26: "Mob"
Air date: October 23, 1978
Director: Corey Allen
Writer: Leon Tokatyan
Guest cast: Nicholas Colasanto (Patsy Reese), Mary Ann Chinn (Charlene), Carmen Argenziano (Anthony Leone), Phillip Pine (Paul Thackery), and Dennis Robertson (assistant manager).

Lou and Rossi visit a resort to set up the *Tribune*'s annual tennis tournament. They stumble onto what appears to be a meeting of organized crime bosses. Lou sends for Animal, who appears clean shaven and nattily dressed in his role as a fashion photographer. The *Tribune* staffers discover a Senate candidate at the resort, which is owned by a reputed mobster. Animal photographs the candidate in the company of alleged crime lords, but later his film is stolen. Without evidence the *Tribune* has no story, and Lou returns to the *Tribune* frustrated.

Episode 27: "Murder"
Air date: October 30, 1978
Director: Mel Damski
Writer: Gary David Goldberg
Guest cast: Alan Fudge (Detective Collins), Jane Rose (Mrs. Walker), Ketty Lester (Sara Marshall), Thalmus Rasulala (S. Chandler), and Ralph Wilcox (Mr. Thomas).

The murder of a young black woman in a Los Angeles ghetto is first viewed as nothing extraordinary in the *Tribune* newsroom. Yet the story of an elderly, affluent white woman who wards off an intruder with a golf club becomes a media event. Billie digs deeper into the murdered woman's life and the problems in the ghetto neighborhood. The woman's young daughter spots the drug addict who killed her mother. He sees her, too, and follows her home where Billie happens to be waiting. Billie screams when the killer faces her, and police nearby arrest him. In the budget meeting Lou successfully pushes for Billie's story to appear on the front page.

Episode 28: "Dying"
Air date: November 6, 1978
Director: Alexander Singer
Writer: Michele Gallery
Guest cast: Geraldine Fitzgerald (Peggy Donovan), Larry Gates (Dr. Relph), Joan Hotchkis (Dr. Rita Chase), Stephen Johnson (Matt Calloway), and Raleigh Bond (Arty Wilcox).

Art refuses to accept a doctor's diagnosis that his mother Peggy is dying of leukemia. He becomes testy at work and refuses to discuss his mother's illness.

When he reads of a miracle cure in Mexico, he plans to take his mother there for treatment. Mrs. Donovan, however, has accepted the fact that she is dying. She refuses to go and asks Art to take her home so she can spend her last days there. They come to terms about death and about their relationship as mother and son.

Episode 29: "Schools"
Air date: November 20, 1978
Director: Burt Brinckerhoff
Writer: Gary David Goldberg
Guest cast: Lee Chamberlin (Jenny Davis), Kevin Hooks (Wesley), Lloyd Hollar (Neil Mahaffey), Justin Lord (Haskell Wynn), and the Reverend Jesse Jackson (himself).

Lou learns about troubled schools when he visits guidance counselor Jenny Davis to help choose *Tribune* scholarship winners. As the newspaper develops a story on education teachers tell Rossi about their fears and the violent atmosphere in schools, but an administrator plays down the problems when interviewed by Billie. Two students rape and beat Jenny, and she quits her job. Scholarship ceremonies at the school are highlighted by a stirring speech by the Reverend Jesse Jackson, who encourages students not to give up hope. Lou later sees Jenny and pleads with her to stay at the school to help the students. They leave the school together, each unsure of what she will do.

Episode 30: "Slaughter"
Air date: November 27, 1978
Director: Roger Young
Writer: Bud Freeman
Guest cast: Stephen Elliot (Chip Murphy), Sandy McPeak (John Harper), Sally Kirkland (Dr. Peterson), Danny Goldman (Dr. Pober), and Sybil Scotford (Lucy Harper).

While on vacation Lou visits old friend Chip Murphy, the crusty editor of a newspaper in a small California town. Murphy suspects that a mysterious epidemic might be responsible for sick cattle in the area. But he fears that if he reports what information he has, the sick livestock will be shipped to market before authorities can impose a quarantine. Lou arranges for an analysis of cattle feed from a farm, which reveals that antifreeze has contaminated the feed and the cattle. A health official hesitates to issue a countywide quarantine until the journalists urge him to read the report on the tainted feed. Lou wants to celebrate their victory, but Murphy says he knows too many townspeople affected by the decision to relish their scoop.

Episode 31: "Singles"
Air date: December 4, 1978
Director: Michael Zinberg

Writer: Gina Frederica Goldman and Sally Robinson
Guest cast: Peter Donat (Michael Barton).

Mrs. Pynchon hires a media consultant, Michael Barton, to help the newspaper increase its circulation. He suggests a series of stories on single life aimed at readers age eighteen to thirty-five. Although they complain about their fluffy assignments, Rossi writes about video dating while Billie looks into a computer dating service. Their various blind dates have humorous consequences, and Barton presses them to write more sensational accounts to boost the *Tribune*'s circulation. Lou resists Barton's attempts to build readership this way. When stories on suicide by lonely people and the problems facing homeless older singles are added to the feature package, Barton accuses Lou and Charlie of sabotaging his efforts. Mrs. Pynchon supports her staff's judgment and dismisses Barton, preferring to stick with the *Tribune*'s reputation as a newspaper of substance.

Episode 32: "Babies"
Air date: December 11, 1978
Director: Alexander Singer
Writer: David Lloyd
Guest cast: Joseph Mascolo (McIntyre), John Carter (Dr. Davidson), Russell Johnson (Karlan), Judyann Elder (Mrs. Hatch), and Robert Broyles (motel clerk).

For a story on black-market adoptions Billie and Rossi pose as a childless couple in search of an infant. On the night they are to receive a baby the attorney handling the adoption raises the price from ten thousand to fifteen thousand dollars. They spend the night at a motel in a small town waiting for the baby. Finally, they get the child and proceed to expose the unscrupulous adoption ring.

Episode 33: "Conflict"
Air date: December 18, 1978
Director: Mel Damski
Writer: Michele Gallery
Guest cast: Normann Burton (Nash), Peggy McCay (Marion Hume), Fred Holliday (Ferguson), Helen Kleeb (Mildred), and Eve Roberts (Mary Alice Roper).

When the *Tribune*'s food editor admits that his trip to Italy was financed by the food industry, Mrs. Pynchon orders an end to "freebies" by the staff. Rossi becomes the *Tribune*'s in-house media critic, quickly angering the staff with his terse memos. It seems that nearly everyone has a conflict of interest. Billie uses her contacts with a city councilman to help a protest group stop the widening of the street in front of her home. Lou is close friends with the owner of a professional basketball team. Mrs. Pynchon supports a charity that uses questionable fund-raising tactics. Donovan performs some work for a Senate candidate. Charlie's wife, Marion, works for a political candidate, but she quits her job rather than see Charlie lose his. Lou angers Mrs. Pynchon by publishing a story critical of the charity drive, arguing that the *Tribune* must remain independent.

Episode 34: "Denial"
Air date: January 1, 1979
Director: Charles Dubin
Writer: Leonora Thuna
Guest cast: Ann Sweeny (Ellen), Robert Pine (Burt), Fred Beir (Dr. Wyatt), Dennis Redfield (Kevin Marshall), and Meeno Peluce (Nick).

A visit by Lou's daughter Ellen and grandson Nick reveals that the boy is losing his hearing. Yet Ellen refuses to admit her son may be handicapped. While Lou tries to persuade her to get help for the boy Rossi is angry that his editors refuse to print his story about faulty building construction, contending he does not have adequate substantiation. Then, Rossi gets in trouble by giving a rival reporter the information. Lou persuades Charlie not to fire Rossi, arguing that Rossi acted out of concern for the construction workers. Encouraged by Lou, Ellen takes Nick to a school for the deaf.

Episode 35: "Fire"
Air date: January 8, 1979
Director: Roger Young
Writer: Seth Freeman
Guest cast: Tom Atkins (Frank Durning), Tom Bower (Lind), Ann Ryerson (Debbie Dexter), William Joyce (fire marshal), and Ellen Bake (Emmaline).

The *Tribune* staff investigates a series of arson fires. An internal report leaked to the *Tribune* by fire investigator Frank Durning, a friend of Lou's, reveals an arson-for-profit ring linked to two fire officials. When the *Tribune* publishes the story, Frank is snubbed at the department for releasing the report. Another fire is set at an older building where Animal lives. He and a girlfriend escape unharmed, but one tenant dies. Firefighters tell Frank they are glad the report was made public. Later, Frank admits to Lou that he would risk his job again if it meant ensuring public safety.

Episode 36: "Vet"
Air date: January 15, 1979
Director: Alexander Singer
Writer: Leon Tokatyan
Guest cast: Lionel Smith (Sutton), George Pentecost (dangler), Charlie Robinson (Don), John Wyler (Howard), and B. J. Bartlett (Jack).

Animal risks his life during a hostage incident to get photos for the *Tribune*, which is one of several acts that cause concern for him among the staff. Lou discovers that the photographer is a Vietnam veteran still haunted by his experiences during the war. Lou later becomes friends with Sutton, a black panhandler and Vietnam vet. He then assigns *Tribune* reporters to stories about the difficulties facing veterans. For his part, Lou tries to get Sutton a job at the *Tribune*, but his dishonorable discharge and bad attitude sink his chances. Lou urges Mrs. Pynchon and the *Tribune*'s personnel director to give Sutton and other veterans a chance. But when Lou looks for Sutton, he learns that the man has disappeared and probably moved on to another city. Animal, however, comes to grips with his problem and becomes determined to face his demons.

Episode 37: "Scam"
Air date: January 22, 1978
Director: Gerald Mayer
Writer: Gary David Goldberg
Guest cast: John Considine (David Milburn), J. Pat O'Malley (Patrick Terhune), Peggy McCay (Marion Hume), Barney Phillips (Dr. Barnes), and Booth Colman (judge).

Lou searches for ways to invest fifteen thousand dollars he receives from his son-in-law as repayment for a loan. He learns that Charlie's investment adviser, David Milburn, is under investigation for fraud. Charlie refuses to believe he might be the victim of a scam, but the *Tribune* reporters turn up a dozen investors who claim Milburn has defrauded them. Charlie becomes obsessed with the case and eventually joins others in a suit against Milburn. Although Milburn is given a ten-year prison term, Charlie must face the fact that he has lost his life savings. Lou, meanwhile, decides to spend his windfall by sponsoring a Little League baseball team.

Episode 38: "Sweep"
Air date: February 5, 1979
Director: Charles Dubin
Writer: Steve Kline
Guest cast: Maureen McCormick (Tiffany), Rafael Campos (Jesus), Jonathan Banks (Cyrus), Cynthia Avila (Consuela), and Maria Elena Cordero (Rosa).

When immigration officers raid a Mexican restaurant where Lou, Rossi, and Billie are dining, the reporters look into the plight of illegal aliens. The story leads them to holding cells for those ordered back to Mexico, government officials who fight an unending tide of illegal immigrants, and people who exploit those who want to live in the United States at any cost. At the same time Lou discovers that Mrs. Pynchon's young niece, the city room's new copygirl, is illiterate. Both he and her aunt encourage the girl to get help.

Episode 39: "Samaritan"
Air date: February 12, 1979
Director: Paul Leaf

Writer: Eliot West

Guest cast: Richard B. Shull (Jack Towne), Ben Piazza (Jim McCrea), Marcia Rodd (Nancy Rhoden), John Larch (Bill Bergin), and Bill Watson (Newsome).

Five years earlier, a serial killer called Samaritan had terrorized Los Angeles by commiting five murders, announcing each in a letter to the press. Now the *Tribune* receives a letter indicating Samaritan is back. Jim McCrea, the *Tribune* reporter who covered the original killings, is put on the story. The letter is turned over to authorities, but the *Tribune* decides not to publish it for fear of causing unwarranted concern. Columnist Jack Towne writes about the letter, however, forcing the *Tribune* to cover the story. Another Samaritan letter arrives, throwing the city into a mild panic. Rossi tracks down the retired detective who investigated the murders, and he contends that the latest letters are phony. Lou suspects Jim is behind the hoax, and the reporter admits he dredged up the Samaritan to return to the limelight.

Episode 40: "Hit"
Air date: February 19, 1979
Director: Peter Levin
Writer: Michele Gallery
Guest cast: Allyn Ann McLerie (Martha), Ed Harris (Warren), Ivan Bonar (Judge Cromwell), Michael Champion (Red), and Paul Sorensen (McPhee).

Rossi meets Martha, a woman as abrasive and single-minded as he. She is investigating the hit-and-run death of her son two years earlier. Her tireless pursuit of justice impresses Rossi, who ignores his *Tribune* assignments to help Martha track down the driver. The trail of small bits of evidence leads to a traffic judge, and Martha brings charges against him.

Episode 41: "Home"
Air date: February 26, 1979
Director: Alexander Singer
Writer: Gary David Goldberg
Guest cast: Jack Gilford (Fred Horton), Ed Grover (John Berrtram), Patricia Smith (Dr. Kalman), Lee Kessler (Leslie), and Jessamine Milner (Mrs. Keaton).

Rossi and Billie investigate a nursing home after an elderly woman is dumped at a county office because her bill has not been paid by the county. When the nursing home administrator refuses to allow Rossi to tour the home, Billie goes undercover by applying for a job as an aide. She discovers that the home is understaffed and apparently overmedicates its residents. When she complains to the administrator about poor care, she is immediately fired. Rossi contributes to her story by investigating alternatives to nursing homes and other problems facing the elderly. Lou sees the human side of the issue through an elderly friend, Fred Horton.

Episode 42: "Convention"
Air date: March 5, 1979
Director: Charles Dubin
Writer: David Lloyd
Guest cast: Kenneth McMillan (Jack Riley), Ivor Francis (Mr. Nelson), Amanda McBroom (Lois Craig), Laurie Heineman (Sandra), and Robert Rothwell (Hanlon).

Authorities fear a radical group is planning to kidnap someone at a newspaper convention in Palm Springs. Mrs. Pynchon, Charlie, and Lou attend the meeting, which takes on a comical air as those present deal with the prospect of a terrorist incident. Despite their fears nothing happens. Later, Billie's interview with a terrorist leader reveals that the plot was merely a ruse to gain publicity.

Episode 43: "Marathon"
Air date: March 19, 1979
Director: Alexander Singer
Writer: Gene Reynolds
Guest cast: Peter Hobbs (Driscoll), Michael Warren (Andrew Turner), John Petlock (Dreyfus), Emilio Delgado (Castillo), and Rebecca Stanley (Moyers).

A busy day puts pressure on everyone at the *Tribune*. The main story is the collapse of a tunnel in the Los Angeles foothills. Besides rescue efforts, the staff also must deal with a "human fly" scaling a downtown building and a crackpot claiming that aliens will land at a nearby Air Force base. Donovan weighs a job offer with the governor's staff, which worries Charlie that he will lose a good editor. Meanwhile, updates in the rescue story demand constant changes in the newspaper through the afternoon and night. A tired staff puts out the final edition at two in the morning.

Episode 44: "Bomb"
Air date: March 26, 1979
Director: Gene Reynolds
Writer: Seth Freeman
Guest cast: Dinah Manoff (Joanie Hume), Joe Spano (Jack Ridgeway), Frank Marth (Robert Oguns), Norbert Weisser (Bovic), and Paul Kent (Roger Winant).

A young man gives Rossi plans for an atomic bomb and a written threat to blow up Los Angeles if certain demands are not met. Federal officials assure the *Tribune* that the plans are a hoax. Yet Lou, Rossi, and Billie are followed by people appearing to be government agents. That spurs them to investigate the possibility that a "garage bomb" could be built by someone with the plans and the proper materials. Rossi meets with the terrorists, who show him the bomb they have built. Federal agents burst in, having followed Rossi, and arrest the terrorists. Later, the staff breathes a collective sigh of relief, but Lou fears such threats are only beginning.

Episode 45: "Skids"
Air date: April 2, 1979
Director: Burt Brinckerhoff
Writer: Steve Kline
Guest cast: Andrew Duggan (Doc), Al Ruscio (Carmine), Virginia Gregg (Dirty Donna), Scoey Michill (Minister), and James Hong (Lee Wong).

Rossi resists an assignment to cover a series of strangulations on skid row, an area populated by drunks and bums. The reason for his discomfort is his father, an alcoholic who occasionally calls on Rossi for help. Lou is shocked to discover that one of the skid-row bums is a surgeon whom he once knew. Doc refuses Lou's help, saying he only worries about how to get his next drink. Billie meets "Dirty Donna," a mentally ill woman who lives on the street. Having learned more about alcoholism, Rossi comes to terms with his father's drinking and calls an uneasy truce with him. After bone-chilling weather hits Los Angeles Lou is saddened by the news that Doc has died of exposure.

Episode 46: "Romance"
Air date: May 7, 1979
Director: Roger Young
Writer: Michele Gallery
Guest cast: Francis Lee McCain (Susan Sherman), Teri Nunn (Wendy), Devon Ericson (Cheryl), Craig Wasson (Aaron), and Robert Costanzo (Tannenberg).

The ups and downs of romance touch *Tribune* staffers at work and at home. Rossi covers a rock star who is being sued by a former girlfriend. Billie writes about a young welfare mother facing charges that she is an unfit mother. She meets another young girl who wants to have a baby so she can receive welfare payments and live away from her mother. Lou and his girlfriend, police officer Susan Sherman, consider living together. Lou would rather be married, but Susan is not ready for such a commitment. They remain together, at least for now.

Third Season, 1979–1980

Executive producer:
  Gene Reynolds.
Producer:
  Seth Freeman.
Executive consultant:
  Allan Burns.
Creative consultant:
  Gary David Goldberg.

Episode 47: "Cop"
Air date: September 17, 1979
Director: Roger Young

Writer: Seth Freeman
Guest cast: Joe Penny (Mike Tynan), Ed Winter (Robert Dennahy), Maxine Kintner (Mariclare Costello), Michael Alldredge (Ted McPhee), and Ron Max (Tony Stiles).

Two stories bring the issue of homosexuality to the *Tribune:* the murder of Lou's gay neighbor and the fire deaths of five people at a gay bar. Investigating patrolman Mike Tynan admits to Lou that he is gay but says that if it were widely known on the force he would be ostracized. Meanwhile, the *Tribune* editors decide to publish the fire victims' names, agreeing that the newspaper cannot withhold information and maintain its reputation. When Tynan's partner, Robert Dennahy, discovers that Tynan is gay, he seeks a transfer because he cannot work with a man he believes is unfit to be a police officer. Before the transfer can take place, however, the officers find the murder suspect. In the ensuing gunfight a wounded Tynan saves Dennahy's life, and Dennahy has a change of heart about his gay partner.

Episode 48: "Exposé"
Air date: September 24, 1979
Director: Gene Reynolds
Writer: David Lloyd
Guest cast: William Schallert (Mark Worth), Louise Troy (Bonita Worth), Richard Brestoff (Mike Norvette), Julie Cobb (Barbara Benedict), and Ivan Bonar (Foreign Editor).

City Supervisor Bonita Worth is a promising politician, but husband Mark Worth has a penchant for alcohol and outrageous behavior. After the *Tribune* publishes a story about his wife, he makes a drunken threat to punch Charlie. Later, a drunken Worth bursts into the *Tribune*'s budget meeting to complain about an editorial critical of him. While the *Tribune* reports Worth's embarrassing escapades the staff finds itself unflatteringly profiled in a local tabloid. Worth gains more notoriety when he is in a car accident in the company of a cocktail waitress. Mrs. Pynchon fears that the *Tribune* and other media have unfairly brought misery to the Worths. Ultimately, Mrs. Worth announces her resignation from public office.

Episode 49: "Slammer"
Air date: October 1, 1979
Director: Alexander Singer
Writer: Johnny Dawkins
Guest cast: Kene Holliday (J.D.), Alan Fudge (David Goffman), J. Jay Saunders (Neil Turner), Robert Davi (Hector), and Danny Glover (Leroy).

Lou and Rossi get a glimpse of prison life when they help a group of inmates start a prison newspaper. Rossi's feature for the *Tribune* on one inmate draws an angry response from the man the prisoner assaulted, setting off a debate between the rights of victims and the rights of inmates. When the inmates try to publish an unsubstantiated story that an inmate was murdered by a prison gang, the warden stops publication. A fight ensues among prisoners, and the warden puts the prison on riot alert. Lou later convinces the warden that the newspaper helps inmates vent their feelings. He also urges the prisoners to act responsibly.

Episode 50: "Charlatan"
Air date: October 15, 1979
Director: Roger Young
Writer: Michael Vittes
Guest cast: Mesach Taylor (Marcus Prescott), Ruth Silveira (Agnes Carson), Kenneth Tigar (Fugene Smithfield), John Carter (Dr. Bunning), and Carmen Argenziano (Arnold Zinner).

Two First Amendment issues, about religion and about the press, divide the *Tribune* staff. Religion writer Marcus Prescott is critical of Rossi's and Billie's investigation of a religious leader accused of fraud by former followers. Yet their stories about irregularities in accounting do not shake the faith of others in the church. Meanwhile, Mrs. Pynchon and Charlie balk at defending the right of a pornographer to publish names and addresses of undercover agents in his magazine. Lou, however, agrees to testify in court on the pornographer's behalf because he believes that prior restraint hurts all journalists.

Episode 51: "Frame-Up"
Air date: October 22, 1979
Director: Burt Brinckerhoff
Writer: Steve Kline
Guest cast: Stephen McHattie (Curtis Folger), Wendy Phillips (Nell Wheeler), Paul Kent (Councilman Naughton), Edward Marshall (Supervisor), and Bill Smillie (Shirley Hagen).

When Billie reports that a company moving to Los Angeles has a history of polluting, the paper is criticized as being anti-industry. The company announces it will not relocate to the city, raising more ire against Billie and the *Tribune*. Then, company officials reverse their decision and agree to move to Los Angeles. A disgruntled secretary gives Billie a memo that shows the company's off-again, on-again plans were merely a ruse to gain more tax breaks and other incentives. After her story appears the secretary disappears, and the company sues the *Tribune* for libel. Billie realizes she has been set up. Rossi tracks down the phony secretary and exposes the elaborate scheme, saving the reputation of Billie and the *Tribune*.

Episode 52: "Hype"
Air date: October 29, 1979
Director: Peter Levin
Writer: Michele Gallery
Guest cast: Harold Gould (Dr. David Duncan), David Huffman (Daniel Todson), Craig Wasson (Michael Avenik), Silvana Gallardo (Rita Silvera), and Paul Sparer (Damon Forrest).

Rossi and Billie discover that research is big business at Los Angeles University Medical Center. Developing new medicines provides critical funding for the facility. Research director Dr. David Duncan pressures young Dr. Daniel Todson to complete his testing of a new arthritis medication, and Todson falsifies his research results, leading to a news conference announcing a medical breakthrough. But the ruse is discovered by other researchers, embarrassing the university.

Episode 53: "Gambling"
Air date: November 5, 1979
Director: Alexander Singer
Writer: Bud Freeman
Guest cast: Charles Lane (Mort Farber), Michael Shannon (Mac McIvor), Sandy Kenyon (Eddie Talbert), Alan Mason (Kingsley), and John Karlem (Ken Navaretti).

A proposed gambling initiative raises the issue of legal and illegal betting. Business reporter Mac McIvor runs afoul of a bookie when he cannot pay off his debts, so he borrows money from Billie on false pretenses. To raise more cash he breaks the *Tribune*'s conflict-of-interest policy by making financial investments on behalf of pressroom employees. Lou fires McIvor over his gambling-related activities. Meanwhile, Lou is shocked when a friend wins thirty-five thousand dollars at the track by betting on a fixed race, which then becomes a news story for the *Tribune*. When Mrs. Pynchon decides to drop sports lines and other features that serve as information for illegal gambling, the paper receives hundreds of complaints.

Episode 54: "Witness"
Air date: November 12, 1979
Director: Peter Levin
Writer: Gary David Goldberg
Guest cast: Peter Marshall (McQueen), Richard Jaeckel (Dan Staley), Charles Hallahan (Chet Wilke), Barlett Robinson (Bauman), and William Bryant (Robinson).

A brutal assault on a lawyer is linked to a grand jury investigation of a game-show host. The assailant contacts Billie and admits that the host hired him to beat the lawyer. When the assailant is murdered and the brakes on Billie's car mysteriously fail, Billie is placed in protective custody by police Detective Dan Staley. Personality clashes mark their time together as Staley guards Billie in a hotel. The watch ends when she testifies before the grand jury. Having gained understanding of each other's points of view, Billie and Staley part friends.

Episode 55: "Kidnap"
Air date: November 26, 1979
Director: Alan Cooke
Writer: Bud Freeman

Guest cast: Parley Baer (Sheriff Burkhardt), Jonathan Banks (Clay Starkes), Jordan Rhodes (Schultz), Stanley Kamel (Marty Niles), and Virginia Bingham (Patty Starkes).

The disappearance of a small town's high school basketball teams turns into a kidnapping. Lou dispatches Billie and Animal and later sends Rossi and another reporter. The story creates a turf battle between Billie and Rossi, each fighting over who gets the main story. Art flies in to coordinate coverage. Billie outsmarts Rossi and the rest of the media by getting the first word that the kids are safe and the kidnappers captured. At the *Tribune* Mrs. Pynchon declines a tempting offer to sell the newspaper to a large chain. She prefers to remain in charge and keep the paper locally owned.

Episode 56: "Andrew, Part 1: Premonition"
Air date: December 3, 1979
Director: Roger Young
Writer: Seth Freeman
Guest cast: Bruce Davison (Andrew Raines), Barbara Barrie (Edna Raines), Joan Hotchkis (Dr. Teresa Myrdal), Nita Talbot (Lana Barkley), and Ellen Regan (Terry Mills).

The series' only two-part episode focuses on Art's cousin Andrew, an emotionally disturbed young man. He has been through therapy and hospitalization, but Art and Andrew's mother, Edna Raines, fear Andrew will do something "really crazy" one day. Andrew admits hearing voices and wanting to stop women from bothering him. He enters a hospital at Art's urging but is released after just three days. The family's fears are realized when Andrew is arrested for killing a friend of his mother's.

Episode 57: "Andrew, Part 2: Trial"
Air date: December 10, 1979
Director: Peter Levin
Writer: Seth Freeman
Guest cast: Bruce Davison (Andrew Raines), Barbara Barrie (Edna Raines), Charles Aidman (Davis Mendelsohn), Joan Hotchkis (Dr. Teresa Myrdal), and Michael McGuire (Bradley Gordon).

How the *Tribune* should cover Andrew's case is debated at the *Tribune*. Art fears that publicity will hurt the chances of a plea bargain for his mentally ill cousin. The *Tribune* editors, concerned that they do not appear biased, assign Billie and Rossi to write news and features about the case. When Andrew escapes from custody, Art criticizes the staff for hurting Andrew's case just to show the *Tribune* is not protecting one of its staff. No plea bargain is offered, and Andrew goes to trial. He is found guilty of second-degree murder and, despite testimony from his psychiatrist, is judged to have been sane. Andrew is sentenced to fifteen years in prison.

Episode 58: "Hollywood"
Air date: December 17, 1979
Director: Burt Brinckerhoff
Writer: Michele Gallery
Guest cast: George Chandler (Caretaker), Laraine Day (Lauran Sinclair), Howard Duff (Wild Man Moran), Nina Foch (Mrs. Polk), and Margaret Hamilton (Thea Taft).

A mystery unfolds in film-noir style when the *Tribune* stumbles over a decades-old murder case. A reclusive woman, Mrs. Polk, still lives above the abandoned cantina where popular Philippine boxer "Baby" Duarte was murdered. A feature story about her spurs an investigation of the case by the *Tribune* staff. Leads take the reporters to faded Hollywood stars and other characters, but the case remains a mystery. In the end Mrs. Polk admits she loved Duarte but could not enter into an interracial marriage. She also says she could not let him return to the Philippines, leaving the impression that she may have been the killer.

Episode 59: "Kids"
Air date: December 24, 1979
Director: Alexander Singer
Writer: Michael Vittes and Shep Greene
Guest cast: Matthew Laborteaux (Mark Donner), Nicholas Pryor (Al Mitchell), Melinda Cordell (Helen Mitchell), Jenny Sullivan (Meg Donner), Elizabeth Bliss (Carly Mitchell), and Michael J. Fox (Paul Stone).

The problems of children confront Lou, Rossi and Billie in their work and in their personal lives. Lou tries to help Mark, a troubled young boy ignored by his mother. Rossi writes about child film star Carly, who cannot take the pressures of acting and her overbearing father. Billie covers the suicides of two teenagers and the trauma suffered by their parents.

Episode 60: "Brushfire"
Air date: January 7, 1980
Director: Donald A. Baer
Writers: Allan Burns and Gene Reynolds
Guest cast: Peggy McCay (Marion Hume), Marshall Thompson (Paul Newman), Jeff Corey (Mr. Bergman), Brian Farrell (Sweeney), and Tony Perez (Ramirez).

A brush fire takes its toll on the Los Angeles area and on the *Tribune* staff. While Rossi, Billie and Animal scurry to cover the fire Charlie and wife Marion struggle to save their home from the flames. Animal's photos lead police to the arsonist responsible for the blaze. A weary Charlie and Marion, who had decided to separate before the fire, reconcile in the wake of the near tragedy.

Episode 61: "Indians"
Air date: January 14, 1980
Director: Ralph Senesky
Writer: April Smith
Guest cast: David Yanez (Raymond White), Ned Romero (Howard Sweetwater), Julie Carmen (Teresa Davis), Ray Tracey (Gordon Davis), Tom Rosqui (Sam Duryea).

Billie and Rossi write about the lives of urban Indians. They meet a boy who has run away from an Indian boarding school, a middle-aged man who cannot adjust to the pressures of white society, and a couple whose marital problems seem fueled by cultural differences.

Episode 62: "Cover-Up"
Air date: January 21, 1980
Director: Gerry Mayer
Writer: Paul Ehrmann
Guest cast: Andrew Rubin (Jeff Lindsey), David Hollander (Bryan Furniss), Edward Power (Brubaker), Ross Bickell (Les Furniss), and William Jordan (Danzinger).

Rossi and Billie pursue two stories that ultimately do not appear in the *Tribune*. Rossi meets Jeff Lindsay, a grade school teacher falsely accused of molesting a male student. Both the boy's parents and the school board keep the incident private. Rather than make his firing public and risk losing a court battle, Lindsay accepts the school board's decision that he leave. Billie discovers that a successful film studio executive has been soliciting kickbacks from suppliers. Although he resigns from the studio, the reason for his resignation is not discussed. The executive also continues working with the studio as an independent producer. In both cases the *Tribune* reporters lack the verification they need to write their stories and make the incidents public.

Episode 63: "Inheritance"
Air date: January 28, 1980
Director: Roger Young
Writer: April Smith
Guest cast: Allyn Ann McLerie (Betty Newman), Marshall Thompson (Paul Newman), Sands Hall (Jessica Downey), Carol Bagdasarian (Sarah Hartounian), and Buck Kartalian (Leon Hartounian).

A young woman, Jessica Downey, sues drug companies that made DES, an artificial hormone linked to cancer in the female children of the women who took it as a pregnancy medication. As Billie covers the story Rossi meets Sarah Hartounian, who is contesting her father's will. She has been ostracized by the family because she, an Armenian, has married a Turk, the enemy of Armenians. Billie, meanwhile, is shocked to learn that she, too, is a DES daughter. Although not in danger, she cannot accept the fact that her mother took the medication in blind faith, but she later realizes that her mother is not to blame and reconciles with her. Although a judge rules that Sarah's father wrongly cut her out of his will, she is unable to reconcile with her family. They continue to believe she has betrayed them and their people.

Episode 64: "Censored"
Air date: February 4, 1980
Director: Alexander Singer
Writer: Joanne Pagliaro
Guest cast: Richard Dysart (Mitchell Webster), Laurie Heineman (Marilyn Keefer), Paul Lambert (Senator Fleming), Dan Spector (Ernie), and James Gallery (Hank Selby).

A book burning by a citizens group in a rural community leads to a *Tribune* story on censorship. A teacher loses her job for using a book that teaches cultural values. A librarian admits that the library board bans books from its shelves. Censorship becomes an issue at the *Tribune* when Charlie refuses to run a controversial political cartoon, fearing a lawsuit. An old friend of Lou's, newspaper editor Mitch Webster, is behind the censorship crusade. The crusade climaxes with a mass burning of books, record albums, and anything else people do not like.

Episode 65: "Lou"
Air date: February 11, 1980
Director: Roger Young
Writer: Michele Gallery
Guest cast: Richard B. Shull (Jack Towne), Elta Blake (Regina Kelly), Michael Bond (Sam Huntington), Ray Oliver (Wayne Burroughs), Billy Beck (Photo Editor).

A day in the life of Lou Grant is full of problems, large and small. Mrs. Pynchon chides him to be more polite to callers. Donovan questions his news judgment. Billie complains about a feature assignment. Animal does not like the way Lou cropped a photograph. Lou must fire a reporter who plagiarized from a college newspaper. A feature writer wants a job on the city desk. Rossi objects to Lou changing the focus of his story. All of the pressures make Lou tense and edgy. Finally, Charlie tells Lou that the *Tribune* should not be his whole life, ordering him to delegate his work and to take a vacation.

Episode 66: "Blackout"
Air date: February 18, 1980
Director: Allen Williams
Writer: Steve Kline
Guest cast: Richard Evans (Walker), Margie Impert (March), Stanley Grover (Jarret Longworth), Paul Jenkins (Kirby), and Walter Brooke (Reggie Washburn).

Shortly after a minor earthquake rocks Los Angeles, there is no electricity and the *Tribune* and the rest of the city goes dark. While Rossi, Billie and Animal cover looting and rioting in the city the staff puts together the paper by candlelight. Mrs. Pynchon, gambling that electrical power will not return in time to publish the paper on the *Tribune*'s presses, approves a truncated edition without ads to be printed at a newspaper in nearby Long Beach. After the staff toasts their triumph over nature, the lights come back on.

Episode 67: "Dogs"
Air date: March 3, 1980
Director: Burt Brinckerhoff
Writer: Seth Freeman
Guest cast: Geoffrey Lewis (Jim Lawrence), Alan Vint (Len Huskie), Michael Jeter (Max Galt), Eric Server (Sgt. Oguns), and Pat Corley (Organizer).

Mrs. Pynchon's beloved Yorkshire terrier, Barney, is stolen. To their horror the staff discovers that Barney was used as training fodder by men who breed fighting dogs. Rossi explores the culture of dog fighting with a humane society investigator. Working undercover at a gas station, he becomes friends with a breeder. Investigators fit him with a transmitter before he attends a dog fight. When Rossi is recognized by one of the spectators, he is beaten until authorities come to his rescue. Despite a bruised face and a broken arm Rossi types his story. Mrs. Pynchon takes home a Yorkie puppy, a gift from the staff.

Episode 68: "Influence"
Air date: March 10, 1980
Director: Gene Reynolds
Writer: April Smith
Guest cast: James Whitmore Jr. (Nick Boyer), Sheila Larken (Rosalie Wilson), Bartlett Robinson (Dutch Van Deusen), Al Ruscio (Carmine Rossi), and Fred Beir (Gig Montgomery).

While a drinking problem takes its toll on financial editor Adam Wilson Mrs. Pynchon joins a club of prominent business people, many of whom favor the construction of a new airport. She later demands that the *Tribune* reevaluate its coverage of the controversial project. Meanwhile, Lou picks up a drunk Adam at a bar and then brings Adam to his home when his wife refuses to take him. Lou also overlooks the bottle of vodka Adam keeps in his desk. Rossi, the son of an alcoholic, urges Lou not to cover up for Adam any longer. When Adam asks Lou to bail him out of jail after an arrest for driving under the influence, Lou refuses and suggests he seek help. Mrs. Pynchon, having discovered that certain businessmen in her group will benefit financially from the airport project, reasserts her independence by quitting the group.

Episode 69: "Guns"
Air date: March 17, 1980

Director: Bob Sweeney
Writer: Seth Freeman
Guest cast: Rue McClanahan (Maggie McKenna), Redmond Gleeson (Francie
  Fitzgerald), Michael Alldredge (Lt. McPhee), Jack Dodson (Walter Parrott),
  and Deirdre Lenihan (Deirdre).

During a St. Patrick's Day celebration at McKenna's Lou meets endearing
Irishman Francie Fitzgerald. He is shocked when federal agents link Fitzgerald to
the theft of weapons from a Los Angeles gun shop. As Rossi and Billie investigate
the American support of Irish insurgency Lou becomes intrigued by Fitzgerald
and his ties to the Irish Republican Army (IRA). He learns that IRA leaders are
unhappy with Fitzgerald's mistakes. Fitzgerald later visits Lou's home and admits
that he has become disenchanted with the random violence inherent in the movement. Short of cash and on the run from American authorities and the IRA, the
amiable Irishman robs Lou at gunpoint. Later, a boobytrap meant for Fitzgerald
kills a child. At McKenna's Lou and others lament the death and the continued
violence in Northern Ireland.

Episode 70: "Hazard"
Air date: March 24, 1980
Director: Burt Brinckerhoff
Writer: Michele Gallery
Guest cast: Tom Rosquim (Kramer), Phillip R. Allen (David Marcus), Ed Harris
  (Rick Reiner), Clete Keith (Kid), and Edward Bell (Talbot).

Rossi investigates allegations that a particular make of motorcycle marketed
for young people is unsafe. Paul Kramer, an official of the motorcycle company,
admits that it is cheaper to pay off death and injury claims than fix the motorcycle's
brake system. To provide documents supporting that charge, however, Kramer
demands four thousand dollars from the *Tribune*. Mrs. Pynchon refuses to engage
in so-called "checkbook journalism." Lou points out that the *Tribune*, meanwhile,
is paying for news by serializing the memoirs of a former government official.
Undaunted by Mrs. Pynchon's decision, Rossi uses his own money to obtain the
documents. Then, Kramer leaks the story to other media, robbing Rossi of his
exclusive. Rossi refuses to strike back by identifying Kramer as his source, retaining his integrity as a journalist.

Fourth Season, 1980–1981

Executive producer:
  Gene Reynolds.
Producer:
  Seth Freeman.
Executive consultant:
  Allan Burns.

Episode 71: "Nightside"
Air date: September 22, 1980
Director: Gene Reynolds
Writer: Michele Gallery
Guest cast: Richard Erdman (Hal), David Paymer (Roy), Millie Slavin (Corinne),
Alexandra Johnson (Kim), and Charles Bloom (Scotty).

When Lou works a rare double shift at the *Tribune*, he discovers that
nightside staffers have a routine all their own. The calm of the evening is broken
when a small plane crashes and a yacht sinks amid rumors of gambling, drugs,
and organized crime. Billie and Donovan pitch in to help cover the yacht accident,
which becomes the *Tribune*'s lead story when it is tied to a wealthy family's son
and a possible scheme to smuggle drugs. With the paper finished but a new day
for the morning staff only hours away a weary Lou falls asleep in the newsroom.

Episode 72: "Harassment"
Air date: September 29, 1980
Director: Roger Young
Writer: April Smith
Guest cast: David Spielberg (Lloyd Bracken), Lynn Carlin (Catherine), Marilyn
Jones (Karen), Michael Talbot (Warren), and Candy Ann Brown (Yvette).

Sexual harassment is a story for the *Tribune* staff and a problem for many of
its employees. Rossi interviews an angry husband who assaults a man accused of
harassing his wife. At the *Tribune*, an advertising executive harasses his female
assistant. Billie, assigned to write a feature about harassment, discovers that half
of the female employees at the newspaper claim they have been harassed by men.
Charlie resists Billie's attempt to use the experiences of *Tribune* employees in her
story, but Mrs. Pynchon supports Lou's belief that the newspaper should admit
to its flaws. She also orders that a grievance board look into the charges.

Episode 73: "Pack"
Air date: October 27, 1980
Director: Burt Brinckerhoff
Writer: Steve Kline
Guest cast: Eileen Heckart (Flo Meredith), Ed Nelson (Jim Carlisle), John Hiller-
man (Sturbridge), James Callahan (Stephens), and Ivor Francis (Haywood).

Billie joins seasoned political reporters covering the campaign of a Senate
candidate. She quickly learns the frustrations of being part of the so-called "pack."
She is criticized by her editors for clichéd writing and coverage; then they question
why she is not reporting what everyone else is reporting. Her story about Carlisle's
temper draws anger from his press secretary and her colleagues, who now must
explain to their editors why they did not have the story. When ostracized by her
fellow reporters, Billie bitterly criticizes them for lazy reporting and forgetting
that the public counts on them for news. They later join Billie in pinning down

Carlisle and pressing him into admitting he supports gun control. Carlisle's honesty boosts his standing with voters, and Billie wins the respect of her colleagues and her editors.

Episode 74: "Sting"
Air date: November 17, 1980
Director: Peter Levin
Writers: Patt Shea and Harriett Weiss
Guest cast: Larry Linville (Thatcher), John Considine (Garvey), Peggy McCay (Marion Hume), Michael Alldredge (Lt. McPhee), and Cliff Norton (Herb Bronner).

Charlie and Marion Hume lease their house to the Thatchers when they move to an apartment to shorten Charlie's commute to work. Suspicious about the couple's odd behavior, Charlie confronts the Thatchers only to be told that they are undercover police operating a "sting" operation from his home. At the *Tribune* Lou and other staffers argue whether such operations catch crooks or entrap them by creating crimes. When the Thatchers mysteriously disappear, Charlie wonders if he was duped by criminals using his home. His fears are laid to rest when Thatcher turns out to be with the state attorney's office. The operation results in charges against three public officials in a bribery scheme. Charlie and Marion, unhappy with their noisy apartment, return to their house.

Episode 75: "Goop"
Air date: November 24, 1980
Director: Alexander Singer
Writer: Seth Freeman
Guest cast: Parley Baer (Haggarty), Dominique Dunne (Teri Wilk), Alex Hentel-off (Marvin Galosh), Jordan Rhodes (Lester Fields), and Med Flory (Doug Traynor).

Bubbling chemicals and other hazardous waste mysteriously appear in a pond and in the yards of several homes. Rossi and Billie trace the waste to the Dillard chemical plant, which they suspect is illegally dumping hazardous materials. Only after debating the merits of using deception to cover a story do Charlie and Mrs. Pynchon allow Billie to take a clerical job at the plant. As she becomes friends with coworkers such as young Teri Wilk, Billie grows increasingly uncomfortable with her role as a spy. When she discovers records indicating a trucking crew is dumping the waste, Rossi and Animal follow the truckers and watch them dump chemicals into a stream. Billie later tries to explain to Teri why she had to deceive her to expose the company's activities. Unmoved, Teri bitterly rejects Billie as a liar.

Episode 76: "Libel"
Air date: December 8, 1980
Director: Burt Brinckerhoff

Writer: William Hopkins
Guest cast: Robin Gammell (Howard Gunther), Alan Oppenheimer (George Lester), Marie Windsor (Janet Hart), Bernard Fox (Clive Whitcomb), and Dean Santoro (Marvin Hartley).

The *Tribune* investigates the *National Spectator*, a tabloid newspaper that has been criticized for sensational, inaccurate, and misleading reporting. Charlie and others and the *Tribune* fear that the *Spectator* will fight back. Indeed, Rossi's and Billie's story results in a sixty million dollar suit against the *Tribune*. Fighting the suit becomes costly both in money and time. It also raises concern that investigative reporting will suffer because of the mere threat of a suit. During a deposition Lou bristles at being asked about his state of mind while editing the *Spectator* piece, arguing that such questions undermine an editor's ability to do his job. Faced with a daily one hundred dollar fine for not answering and urged by Mrs. Pynchon to allow the process to continue, Lou reluctantly cooperates.

Episode 77: "Streets"
Air date: December 15, 1980
Director: Bud Freeman
Writer: Don Baer
Guest cast: Carl Franklin (Milt), Mark Bell-James (Eddie), Larry B. Scott (Oscar), Beverly Todd (Gloria), Lawrence Cook (Hughes).

A policeman's slaying and the subsequent shooting death of a suspect focus the *Tribune* staff on inner-city tensions. Black reporter Milt Carmichael joins Rossi in covering the controversy, and they clash at times over how the story should be reported. As they interview police and people who live in the ghetto, Milt fears that he is on the story simply because he is black. Rossi argues that Milt's perspective is important to the story. By the time their story is published Milt and Rossi respect each other.

Episode 78: "Catch"
Air date: January 5, 1981
Director: Roger Young
Writer: Michele Gallery
Guest cast: Cliff Potts (Ted McCovey), Jordan Charney (Karl Buckner), Robert Hirschfeld (Vern Eggly), Eve McVeagh (Clare), and Erin Donovan (Laurel).

While the *Tribune* struggles with its new computer system, Billie meets baseball player Ted McCovey. He is an investor in a real estate corporation she is investigating. They seem smitten with each other, but Billie worries that she is growing too close to a source for her story. When Ted is cut by his baseball team, she comforts him. His plans to leave Los Angeles change when he lands a job as a scout. With a concerned (and perhaps jealous) Lou and Art looking on, Ted and Billie kiss in the *Tribune* newsroom.

Episode 79: "Rape"
Air date: January 12, 1981
Director: Seth Freeman
Writer: Seth Freeman
Guest cast: Lynne Moody (Sharon), Linda Carlson (Carol), Jonathan Banks (man), Julia Duffy (Charlene), and Macon McCalman (Kibbee).

Rossi enjoys working with Sharon, another reporter at the *Tribune*. Her life is thrown into turmoil when she is robbed and raped at knifepoint at her home. Later, Rossi helps Sharon decide to report the rape to police. *Tribune* staffers react differently to the incident. Art discovers his girlfriend had been raped; he is not sure how to treat her. Rossi is angry and wants to do something, such as beat Sharon's assailant. Mrs. Pynchon demands that the *Tribune* improve its coverage of rape and the legal system. Sharon grapples with emotions and feelings resulting from the attack, finally asking for time off.

Episode 80: "Boomerang"
Air date: January 19, 1981
Director: Alexander Singer
Writer: Steve Kline
Guest cast: Michael Constantine (Sidney Kovac), Roger Newman (Hollingsworth), Drew Snyder (Kirkwood), Charles Parks (Loggins), and Emilio Delgado (Rubin Castillo).

A faulty respirator contributes to the death of the *Tribune*'s Central America correspondent. Billie discovers that the respirator was recalled in the United States but still shipped to international markets. She investigates "dumping," in which U.S. firms sell defective products to foreign markets. Members of the staff, urged by guest columnist Sidney Kovac, use all their foreign connections to gather information for the dumping story. Lou clashes with Sidney because Rossi and Billie are not spending enough time on their regular assignments. In turn, the reporters resent Lou for not allowing them more time for the dumping story. Sidney writes about dumping in his national column, ruining the *Tribune*'s exclusive. Rossi and Billie, seeing Sidney as an opportunist, later apologize to Lou for snubbing him.

Episode 81: "Generations"
Air date: January 26, 1981
Director: Harvey Laidman
Writer: Johnny Dawkins
Guest cast: Arthur Space (Harvey), Charles Lane (Rupert Hume), Whitman Mayo (Fred Jenkins), Peggy McCay (Marion Hume), and Shirley Jo Finney (Donna).

Problems between the young the middle-aged and the elderly are brought to *Tribune* attention through news and personal experiences. Irrascible, attention-seeking Rupert Hume moves in with son Charlie after he is caught shoplifting. Bus driver Fred Jenkins, elderly and a bit eccentric, awards small amounts of money to people through a foundation he has established in his late wife's name. Harvey, an elderly neighbor of Lou's, is constantly taunted by neighborhood kids. Fearful when they shine lights into his house and break his windows one night, he fires a handgun and kills one of the boys.

Episode 82: "Search"
Air date: February 9, 1981
Director: Allen Williams
Writer: Everett Greenbaum and Elliott Reid
Guest cast: Alley Mills (Lisa), Millie Slavin (Corinne), Carolyn Coates (Margaret), Juliana McCarthy (Augusta), and Antony Ponzini (Mario).

Lisa, a *Tribune* photographer, is inspired by Rossi's story of the happy reunion of a mother and the daughter she had given up for adoption. An adopted daughter herself, Lisa decides to find her natural mother. Rossi helps her pour through records and eventually locate the woman in Virginia. Instead of a joyous reunion, Lisa's natural mother coldly admits she had made a mistake by becoming pregnant and does not want to be reminded of it. Rejected, Lisa tells Rossi she expected too much and now realizes that her adoptive mother is her "real" mother after all.

Episode 83: "Strike"
Air date: February 16, 1981
Director: Gene Reynolds
Writer: April Smith
Guest cast: Nancy Malone (Ivy Norris), Tom Atkins (Jim Bronsky), Bruce Kirby (Gus Murray), Ray Wise (Bart Franklin), and Phillip Pine (George MacManus).

A new computer system will save the *Tribune* money but cost jobs in its composing and printing operation. Unable to come to terms with *Tribune* management about job security, the printers vote to strike. Employees in editorial and other divisions of the paper support the printers and picket the *Tribune* building. The strike creates mixed feelings among members of the news staff, particularly Lou, who reluctantly remains at work because he is a part of management. Early in the strike a printer dies of a heart attack on the picket line. Feelings become bitter over the next three weeks. Then, Billie is hurt by a wrench hurled from a *Tribune* truck. No longer able to oppose his friends, Lou joins the striking employees. Mrs. Pynchon, against the advice of her business manager, meets the demands of the union to end the divisive strike.

Episode 84: "Survival"
Air date: February 23, 1981
Director: Burt Brinckerhoff

Writer: April Smith
Guest cast: Keene Curtis (Wild Bill), Ed Harris (Ralph Cooper), Doreen Lang (Henrietta), Ray Oliver (Burroughs), and Marc Bentley (Jesse).

After visiting Art's posh cabin in rural California Rossi encounters Ralph Cooper, a survivalist who plans for the eventual breakdown of American society. Rossi begins gathering information for a story on survivalists and why they stockpile food, ammunition, and precious metals. When a storm threatens the area with flash flooding, Lou and Rossi drive to Art's house to cover the hillside with plastic as a favor to their vacationing friend. They become stranded at the remote house when their car breaks down. Cooper shows up and takes all of the plastic from Lou and Rossi at gunpoint. Before he can return to his home, Cooper is injured when his Jeep overturns. Lou and Rossi save Cooper's life by going for help.

Episode 85: "Venice"
Air date: March 9, 1981
Director: Paul Stanley
Writers: Patt Shea and Harriett Weiss
Guest cast: James Callahan (John Becker), Frank Aletter (David Ellison), Claire Malis (Helen), Colby Chester (Jim Bishop), and Elizabeth Halliday (Carol Bishop).

While photographing the free spirits of Venice Beach Animal witnesses the discovery of a drowning victim. When Leslie's death is ruled a suicide, he wonders why a beautiful young woman would kill herself. The *Tribune* photographer becomes almost obsessed with finding the answer, even questioning whether the death was indeed a suicide. By piecing together information from her friends and relatives, Animal discovers that the woman had felt rejected throughout her life. She had become infatuated with her best friend—a woman—only to be rejected again.

Episode 86: "Campesinos"
Air date: March 16, 1981
Director: Peter Levin
Writer: Michael Vittes
Guest cast: James Victor (Tommy Hernandez), Bill Lucking (Paul Geyer), Jeff Corey (Hugh Holstrum), Pepe Serna (Frank Garcia), and Emilio Delgado (Castillo).

A strike by farm workers brings Rossi to the fields of central California. Labor leader Tommy Hernandez hopes publicity will help the striking workers break a stalemate with growers. He enlists the help of legendary activist Hugh Holstrum, who leads pickets into the fields and is arrested for trespassing. Rossi and other *Tribune* reporters interview growers, striking workers, and undocumented workers from Mexico who need work to feed their families. Another demonstration turns violent: Tommy is shot and killed by the growers' guards.

His death leads to a settlement between growers and workers. No longer needed, the immigrants pack up and head for other fields, their lot in life no better.

Episode 87: "Business"
Air date: March 23, 1981
Director: Alan Cooke
Writer: Steve Kline
Guest cast: Ed Winter (Russell Davidson), David Spielberg (Rich Havens), Richard Erdman (Hal Hennecker), Philip Abbott (Lester Sorenson), and Paul Kent (Glen Maris).

Rossi and Billie cover a suspicious fire at Cal Electronics, a manufacturing firm. Their story suggesting a link between the fire and safety violations turns out to be wrong when fire officials blame city street workers for the blaze. Cal Electronics chief Russell Davidson complains to the *Tribune* editors that the newspaper is antibusiness in its coverage. Lou and Charlie, in turn, criticize business for blaming the media for its problems and for not being open and cooperative with the press. Later, each side attempts to improve relations. The *Tribune* begins publishing guest columns by people in business and industry, and Davidson is more open and cooperative when announcing a company restructuring.

Episode 88: "Violence"
Air date: April 4, 1981
Director: Georg Stanford Brown
Writer: Johnny Dawkins
Guest cast: Fred Williamson (Crusher Carter), Tyne Daly (Melissa Cummings), Fred Dryer (Mike Hauser), Chick Hearn (Clarence Harvey), and Faye Hauser (Jacquie Templeton).

Violence in society is explored by the *Tribune* staff when they examine football and movies. Rossi covers the story of "Crusher" Carter, a hard-hitting football player sued for crippling an opponent. Billie learns how dangerous football can be by speaking to doctors and the wife of the injured player, who contends that Carter is nothing more than a criminal. Meanwhile, Lou clashes with *Tribune* film critic Melissa Cummings over violence in film. He finds it unnecessary and not entertaining while she defends violence as art.

Episode 89: "Depression"
Air date: April 13, 1981
Director: Peter Levin
Writer: Gene Reynolds
Guest cast: Peter Hobbs (George Driscoll), James Sloyan (Hank Dougherty), Priscilla Pointer (Elizabeth Driscoll), Sanda Hall (Amanda Driscoll), and Ivan Bonar (Ted Schlosser).

Charlie and veteran reporter George Driscoll face disappointment and frustration. Driscoll, a recovering alcoholic who never achieved his potential as a journalist, attempts suicide when his marriage breaks up. Charlie becomes testy and depressed when Mrs. Pynchon seeks an executive editor without considering him for the job. Driscoll comes to terms with his estranged daughter, apparently agreeing with her that he must face his problems. Charlie finally tells Mrs. Pynchon he is unhappy that she did not consider him for the new job. Both are satisfied that he at least has aired his feelings.

Episode 90: "Stroke"
Air date: May 4, 1981
Director: Roger Young
Writer: April Smith
Guest cast: Alan Fudge (Fred Hill), Philip Allen (Marvin Hartley), Jim Antonio (Prof. Williams), Paul Sparer (Dr. Walter Goren), and Harris Kal (Rick Henshaw).

Mrs. Pynchon suffers a stroke at the *Tribune*. While expressing concern for her Charlie and Lou also fear that her nephews will close the paper if she remains incapacitated. In the newsroom Billie covers a controversy stemming from a magazine's plan to take pictures of female students in nude poses. Mrs. Pynchon struggles with paralysis and the loss of speech. Lou and Charlie clash with her nephews over the purchase of a magazine planned by Mrs. Pynchon before she became ill. Encouraged by the *Tribune* editors, her lawyer successfully bids for the magazine. Two months after her stroke Mrs. Pynchon returns to the *Tribune* with a leg brace, an arm in a sling, and a cane. She haltingly complains about a story, signaling that she is back at work.

Fifth Season, 1981–1982

Executive producer:
  Gene Reynolds.
Producer:
  Seth Freeman.
Executive consultant:
  Allan Burns.

Episode 91: "Wedding"
Air date: November 2, 1981
Director: Alexander Singer
Writer: Seth Freeman
Guest cast: Cliff Potts (Ted McCovey), Parley Baer (Carlton Stiefel), Barbara Dirickson (Janie), Arthur Rosenberg (Chetwynd), and Michael Griswold (Tyler).

Billie's romance with baseball player Ted McCovey leads him to propose marriage. She hesitates to accept, fearing that her career will not allow her enough time to make a marriage work. Indeed, the demands of a career have strained

Lou's relationship with daughter Janie. Billie, having thought of all of the reasons not to marry Ted, realizes she wants to make it work. The day before the marriage, the *Tribune* computer crashes and forces everyone to reassemble that day's paper. Lou must cancel a reunion in Chicago with Janie and his other two daughters. Billie and the rest of the *Tribune* staff are exhausted as she and Ted marry at Charlie's home. Lou finds a surprise at his home: his daughters have shifted the reunion to Los Angeles to be with him.

Episode 92: "Execution"
Air date: November 9, 1981
Director: Burt Brinckerhoff
Writer: April Smith
Guest cast: Terri Nunn (Kitty Larsen), Christopher Cazenove (Peter Witter), George Wyner (Jeff Benedict), Mariclare Costello (Louise Larsen), and Sharon Spelman (Jeanette Pepper).

Convicted killer Kitty Larsen asks to be executed for shooting four people in a holdup. She picks Rossi to tell her unusual story, saying she trusts him to be fair and accurate. As Billie contacts relatives of her victims as well as Kitty's mother Rossi becomes friends with Kitty and later urges her not to seek execution. The condemned woman then signs an exclusive deal with an agent to handle book and movie rights to her life. When a false report of a love affair between Kitty and Rossi is leaked to the press, Rossi realizes he has been used to promote her story. He covers the execution only after Kitty asks him to be there. Rossi seems dispassionate as he calls in his execution report to the *Tribune*.

Episode 93: "Reckless"
Air date: November 16, 1981
Director: Alexander Singer
Writer: Steve Kline
Guest cast: Michael McGuire (Roger Sandler), William Schilling (Bob Jurgenson), Michael Tucci (Marvin), Chip Lucia (Cop), and Milt Kogan (McElwain).

After Charlie's car is vandalized he suggests that the *Tribune* set up a crime hotline that offers a reward to readers who call with tips. Meanwhile, Lou begins a trek through the legal system when he is arrested for driving while intoxicated. When a hotline tip leads police to a murder suspect, the suspect's lawyer accuses the *Tribune* of encouraging anonymous accusations to play up its importance in the community. Charlie slowly realizes that the hotline is, in effect, paying people for stories. He agrees that a citizens group should take over the hotline to allow the *Tribune* to remain independent. Lou's conviction for drunk driving leads to a story by Billie about the dangers of drinking and driving.

Episode 94: "Hometown"
Air date: November 23, 1981

Director: Gene Reynolds
Writer: Michele Gallery
Guest cast: Robert Prosky (Paul Policzinski), Georgann Johnson (Carol Kuzik), Kenneth Kimmins (Howard Cutler), Anthony Costello (Tim Switzer), and Sandy Ward (Skip Rogers).

The death of Lou's aunt sends him on a sentimental trip to his hometown of Goshen, Michigan. Much has changed, and the town is on the verge of losing a glass factory that is a major employer. When Lou discovers that the glass factory is owned by a Los Angeles firm, he writes about the closing for the *Tribune*. He also is reunited with Georgann, an old girlfriend. In a bittersweet reunion, Lou recalls how his parents objected to their romance because she was Catholic. Employees of the glass factory successfully buy the company and keep it open. Kissing Georgann goodbye, Lou returns to Los Angeles.

Episode 95: "Risk"
Air date: November 30, 1981
Director: Allen Williams
Writer: Seth Freeman
Guest cast: Lynne Moody (Sharon McNeil), J. Jay Saunders (Frederick Gibbs), Michael Alldredge (Lt. McPhee), Kario Salem (Mike Schrader), and Sandy Martin (Gloria).

While investigating a pornography ring Rossi and reporter Sharon McNeil promise confidentiality to their sources. A mother tells Sharon she allows her nine-year-old daughter to appear in pornographic movies to pay the rent. When the story is published, police demand that Sharon reveal the identity of the girl and her mother. She refuses, citing her promise of anonymity. Mrs. Pynchon and Lou reluctantly support her but point out that she should not have made the promise so quickly. Police discover where the mother and daughter live, but they arrive after the two have left. Sharon, guilty over her role in failing to help the girl, is determined not to promise anonymity so easily in the future.

Episode 96: "Double-Cross"
Air date: December 7, 1981
Director: Roger Young
Writer: Michele Gallery
Guest cast: Lin McCarthy (Alex Matheson, Sr.), Nigel Bullard (Michael Shepherd), Barbara Cason (Jinx Matheson), Peter Fox (Ed Matheson), and Roger Kern (Brad Matheson).

Billie covers the story of a valuable gold cross supposedly contained in a 100-year-old time capsule. The cross is at the center of a family feud involving the Matheson clan. The family decides to donate the cross to the city. Yet when the capsule is opened, the cross is not as ornate as it had been described in old documents. Working with local historian Michael Shepherd, Billie determines that the cross is a fake. Indeed, the real cross is in the hands of one of the Mathesons—until someone steals it. When a new time capsule is buried, Shepherd reveals that he has the cross. It seems that his family had made the cross and had been swindled out of their land by the Mathesons. The cross then is buried again. Later, Shepherd admits to Mrs. Pynchon that the cross he buried also was a fake. The real one is on a statue of the Virgin Mary at a local church.

Episode 97: "Drifters"
Air date: December 14, 1981
Director: Peter Levin
Writer: Bud Freeman
Guest cast: W. K. Stratton (Scott Hume), Tom Atkins (Dr. Sorenson), Conchata Ferrell (Myra Wexler), James Callahan (Steve Hume), and Peggy McCay (Marion Hume).

Charlie's nephew Scott is still drifting from job to job at age thirty. Charlie and his wife try to help the young man, letting him stay at their home and finding a job for him. When Scott acts strangely, Charlie discovers that he has been treated for a nervous breakdown and is supposed to be on medication. Steve Hume, Charlie's brother and Scott's father, says that his son has had a history of emotional problems, which have been tough on the family. Later, Scott is fired from his job and begins to unravel. Steve finds Scott staying with an old girlfriend. Father and son come to terms about the latter's problems, and Scott agrees to seek therapy again.

Episode 98: "Friends"
Air date: December 28, 1981
Director: Seth Freeman
Writer: Seth Freeman
Guest cast: Larry Breeding (Burt Cary), Dick Anthony Williams (Tyler Humphries), Logan Ramsey (Jerry Hollister), Paul Kent (Ralph Shillitoe), and Murphy Dunne (Price Townsend).

Rossi is pleased that his friend and jogging partner Burt Cary is a candidate for the board of supervisors. He declines Lou's offer to cover the board, saying he wants to retain his objectivity as a reporter and his friendship with Cary. But Rossi is disturbed when he discovers that Cary has helped frame his opponent by linking him to a cocaine purchase. Faced with losing a friend or seeing the *Tribune* fail to report the facts, Rossi gives the story to the *Tribune* reporter and looks for a new jogging partner.

Episode 99: "Jazz"
Air date: January 4, 1982
Director: Burt Brinckerhoff
Writer: Rogers Turrentine

Guest cast: Todd Susman (Jed Crosley), Richard Erdman (Gary Banks), Joe Williams (Sonny Goodman), Med Flory (Ron Rickell), and Louis Bellson (Johnny Albert).

After meeting jazz musician Sonny Goodman at a nightclub Rossi tries to reunite Goodman's legendary jazz group. Despite their misgivings and old wounds, the musicians finally play together at the club. Meanwhile, *Tribune* investigative reporter Jed Crosley struggles in his effort to work on his own after his longtime partner retires. He ultimately tracks down enough evidence to show how a public official has diverted funds to refurbish his home.

Episode 100: "Ghosts"
Air date: January 11, 1982
Director: Roger Young
Writer: April Smith
Guest cast: Jacqueline Brooks (Dr. Haas), Milton Selzer (Claude Cunningham), Penelope Windust (Josephine), Lionel Smith (Sgt. Roche), and Peter Maloney (Alex Conrad).

Billie covers the investigation of the death of a woman who fell from a second-floor railing inside a house that neighbors say is haunted. She discovers that reports of a haunting began after a ten-year-old girl was murdered there. The lawyer defending the dead woman's husband on a murder charge says he will argue that a poltergeist was responsible. Billie attends a spooky seance at the house, but she and Lou remain skeptical about ghosts. Later, a young girl who had been inside the house at the time of the woman's death tells police the couple had argued over the husband's affair with his sister-in-law. He then pleads guilty to the slaying. Oddly, after a child's battered doll is taken from the house, no more supernatural events are reported.

Episode 101: "Cameras"
Air date: January 25, 1982
Director: Peter Levin
Writer: David Lloyd
Guest cast: Marcia Rodd (Vivian Hamlin), Jack Collins (Judge Strohmemer), Robin Rose (Peggy Daye), Kenneth Tigar (defense attorney), and Corinne Michaels (prosecutor).

Two gunmen hold several children hostage at a restaurant during a birthday party. The *Tribune* staff grudgingly watches television coverage of the event, knowing they cannot compete with the immediacy television news provides the public. A judge's decision to allow cameras in the courtroom during the gunmen's trial leads to a debate among *Tribune* journalists over the impact of televised court proceedings. Billie writes a story about whether some mothers are exploiting their children for monetary gain. When Lou and Art change a sentence in the story to make a mother look more manipulative, the woman accuses Billie of unfair reporting. She admits later, however, that the story was accurate. In the end a furious Billie criticizes Lou for slanting her story at the expense of accuracy and her reputation. Although not apologizing to her, Lou accepts the criticism.

Episode 102: "Review"
Air date: February 2, 1982
Director: Nell Cox
Writer: Jeffrey Lane
Guest cast: Margaret Hamilton (Thea Taft), Karen Carlson (Meredith Hall-Sutton), Diana Douglas (Carole Fuller), Don Plumley (Frank Laven), and Yolanda Marquez (Amalia Castillo).

With the help of Rossi and another reporter, the *Tribune* publishes a story about a councilman's penchant for telling racial jokes. He complains to the Western States News Council, a panel of journalists and community members who listen to complaints about news coverage. Charlie is a member, as is Meredith Hall-Sutton, the daughter of a *Tribune* editor fired years earlier by Mrs. Pynchon. Hall-Sutton is highly critical of the *Tribune*'s story. In private Charlie suggests that she has a bias against the *Tribune* and should abstain from voting on whether the *Tribune* treated the councilman fairly. Although she does not vote, the council agrees that the councilman's complaint is warranted. At the newspaper the editors agree to publish a story about the council's action, believing the *Tribune* can stand the criticism.

Episode 103: "Immigrants"
Air date: February 15, 1982
Director: Alexander Singer
Writer: Steve Kline
Guest cast: Raleigh Bond (Cy Wood), John Carter (Gunther Larsen), Kieu Chinh (Tam), Doan Chau Mau (Col. Eyen Van Long), and J. D. Hall (Norman Diggs).

As a Vietnamese refugee, Tam faces a variety of problems adjusting to life in Los Angeles. He is hired as the *Tribune*'s new photographer and becomes friends with Animal. Despite his excellent skills with a camera he does not follow *Tribune* rules and runs afoul with the editors. Meanwhile, Tam's family is pressured by thugs who want to use their grocery as part of a food stamp fraud operation. His neighbor, a Vietnam veteran, criticizes Tam for even being in the United States. At night a grenade explodes outside of Tam's house, destroying the porch. Tam then aids Rossi by providing information about the food stamp crooks. After the story appears friends and neighbors (including the Vietnam veteran) help Tam rebuild his porch. Later, Lou congratulates Tam for passing probation. Tam asks for a raise—and gets it.

Episode 104: "Hunger"
Air date: March 1, 1982

Director: Peter Levin
Writer: Gene Reynolds
Guest cast: Uta Hagen (Louise Frawley), Tonyo Melendez (Juan), Ivan Bonar (Phil Springerman), Alan Haufrect (Chope), and Stanley Grover (Charles Keefer).

Rossi bets Lou that he can find a good story by talking to anyone Lou points out on the street. Louise Frawley, the middle-aged woman Lou chooses, sparks a *Tribune* story on the problems in feeding the hungry. Louise, a nun, operates a soup kitchen and delivers meals to shut-ins. She then pushes Rossi to investigate the problem of hunger in Malagua, a Central American nation. The complexity of the story concerns the *Tribune* editors at a budget meeting, and Lou later tells Rossi to drop it. But Sister Louise persuades Rossi to pursue it, and he does so on his own time. Finally finished with the story, Rossi is ecstatic when it is scheduled for the front page.

Episode 105: "Recovery"
Air date: March 8, 1982
Director: Roger Young
Writer: Michele Gallery
Guest cast: Clyde Kusatsu (Ken Watanabe), Clint Howard (Jerry Kovacovich), Pat Morita (Ike Tatsumi), Lee McDonald (Leland Willoughby), and Arthur Taxier (Dale Tollifer).

Rossi and Billie cover two scandals that threaten to harm innocent parties through guilt by association. Rossi looks into how profiteers took advantage of Japanese Americans interned during World War II. His investigation reveals that Mrs. Pynchon's husband made a fortune by buying land from Japanese Americans headed for the camps. Meanwhile, Billie covers a Medicaid scandal in which a doctor flees the country. His alleged criminal activities cast a shadow on his wife, recently appointed to the police review board. Later, however, she is arrested at the airport with $350,000 in gold, apparently planning to join her husband. Charlie orders Rossi to drop the Pynchon angle from his story, but Rossi still tells his publisher about her husband's activities. Shocked, Mrs. Pynchon refuses at first to publish the story but later relents. She also establishes a foundation for Japanese Americans and returns to a family the Japanese-inscribed ring her husband had given her during the war.

Episode 106: "Obituary"
Air date: March 22, 1982
Director: Paul Stanley
Writer: April Smith
Guest cast: Michael Bond (Keith Wilbert), Simon Oakland (Col. Taylor), Barney Phillips (Jerry Ellison), Rae Allen (Helen Patterson), and Peter Michael Goetz (Bob O'Brien).

A last-minute change in assignments saves Billie from an ill-fated flight on a chartered plane. The craft crashes, killing the three journalists aboard. Lou, Rossi, and Billie set out to write profiles of their dead colleagues. They soon discover that each was a complicated person. One had few friends. Another ignored her family to focus on her work. The third was disciplined and dedicated to his work but unhappy. As they write their stories Animal struggles with an assignment to photograph a rare moth. If his pictures appear in the *Tribune,* insect collectors will find the field where the moths live and further endanger the species. He decides the assignment is not worth the harm it would cause the tiny creatures.

Episode 107: "Blacklist"
Air date: April 5, 1982
Director: Burt Brinckerhoff
Writer: Seth Freeman
Guest cast: Freddye Chapman (Abby McCann), William Schallert (Frank Obler), Graham Brown (Price McCann), Jeff Corey (Larry Hill), and Rick Lenz (Sam Valentine).

When the *Tribune* publishes "Dr. Valentine," a syndicated sex column for teens, angry readers respond with protests and a call for a boycott. Rossi learns that the father of his girlfriend, *Tribune* reporter Abby McCann, was blacklisted during the 1950s. Mr. McCann later tells them that Frank Ober, another *Tribune* reporter, was an FBI informant during the blacklist days. Frank later admits to Lou that cooperating with the FBI saved him from the blacklist but was a mistake he regrets. Despite sharp criticism of the *Tribune* and the loss of some advertisers the editors and Mrs. Pynchon refuse to pull the column.

Episode 108: "Law"
Air date: April 12, 1982
Director: Burt Brinckerhoff
Writer: Steve Kline
Guest cast: Charles Cioffi (Councilman Garbers), Harold J. Stone (Fred Gruber), Charles Hallahan (Chuck), Mary Louise Wilson (Elvira Wissler), Bartlett Robinson (Jacob Bauman), and Sally Kirkland (Vicky Doppler).

Tribune staff members as well as the people they cover increasingly turn to lawsuits to solve their disputes. Lou sues a plumber for shoddy work at his home. A councilman facing a failed effort to recall him sues some of the petitioners, chilling the efforts of a community group to participate in the political process. When the plumber countersues Lou, he reluctantly drops his lawsuit to avoid higher legal fees. Later, though, Lou pickets outside the plumber's business as a way of protesting his workmanship.

Episode 109: "Fireworks"
Air date: April 19, 1982
Director: Jeff Bleckner

Writer: Michele Gallery
Guest cast: Vincent Baggetta (Greg Serantino), Parley Baer (Ray Elders), Sandy McPeak (Matt Lupton), Lance Guest (Lance), and Emilio Delgado (Castillo).

Billie's story about lobbying and fireworks legislation sends her to Sacramento to deal with her ex-husband, lobbyist Greg Serantino. He proves to be uncooperative, especially when she discovers that he is the author of a bill easing restrictions on fireworks. She denies his charge that she is pursuing the story because he is involved. At the *Tribune* the staff is divided over the newspaper's bid for a Greenwood Foundation award. The foundation was established by a company with a poor environmental record and a history of selling overseas products banned in the United States. Charlie argues that the award would help the *Tribune*. The decision is left to the staff, which decides not to pursue the award. Billie returns to the newsroom with her story, despite her ex-husband's effort to thwart her.

Episode 110: "Unthinkable"
Air date: May 3, 1982
Director: Allen Williams
Writer: April Smith
Guest cast: Lane Smith (Dr. Lawrence), Bonnie Bartlett (Claire), Warren Kemmerling (Gen. Sutherland), Dean Santoro (Dvorak), and Peggy McCay (Marion Hume).

A series of events in the Middle East creates an oil crisis in the United States. As U.S. forces trade shots with the nation of Kulari concern grows that the United States may resort to nuclear war to preserve its access to oil fields. While Lou, Rossi, and other journalists cover preparations for a possible nuclear strike Billie writes about a young girl's struggle to survive burns suffered in a school bus crash. Anxiety grows after reports of leftists taking over the Kulari government in the wake of an explosion and the destruction of a U.S. oil tanker. At the hospital the girl improves slightly. Her doctor says the prognosis for her recovery is guarded but optimistic.

Episode 111: "Suspect"
Air date: May 17, 1982
Director: Alan Cooke
Writer: Seth Freeman
Guest cast: Lance Guest (Lance Reineckee), Dixie Carter (Jessica Lindner), Ren Woods (Karly), Christina Pickles (Elsa), and Roxanne Reese (Delia).

The *Tribune's* newest reporter, Lance Reineckee, is eager to cover the death of an environmental activist struck by a hit-and-run driver. He questions whether the death was an accident because the safety-conscious victim was not wearing a helmet and because a computer disk at the man's home showed he was setting up friends with prostitutes. Lou, testy because of problems with his girlfriend, orders Lance to turn his information over to police. Later, the young reporter decides that police are not working fast enough. He tracks down a prostitute but is threatened when her pimp catches them. Police intervene just in time. Lance later learns that his murder theory was wrong and that the death was indeed an accident. He is discouraged until Lou assures him that trying to find out what happened was worthwhile even if he was proved wrong in the end.

Episode 112: "Beachhead"
Air date: May 24, 1982
Director: Roy Campanella
Writer: Gene Reynolds
Guest cast: Cliff Potts (Ted McCovey), Michael Constantine (Joe Lombardi), Robert Pierce (Panface), Bill Ostrander (Moose), and William Traylor (chairman).

After Lou witnesses surfers running roughshod over other people at the beach Rossi writes a story about surfer gangs. When a fight breaks out among rival gangs, the *Tribune* is criticized by the city council for stirring up trouble with the story. Billie has problems at home when she and husband Ted disagree whether a halfway house for the mentally ill should remain in their neighborhood. Although uncomfortable at first, Billie decides that the house is needed to help people. A visit to the house eases Ted's concern. Lou, who had opposed placing the surfer story on the front page, must take the wrath of the city council when they ask for a *Tribune* representative to appear at a meeting. Later, he tells Charlie that he erred in playing up the story. Charlie suggests that Lou should have spoken up before the story appeared.

Episode 113: "Victims"
Air date: August 30, 1982
Director: Peter Bogar
Writer: Steve Kline
Guest cast: Steve Marachuk (Vince DeMayo), Bruce Kirby (Capt. Shackley), Barry Primus (Sgt. Stapler), James Gallery (Dave Rabowsky), and Lincoln Kirkpatrick (Dr. Turner).

Two acts of violence draw the *Tribune* staff's attention. Lou is robbed and shot in the parking lot after leaving work. During a liquor store holdup police officer Vince DeMayo shoots and kills a man robbing a liquor store. Although he feels the shooting is justified, he becomes irritable, depressed and abusive toward his family. Finally, DeMayo seeks counseling and joins a group of officers who have killed in the line of duty. Lou's recuperation from his wounds takes weeks in the hospital and more at home. When he returns to the newsroom for a short visit, he seems cheered by the prospects of going back to work.

Episode 114: "Charlie"
Air date: September 13, 1982
Director: Seth Freeman

Writer: Michele Gallery
Guest cast: Lance Guest (Lance), Macon McCalman (Dolph Masterson), Freddye
  Chapman (Abby McCann), Joanna Cassidy (Barbara Costigan), and Betty
  Kennedy (Cheryl).

A day in the life of Charlie Hume is filled with problems at work and at home.
He clashes with Mrs. Pynchon when she overrules his decision to force a staffer
with a drinking problem into retirement and fire another over a conflict of interest.
He counsels Art when the assistant city editor fears his girlfriend may be pregnant.
He faces the prospect of losing Billie, who is considering moving to Sacramento to
be able to spend more time with her husband. With quiet strength and wisdom
Charlie handles it all.

APPENDIX E

PRESS AND JERK DEPT.

Remember the terrific "Mary Tyler Moore Show" of a couple of seasons back? It took place in the newsroom of a mythical TV station, where a funny Editor and his funny Staff got involved in a different funny story every week. Well, that Editor now has a TV show of his own where he plays a similar role as the City Editor of a mythical newspaper. The only difference is that now he's no longer surrounded by a funny Staff . . . and the stories he gets involved in every week aren't very funny either. Which may help to explain why he's now known as . . .

Lou Grouch

ARTIST: ANGELO TORRES   WRITER: TOM KOCH

218

I don't **get** it! I'm the boss of **200** people here in the City Room, and not **one** of them ever **speaks** to me! **Why?**

Because they're **Extras** who are hired just to sit there! See, our Producer thinks they make it **more believable** when **you** and **I** and **two reporters** seem to be putting out the paper **all by ourselves!**

These Editorial meetings **ALWAYS** vote to feature my **hottest local story** on page one! But today, **you** want to headline some dull item about **Portugal sinking into the ocean?!?** And you call yourself a **Newspaperman?!?**

No, I call myself the **Janitor!** But you **asked** for my opinion, so **I gave** it to you!

When I was News Editor on the **Mary Tyler Moore Show,** I **never** had this kind of trouble . . . finding local stories that make me look good!

That's because **your staff** were **talented performers** who'd make **ANYBODY** look good! But **now,** you've only got **US!!**

CRASH

Cheer up, Lou! **We'll** think of a big story! How about finding a **kidnapped millionaire** . . . or impeaching an incompetent judge . . . or having Raunchi pose as a **mental patient** to expose conditions in our **State Hospitals?**

Nahh! We did all that stuff last week! Besides, it was **unbelievable!**

WHAT was . . . ?

Well . . . for **one thing** . . . the Hospital **Psychiatrists** tried to tell us Raunchi was **SANE!**

Remember how **great** it was when we were **just starting out** in the newspaper business 25 years ago! **Those were the good old days!**

But we only got paid **40 bucks a week** then! How can you call those **"the good old days"?**

Because I still had a bushy head of hair, weighed **150 pounds** and made out with **chicks** at least twice a year!

Engine Co. 24, investigate a **small fire** in a **tool shed** at **18th** and **Oak** . . .

That's it!! Our **big story!!** Can't you **see?** They're calling it a **small fire** because they don't want us to send a **Reporter!** But my nose for news smells something **funny!**

I smell something funny, **too!** But then, I **always do** when I get trapped in the same room with **The Beast!**

You guys can't make me divulge my **sources,** but I got word that this is a **fire!**

Psst! Psst! I seen the **whole thing,** and—

The past tense is **not "I seen",** you idiot! It's **"I saw"!** That's **elementary grammar!** And you call yourself a **Newspaperman?!?**

No . . . I call myself an **Arsonist!** That's how come I seen the **whole thing!**

44

Notes

Introduction

1. A review of prime-time television series about newspapers shows that only *The Big Story* (1949–57, NBC) and *Big Town* (1950–56, CBS, Dumont, NBC) aired longer than *Lou Grant*.

2. Arnold Becker, letter to the author, Jan. 30, 1992. Becker, vice-president of television research for CBS, provided ratings information based on the Nielsen Television Index.

3. George E. Delury, ed., *The World Almanac and Book of Facts 1980* (New York: Newspaper Enterprise Association, 1980), 427–28.

4. Mike Kaplan, ed., *Variety's Directory of Major U.S. Show Business Awards* (New York: R. R. Bowker, 1989), 198–244.

5. Cobbett Steinberg, *TV Facts* (New York: Facts on File, 1985), 360.

6. Jon Katz, "What TV Makes of the Fourth Estate," *New York Times*, Mar. 17, 1991.

7. Marc Gunther, "The Power of the Press," *Detroit News and Free Press*, Apr. 8, 1990.

8. Colin Covert, "Lou Grant: He Was Quite a Character," *Detroit Free Press*, May 13, 1982.

9. "We'll Miss Good Old Lou," *Lansing State Journal*, May 23, 1982.

10. John J. O'Connor, "TV: A Characteristic Finale from 'Lou Grant'," *New York Times*, Sept. 13, 1982.

1. The Newspaper Drama on Television

1. Robert Walden, interview with the author, Los Angeles, Calif., Dec. 5, 1991. Walden declined to identify the executive.

2. Alfred Brenner, *The TV Scriptwriter's Handbook* (Cincinnati Ohio: Writer's Digest Books, 1985), 43.

3. Walden interview, Dec. 5, 1991.

4. Ibid.

5. See David Shaw, "Actor Wants Byline," *TV Guide*, Jan. 21, 1978, 18; and David Inman, *The TV Encyclopedia* (New York: Perigee, 1991), 760.

6. Walden interview, Dec. 5, 1991.

7. Ibid.

8. Ibid.

9. For the purposes of this study a *newspaper drama* is defined as a dramatic television series with a newspaper as its primary setting or a newspaper or wire service reporter as its main character. Hence, comedies and fantasies with such settings or characters have been excluded.

10. Tim Brooks and Earle Marsh, *The Complete Directory to Prime Time Network TV Shows, 1946-Present*, 5th ed. (New York: Ballantine Books, 1992), xii.

11. Alex McNeil, *Total Television: A Comprehensive Guide to Programming from 1948 to the Present*, 3d ed. (New York: Penguin Books, 1991), 89.

12. Ibid., 280.

13. The twenty-three newspaper dramas were culled from a review of Brooks and Marsh; and McNeil.

14. Alex Barris, *Stop the Presses! The Newspaperman in American Film* (South Brunswick: A. S. Barnes, 1976), 12.

15. See Thomas H. Zynda, "The Hollywood Version: Movie Portrayals of the Press, *Journalism History* 6 no. 1 (Spring 1979); 16–25; Nora Sayre, "Falling Prey to Parodies of the Press," *New York Times*, Jan. 1, 1975; Debra Gersh, "Stereotyping Journalists," *Editor & Publisher*, Oct. 5, 1991, 18–19; and Loren Ghiglione, *The American Journalist: Paradox of the Press* (Washington, D.C.: Library of Congress, 1990), 97–113. In addition, Barris offers an extensive survey of the genre.

16. *The Front Page* (1931) was remade for film as *His Girl Friday* (1940), *The Front Page* (1974), and *Switching Channels* (1988). The latest remake changed the setting from a newspaper to a satellite television station.

17. Christopher H. Sterling and John M. Kittross, *Stay Tuned: A Concise History of American Broadcasting*, 2d ed. (Belmont, Calif.: Wadsworth Publishing, 1990), 278–87.

18. The ten programs were culled from John Dunning, *Tune In Yesterday: The Ultimate Encyclopedia of Old-Time Radio, 1925–1976* (Englewood Cliffs, N.J.: Prentice-Hall, 1976). They are *The Adventures of Christopher Wells* (1947–48); *The Big Story* (1947–54); *Big Town* (1937–52); *Casey, Crime Photographer* (1943–55); *Foreign Assignment* (1943); *Front Page Farrell* (1941–54); *Jane Arden* (1938–39); *Passport for Adams* (1943); *The Story of Sandra Martin* (1945); and *Wendy Warren and the News* (1947–58).

19. Dunning, 68–69.

20. See Brooks and Marsh, 94; and McNeil, 89.

21. See television reviews published in *Variety* on Sept. 21, 1949, Apr. 26, 1950, Sept. 3, 1952, Sept. 2, 1953, Sept. 15, 1954, Sept. 14, 1955, Sept. 12, 1956, and Oct. 10, 1957. The series also was reviewed in *TV Guide*, Feb. 11, 1956, 19.

22. Jack Gould, "Television in Review," *New York Times*, June 11, 1954.

23. Ibid.

24. Thomas O'Neil, *The Emmys: Star Wars, Showdowns, and the Supreme Test of TV's Best* (New York: Penguin Books, 1992), 35.

25. Three episodes of the series were viewed by the author on Aug. 4, 1992, at the Museum of Television and Radio in New York.

26. Episode aired Oct. 20, 1949, cataloged at the Museum of Television and Radio as T86:0279.

27. Episode aired Nov. 24, 1949, cataloged at the Museum of Television and Radio as T86:0280.

28. Episode aired Jan. 15, 1950, cataloged at the Museum of Television and Radio as T86:0282.

29. Television review, *Variety*, Oct. 5, 1949.

30. Jack Gould, "Television in Review," *New York Times*, Oct. 9, 1949.

31. Tim Brooks, *The Complete Directory to Prime Time TV Stars, 1946–Present* (New York: Ballantine Books, 1987), 223–24.

32. John Daly, telephone interview with the author, Dec. 10, 1990.

33. Brooks, 223–24.

34. Dunning, 69–70.

35. See Brooks and Marsh, 95; and McNeil, 90.

36. Television review, *Variety*, Oct. 11, 1950.

37. Television review, *Variety*, Apr. 8, 1952.

38. Television review, *Variety*, Oct. 13, 1954.

39. Television review, *TV Guide*, Dec. 18, 1954.

40. " 'Big Town's' Big Boss," *TV Guide*, Oct. 8, 1955, 8–9. The name of the author of the article was not published.

41. "Case History of a Star," *TV Guide*, Oct. 13, 1956, 17–19. The name of the author of the article was not published.

42. Television review, *Variety*, Oct. 13, 1955.

43. Television review, *Variety*, Feb. 23, 1956.

44. Dunning, 117.

45. See television review, *Variety*, Apr. 25, 1951; Brooks and Marsh, 192–93; and McNeil, 170.

46. See Val Adams, "Foreign Intrigue," *New York Times*, Nov. 4, 1951; television review, *Variety*, Oct. 10, 1951; Brooks and Marsh, 317; and McNeil, 272.

47. Television review, *Variety*, Dec. 17, 1951. The name of the critic was not published.

48. Jack Gould, "Radio and Television," *New York Times*, Oct. 10, 1951.

49. Television review, *Variety*, May 7, 1952.

50. Television review, *Variety*, Oct. 8, 1952.

51. "Location: Europe," *TV Guide*, Aug. 14, 1954, 13–15. The name of the author of the article was not published.

52. See television review, *Variety*, Oct. 13, 1954; and television review, *TV Guide*, Feb. 26, 1955, 14.

53. O'Neil, 35, 38, and 41.

54. Television review, *Variety*, Mar. 21, 1951.

55. Television review, *Variety*, July 2, 1952.

56. See Brooks and Marsh, 325–26; and McNeil, 380.

57. Television review, *Variety*, May 30, 1951.

58. Television review, *Variety*, Dec. 26, 1951.

59. See Brooks and Marsh, 653; and McNeil, 554.

60. See Brooks and Marsh, 646; and McNeil, 549.

61. Television review, *Variety*, Mar. 17, 1954.

62. See " 'Wire Service' Brought George Brent Out of Retirement," *TV Guide*, Mar. 16, 1957, 17–19; "Dateline: Anywhere," *TV Guide*, Mar. 30, 1957; Brooks and Marsh, 985–86; and McNeil, 838. The names of the authors of the *TV Guide* articles were not published.

63. Television review, *Variety*, Oct. 10, 1956.

64. Jack Gould, "TV: 'Forbidden Area'," *New York Times*, Oct. 5, 1956.

65. Review, *TV Guide*, Feb. 16, 1957, 27.

66. Television review, *Variety*, Oct. 22, 1956.

67. Television review, *Variety*, Oct. 15, 1956.

68. Television review, *Variety*, Mar. 13, 1957.

69. Brooks and Marsh, xvii.

70. See Brooks and Marsh, 449, and McNeil, 390.

71. Television review, *TV Guide*, June 21, 1958, 27.

72. Television review, *Variety*, Apr. 30, 1958.

73. Ibid.

74. Television review, *Variety*, Sep. 29, 1958.

75. See Brooks and Marsh, 548, and McNeil, 470.

76. Television review, *Variety*, Jan. 26, 1959.

77. Television review, *Variety*, Oct. 15, 1958.

78. McNeil, 188.

79. Television review, *Variety*, Sep. 30, 1959.

80. Television review, *Variety*, Oct. 9, 1958.

81. McNeil, 241.

82. Television review, *Variety*, Sep. 28, 1960.

83. See Brooks and Marsh, 756–57, and McNeil, 640.

84. Television review, *TV Guide*, Mar. 4, 1961, 23.

85. See reviews published in *Variety* on Sep. 29, 1960, Oct. 5, 1960, Nov. 3, 1960, and Jan. 11, 1961; Brooks and Marsh, 409; and McNeil, 353.

86. Television review, *Variety*, Jan. 11, 1961.

87. See Lester Velie, "Confessions of a TV Novice," *TV Guide*, June 2, 1962, 4–7; Brooks and Marsh, 877; and McNeil, 744–45.

88. Velie, 6–7.

89. Television review, *Variety*, Oct. 4, 1961.

90. Velie, 7.

91. See Brooks and Marsh, 774–75; and McNeil, 656.

92. Television review, *Variety*, Sep. 19, 1962.

93. Ibid.

94. Gilbert Seides, television review, *TV Guide*, Nov. 3, 1962, 14.

95. Richard F. Shepard, "Scoops (for Reporters) and Hints for Hatchet Men (Editors)," *New York Times*, Aug. 16, 1964.

96. Ibid.

97. "A Room with a Past," *TV Guide*, Nov. 30, 1968, 26–27.

98. Jack Gould, "TV: Freshness in Old Military Tale," *New York Times*, Sep. 26, 1964.

99. Television review, *Variety*, Oct. 7, 1964.

100. See Brooks and Marsh, 748; and McNeil, 632.

101. See Brooks and Marsh, 484–85; and McNeil, 550.

102. Television review, *Variety*, Sep. 18, 1974.

103. See Brooks and Marsh, 341; and McNeil, 298.

104. See John J. O'Connor, "TV: 'Gibbsville' on NBC Tonight," *New York Times*, Nov. 11, 1976; television review, *Variety*, Nov. 17, 1976; and John Carmody, "In O'Hara's 'Gibbsville'," *Washington Post*, Nov. 11, 1976.

105. For a more complete discussion of the book and movie, see Michael Schudson, *Watergate in American Memory: How We Remember, Forget, and Reconstruct the Past* (New York: Basic Books, 1992). Consult also Barris; Zynda; and Ghiglione.

106. Jack Hirshberg, *A Portrait of All the President's Men* (New York: Warner Books, 1976), 39.

107. William Goldman, the author of the screenplay, offers a genesis of the script in *Adventures in the Screen Trade: A Personal View of Hollywood and Screenwriting* (New York: Warner Books, 1983), 232–44.

108. Steven Brill, "Back on the Beat with Woodward and Bernstein," *Esquire*, Dec. 1983, 503.

109. Cobbett S. Steinberg, *Film Facts* (New York: Facts on File, 1980), 27. *One Flew over the Cuckoo's Nest* earned $56.5 million, whereas *All the President's Men* took in $29 million.

110. See Steinberg, *Film Facts*, 378–79; and Mason Wiley and Damien Bona, *Inside Oscar: The Unofficial History of the Academy Awards* (New York: Ballantine Books, 1986), 788–90. *All the President's Men* won Oscars for supporting actor (Jason Robards), screenplay based on material from another medium, art direction, and sound. In addition, the film was nominated in the categories of best picture, director (Alan J. Pakula), supporting actress (Jane Alexander), and film editing.

111. Vincent Canby, " 'President's Men,' Spellbinding Film," *New York Times*, Apr. 8, 1976.

112. Thomas Fox, " 'All the President's Men' Finds Honest Drama in Newsroom," *Memphis Commercial Appeal*, Apr. 9, 1976.

113. Richard Cuskelly, "Woodstein and Watergate," *Los Angeles Herald Examiner*, Apr. 4, 1976.

114. Roger Ebert, "Watergate on Film—Facts Not Stardust," *Chicago Sun-Times*, Apr. 9, 1976.

115. See Brooks and Marsh, 43; and McNeil, 43.

116. Steve Goldstein, "Making of 'Andros'," *More*, April 1977, 49.

117. Tom Shales, "Just a Cop Show in Disguise," *Washington Post*, Jan. 31, 1977.

118. See Lee Margulies, "Woodstein Spinoffs," *Los Angeles Times*, Jan. 31, 1977; and television review, *Variety*, Feb. 2, 1977.

119. Gary Deeb, " 'Andros Targets' Doesn't Merit Stopping the Presses," *Chicago Tribune*, Jan. 31, 1977.

120. Nicholas Gage, "Where 'Andros' Hits—and Misses—the Target," *TV Guide*, May 17, 1977, 13–17.

121. Lee Margulies, "Andros' Target: Series Renewal," *Los Angeles Times*, Nov. 1, 1977.

122. See Brooks and Marsh, 479; and McNeil, 414.

123. See Cecil Smith, "A Burr under Angels' Saddle?" *Los Angeles Times*, Mar. 23, 1977; and C. W. Skipper, "If Kingston's Start Is Slow, It Won't Surprise Burr," *Houston Post*, Mar. 22, 1977.

124. Television review, *Variety*, Mar. 30, 1977.

125. John J. O'Connor, "TV: Bad Times Hit 'Good Times'," *New York Times*, Mar. 23, 1977.

126. "What's RB Stand For?" *New Orleans Times-Picayune*, Mar. 23, 1977.

127. Lee Margulies, "Woodstein Spinoffs," *Los Angeles Times*, Jan. 31, 1977.

2. From Classic Comedy to Realistic Drama

1. Allan Burns, interview with author, Los Angeles, Calif., Dec. 17, 1991.

2. Ibid.

3. Jane Feuer, Paul Kerr, and Tise Vahimagi, eds., *MTM: Quality Television* (London: BFI Publishing, 1984), 4–6.

4. See Les Brown, *Les Brown's Encyclopedia of Television*, 3d ed. (Detroit, Mich.: Gale Research, 1992), 665–66; and Steven H. Scheuer, ed., *Who's Who in Television and Cable* (New York: Facts on File Publications, 1982), 482.

5. Feuer, Kerr, and Vahimagi, 5.

6. Inman, 141–42.

7. *Who's Who in Entertainment, 1989–1990* (Wilmette, Ill.: Macmillan Directory Division, 1990), 81.

8. See Inman, 141–42; and *Who's Who in Entertainment*, 79.

9. Robert S. Alley and Irby B. Brown, *Love Is All Around: The Making of "The Mary Tyler Moore Show"* (New York: Delta, 1989), 3–6.

10. See Alley and Brown, 225–27; and Brooks and Marsh, 1101–3.

11. Feuer, Kerr, and Vahimagi, 8–11.

12. Brooks and Marsh, 561–62.

13. Edward Asner, interview with author, Los Angeles, Calif., Dec. 9, 1991.

14. Charles Moritz, ed., *Current Biography Yearbook 1978* (New York: H. W. Wilson 1978), 22–23.

15. See Inman, 57–8; and McNeil, 695–96.

16. Linda S. Hubbard and Owen O'Donnell, eds., *Contemporary Theatre, Film, and Television*, vol. 6 (Detroit, Mich.: Gale Research, 1989), 11–12.

17. Moritz, 23.

18. Alley and Brown, 19–20.

19. Ibid., 18–19.

20. Ibid., 14–15.

21. Ibid., 19–20.

22. Inman, 57–58.

23. Burns interview, Dec. 17, 1991.

24. "Abraham Geller, Justice, Is Dead," *New York Times*, Mar. 9, 1969.

25. Burns interview, Dec. 17, 1991.

26. Ibid.

27. Sander Vanocur, "Ed Asner and Lou Grant, Newsroom to Newsroom," *Washington Post*, May 26, 1976.

28. Burns interview, Dec. 17, 1991.

29. Alley and Brown, 100–103.

30. Grant Tinker, telephone interview with author, Feb. 26, 1992.

31. Burns interview, Dec. 17, 1991.

32. Ibid.

33. Ibid.

34. Ibid.

35. Ibid.

36. David S. Reiss, *"M*A*S*H": The Exclusive Inside Story of TV's Most Popular Show* (Indianapolis: Bobbs-Merrill, 1980), 119–21.

37. Ibid.

38. Gene Reynolds, interview with author, Los Angeles, Calif., Dec. 4, 1991.

39. Burns interview, Dec. 17, 1991.

40. Ibid.

41. Reynolds interview, Dec. 4, 1991.

42. Ibid.

43. Ibid.

44. Ibid.

45. Burns interview, Dec. 17, 1991.
46. Reynolds interview, Dec. 4, 1991.
47. Ibid.
48. George Cotliar, telephone interview with author, Feb. 13, 1992.
49. Ibid.
50. Ibid.
51. Ibid.
52. Mark Murphy, telephone interview with author, Jan. 22, 1992.
53. Ibid.
54. Ibid.
55. Narda Zacchino, telephone interview with author, Jan. 16, 1992.
56. David Shaw, telephone interview with author, Jan. 28, 1992.
57. Boris Yaro, telephone interview with author, Jan. 28, 1991.
58. Ibid.
59. Cotliar interview, Feb. 13, 1992.
60. Murphy interview, Jan. 22, 1992.
61. Al Martinez, telephone interview with author, Jan. 14, 1992.
62. Ibid.
63. Ibid.
64. Ibid.
65. Ibid.
66. Ted Thackrey Jr., telephone interview with author, Jan. 10, 1992.
67. Ibid.
68. Ibid.
69. Ibid.
70. Leon Tokatyan, interview with author, Los Angeles, Calif., Dec. 3, 1991.
71. Ibid.
72. Sydney Z. Litwack, telephone interview with author, July 20, 1992.
73. Ibid.
74. Ibid.
75. Ibid.
76. Ibid.
77. Ibid.
78. Ibid.
79. Ibid.
80. Ibid.

3. Characters and Casting

1. Frank Swertlow, "How Jack Bannon Hates His Hot Tub," *TV Guide*, June 12, 1982, 20.
2. Jack Bannon, interview with author, Los Angeles, Calif., Dec. 4, 1991.
3. Ibid.
4. The sketches, which carry the title "The Trib," are among actor Daryl Anderson's mementos of the series. He recalled that the sketches were distributed by the production staff early in the series.
5. Tokatyan said he probably contributed to the sketches and may have written them, but he added that he could not remember.
6. Brooks and Marsh, 561–62.

7. Alley and Brown, 100–107.
8. Reynolds interview, Dec. 4, 1991.
9. Ibid.
10. Tokatyan interview, Dec. 3, 1991.
11. Asner interview, Dec. 9, 1991.
12. Reynolds interview, Dec. 4, 1991; and Tokatyan interview, Dec. 3, 1991.
13. Asner interview, Dec. 9, 1991.
14. Reynolds interview, Dec. 4, 1991.
15. Ibid.
16. Tokatyan interview, Dec. 3, 1991.
17. Asner interview, Dec. 9, 1991.
18. Ibid.
19. Ibid.
20. Reynolds interview, Dec. 4, 1991.
21. Tokatyan interview, Dec. 3, 1991.
22. Ibid.
23. Ibid.
24. Copies of the character sketches were provided by Daryl Anderson. Used with permission.
25. Ibid.
26. Reynolds interview, Dec. 4, 1991.
27. Ibid.
28. Tokatyan interview, Dec. 3, 1991.
29. Reynolds interview, Dec. 4, 1991; and Tokatyan interview, Dec. 3, 1991.
30. Tokatyan interview, Dec. 3, 1991.
31. Character sketches.
32. Shaw interview, Jan. 28, 1992.
33. Ibid.
34. Ibid.
35. Ibid.
36. Ibid.
37. Ibid.
38. Shaw, "Actor Wants Byline," 18.
39. Ibid.
40. See Inman, 760; and Shaw, "Actor Wants Byline," 19.
41. Inman, 760.
42. Walden interview, Dec. 5, 1991.
43. Ibid.
44. Ibid.
45. Ibid.
46. Ibid.
47. Ibid.
48. Ibid.
49. Character sketches.
50. Ibid.
51. Reynolds interview, Dec. 5, 1991.
52. Linda Kelsey, interview with author, Los Angeles, Calif., Dec. 12, 1991.
53. Ibid.
54. Rebecca Balding, telephone interview with author, Jan. 14, 1992.

55. Ibid.

56. Ibid.

57. Ibid.

58. Ibid.

59. Zacchino interview, Jan. 16, 1992.

60. Ibid.

61. Ibid.

62. Ibid.; and Reynolds interview, Feb. 14, 1992.

63. Shaw interview, Jan. 28, 1992.

64. Martinez interview Jan. 14, 1992; and Thackrey interview, Jan. 10, 1992.

65. Reynolds interview, Feb. 14, 1992; and Leon Tokatyan, telephone interview with author, January 16, 1992.

66. Reynolds interview, Feb. 14, 1992.

67. Reynolds interview, Dec. 4, 1991.

68. Tokatyan interview, Dec. 3, 1991.

69. William H. Taft, *Encyclopedia of Twentieth-Century Journalists* (New York: Garland Publishing, 1986), 306–7.

70. Taft, 133–34.

71. Tokatyan interview, Dec. 3, 1991.

72. Character sketches.

73. Ibid.

74. See Inman, 562–63; and Kay Mills, "Nancy Marchand's Role-Model Role," *Los Angeles Times*, Sept. 17, 1980.

75. Inman, 562–63.

76. Nancy Marchand, telephone interview with author, Jan. 13, 1992.

77. Ibid.

78. Ibid.

79. Thackrey interview, Jan. 10, 1992.

80. Marchand interview, Jan. 13, 1992.

81. Ibid.

82. Ibid.

83. Ibid.

84. Reynolds interview, Dec. 4, 1991.

85. Character sketch.

86. Ibid.

87. Ibid.

88. See Inman, 16; and Lisa See, "Now the Voice Has Authority," *TV Guide*, Oct. 4, 1980, 28.

89. See, 30.

90. Ibid., 27.

91. Mason Adams, telephone interview with author, Feb. 12, 1992.

92. See, 27.

93. Adams interview, Feb. 12, 1992.

94. Ibid.

95. Bill Brink, telephone interview with author, Feb. 13, 1992.

96. Ibid.

97. Adams interview, Feb. 12, 1992.

98. Ibid.

99. Tokatyan interview, Dec. 3, 1991.

100. Character sketch.
101. Ibid.
102. Ibid.
103. Ibid.
104. Reynolds interview, Dec. 4, 1991.
105. Tokatyan interview, Dec. 3, 1991.
106. Inman, 76–77.
107. Swertlow, 20.
108. Ibid.
109. Bannon interview, Dec. 4, 1991.
110. Ibid.
111. Eric Malnic, telephone interview with author, Mar. 16, 1992.
112. Bannon interview, Dec. 4, 1991.
113. Ibid.
114. Character sketch.
115. Ibid.
116. Ibid.
117. Inman, 38.
118. Jerry Buck, " 'Lou Grant' Photographer Thinks Criticism out of Focus," Kansas City Star, May 24, 1981.
119. Tokatyan interview, Dec. 3, 1991.
120. Ibid.
121. Daryl Anderson, interview with author, Los Angeles, Calif., December 3, 1991.
122. Ibid.
123. Yaro interview, Jan. 28, 1992.
124. Ibid.
125. Ibid.
126. Anderson interview, Dec. 3, 1991.
127. Yaro interview, Jan. 28, 1992.
128. Martinez interview, Jan. 14, 1992.
129. J. Robert Mantler, an official of the Professional Photographers Society of New York, sent an angry letter to producer Gene Reynolds regarding the character Dennis "The Animal" Price. A copy of the letter, dated Oct. 16, 1978, is among Anderson's papers. Such protests are discussed in detail in chapter 5.
130. Yaro interview, Jan. 28, 1992.
131. Tokatyan interview, Dec. 3, 1991.
132. Zacchino interview, Jan. 16, 1992.
133. Murphy interview, Jan. 22, 1992.
134. Tokatyan interview, Dec. 3, 1991.

4. Series Production and Censorship

1. Interviews with cast members, writers, and directors support the contention that Reynolds had the most influence.
2. Seth Freeman, telephone interview with author, July 8, 1992.
3. See Steinberg, 383–84; and Kaplan, 198–244.
4. Kaplan, 198–244.
5. Freeman interview, July 8, 1992.
6. Michele Gallery, interview with author, Los Angeles, Calif., Dec. 5, 1991.

7. Gene Reynolds, interview with author, Los Angeles, Calif., December 16, 1991.

8. Ibid.

9. Notebook no. 1, Box 22, Gene Reynolds Collection, Arts Special Collection, Univ. of California at Los Angeles (hereinafter cited as GRC).

10. Notebook no. 2, Box 22, GRC.

11. "Blackout" file, Box 22, GRC.

12. "Dumping" file, Box 24, GRC.

13. "Boys on the Bus" file, Box 24, GRC.

14. Gallery interview, Dec. 5, 1991.

15. Reynolds interview, Dec. 16, 1991.

16. Steve Kline, telephone interview with author, Nov. 16, 1992.

17. April Smith, telephone interview with author, Nov. 18, 1992.

18. The process was described in Reynolds interview, Dec. 16, 1991.

19. Ibid.

20. Gail Abarbanel to Seth Freeman, letter dated Nov. 11, 1980, in file labeled "Rape," Box 56, GRC.

21. Ronald M. Sohigian to Gene Reynolds, letter dated Nov. 6, 1979, in file labeled "Inheritance," Box 52, GRC.

22. Reynolds interview, Dec. 16, 1991.

23. Peter Levin, telephone interview with author, Dec. 29, 1992.

24. Ibid.

25. For views of the roles of producer and director in episodic television see Horace Newcomb and Robert S. Alley, *The Producer's Medium: Interviews With Creators of American TV* (New York: Oxford Univ. Press, 1983), 3–45; and John W. Ravage, *Television: The Director's Viewpoint* (Boulder, Colo.: Westview Press, 1978), 1–19.

26. Alexander Singer, telephone interview with author, July 18, 1992.

27. Newcomb and Alley, 18.

28. Ibid., 209.

29. Reynolds interview, Dec. 16, 1991.

30. Ibid.

31. Roger Young, telephone interview with author, July 9, 1992.

32. Freeman interview, July 8, 1992.

33. Singer interview, July 18, 1992; Levin interview, Dec. 29, 1992; Young interview, July 9, 1992; and Burt Brinckerhoff, telephone interview with author, July 7, 1992.

34. Brinckerhoff interview, July 7, 1992.

35. Young interview, July 9, 1992.

36. Levin interview, Dec. 29, 1992.

37. Singer interview, July 18, 1992.

38. Brinckerhoff interview, July 7, 1992.

39. Mel Damski, telephone interview with author, Dec. 10, 1992.

40. Singer interview, July 18, 1992.

41. Brinckerhoff interview, July 7, 1992.

42. Singer interview, July 18, 1992

43. Young interview, July 9, 1992.

44. Damski interview, Dec. 10, 1992.

45. Steinberg, 389.

46. Kaplan, 198–244.

47. Ibid.

48. Patrick Williams, telephone interview with author, July 6, 1992.

49. Ibid.
50. Ibid.
51. Ibid.
52. Ibid.
53. Ibid.
54. For a concise explanation of standards and practices departments at the three major networks see the entry in Brown, 530. For views of censorship from within the industry see Bob Shanks, *The Cool Fire: How to Make It in Television* (New York: Vintage Books, 1977) 77–81; and Bob Shanks, *The Primal Screen: How to Write, Sell, and Produce Movies for Television* (New York: W. W. Norton, 1986), 328–34. For a view of censorship by television critics and journalists as well as industry professionals see Saul Braun, "How Television Cuts the Bleep out of Shows," *TV Guide*, May 5, 1973, 6–10; Eric Levin, "Censors in Action," *TV Guide*, Dec. 10, 1977, 4–10; "You Can't Go at This Job with a Meat Cleaver," *TV Guide*, Dec. 17, 1977, 18–22; Dick Russell, "Leave It to the Merry Prankster," *TV Guide*, Dec. 16, 1978, 39–42; L. J. Davis, "Looser, Yes, but Still the Deans of Discipline," *Channels*, July-August 1987, 32–38; and "Making the Rules in Prime Time," *Channels*, May 7, 1990, 23–27.
55. Carol Isaacs, telephone interview with author, May 12, 1992.
56. Ibid.
57. Ibid.
58. Ibid.
59. Seth Freeman, telephone interview with author, May 11, 1992.
60. Isaacs interview, May 12, 1992.
61. Freeman interview, May 11, 1992.
62. Isaacs interview, May 12, 1992.
63. Ibid.
64. Ibid.
65. Ibid.
66. In an interview with the author on Dec. 16, 1991, in Los Angeles, California, Reynolds said he did not know what became of the Program Practices reports for the other episodes. They may not have been kept during the time the series was on the air, for he recalled turning over whatever *Lou Grant* materials remained in his files to UCLA.
67. Reynolds interview, December 16, 1991; and Freeman interview, May 11, 1992.
68. Carol Isaacs to Gene Reynolds, Program Practices memo for episode titled "Renewal," Dec. 19, 1977, GRC. All Program Practices memos cited in this study are held in the GRC.
69. Carol Isaacs to Gene Reynolds, Program Practices memo for episode titled "Sect," Dec. 12, 1977.
70. Isaacs interview, May 12, 1992.
71. Freeman interview, May 11, 1992.
72. Kellam de Forest, telephone interview with author, May 22, 1992.
73. The de Forest research report, dated June 27, 1978, is included in the folder for the episode "Mob," GRC.
74. Isaacs interview, May 12, 1992.
75. Carol Isaacs to Gene Reynolds, Program Practices memo for episode titled "Sect," Dec. 12, 1977.
76. Carol Isaacs to Gene Reynolds, Program Practices memo for episode titled "Renewal," Dec. 19, 1977.
77. Michele Brustin to Gene Reynolds, Program Practices memo for episode titled "Housewarming," Oct. 5, 1977.

78. Carol Isaacs to Gene Reynolds, Program Practices memo for episode titled "Barrio," May 25, 1977.

79. Carol Isaacs to Gene Reynolds, Program Practices memo for episode titled "Schools," Aug. 23, 1978.

80. Carol Isaacs to Gene Reynolds, Program Practices memo for episode titled "Coverup," Oct. 31, 1979.

81. Carol Isaacs to Gene Reynolds, Program Practices memo for episode titled "Pills," June 7, 1978.

82. Isaacs interview, May 12, 1992.

83. Carol Isaacs to Gene Reynolds, Program Practices memo for episode titled "Nazi," Aug. 12, 1977.

84. Isaacs interview, May 12, 1992.

85. Freeman interview, May 11, 1992.

86. Isaacs interview, May 12, 1992.

87. Holly Traister to Gene Reynolds, Program Practices memo for episode titled "Hoax," May 31, 1977.

88. Carol Isaacs to Gene Reynolds, Program Practices memo for episode titled "Scandal," Jan. 6, 1978.

89. See Michele Brustin to Gene Reynolds, Program Practices memo for episode titled "Housewarming," Oct. 5, 1977; and Carol Isaacs to Gene Reynolds, Program Practices memo for episode titled "Cop," June 19, 1979.

90. Isaacs interview, May 12, 1992.

91. Carol Isaacs to Gene Reynolds, Program Practices memo for episode titled "Spies," Jan. 18, 1978.

92. See Carol Isaacs to Gene Reynolds, Program Practices memos for episode titled "Hooker," July 14, 1978; and Carol Isaacs to Seth Freeman, Program Practices memo for episode titled "Execution," Sep. 15, 1981.

93. Isaacs interview, May 12, 1992.

94. Carol Isaacs to Gene Reynolds, Program Practices memo for episode titled "Aftershock," Aug. 12, 1977.

95. Carol Isaacs to Gene Reynolds, Program Practices memo for episode titled "Babies," Sep. 18, 1978.

96. Carol Isaacs to Gene Reynolds, Program Practices memo for episode titled "Murder," June 20, 1978.

97. Carol Isaacs to Gene Reynolds, Program Practices memo for episode titled "Charlatan," July 16, 1979.

98. Carol Isaacs to Gene Reynolds, Program Practices memo for episode titled "Henhouse," July 19, 1977.

99. Isaacs interview, May 12, 1992.

100. Ibid.

101. Carol Isaacs to Seth Freeman, Program Practices memo for episode titled "Harassment," June 9, 1980.

102. Isaacs interview, May 12, 1992.

103. Carol Isaacs to Gene Reynolds, Program Practices memo for episode titled "Renewal," Dec. 19, 1977.

104. Holly Traister to Gene Reynolds, Program Practices memo for episode titled "Hoax," May 31, 1977.

105. Carol Isaacs to Gene Reynolds, Program Practices memo for episode titled "Barrio," May 25, 1977.

106. Ibid.

107. Carol Isaacs to Gene Reynolds, Program Practices memo for episode titled "Prisoner," June 5, 1978.

108. Carol Isaacs to Seth Freeman, Program Practices memo for episode titled "Rape," Nov. 10, 1980.

109. Isaacs interview, May 12, 1992.

110. Carol Isaacs to Gene Reynolds, Program Practices memo for episode titled "Slammer," June 8, 1979.

111. Carol Isaacs to Seth Freeman, Program Practices memo for episode titled "Harassment," June 9, 1980.

112. Carol Isaacs to Seth Freeman, Program Practices memo for episode titled "Suspect," Mar. 12, 1982.

113. See Holly Traister to Gene Reynolds, Program Practices memo for episode titled "Hoax," May 31, 1977; and Holly Traister to Gene Reynolds, Program Practices memo for episode titled "Christmas," May 31, 1977.

114. Carol Isaacs to Gene Reynolds, Program Practices memo for episode titled "Scandal," Jan. 6, 1978.

115. See Carol Isaacs to Gene Reynolds, Program Practices memo for episode titled "Cop," June 19, 1979; and memo for episode titled "Slammer," June 8, 1979.

116. Holly Traister to Gene Reynolds, Program Practices memo for episode titled "Cophouse," Apr. 25, 1977.

117. Carol Isaacs to Gene Reynolds, Program Practices memo for episode titled "Nazi," Aug. 12, 1977.

118. Isaacs interview, May 12, 1992.

119. Carol Isaacs to Seth Freeman, Program Practices memo for episode titled "Recovery," Jan. 12, 1982.

120. Ibid. The de Forest Research reports carried out that function, checking facts and references to historical events.

121. Isaacs interview, May 12, 1992.

122. Freeman interview, May 11, 1992.

123. Isaacs interview, May 12, 1992.

124. Freeman interview, May 11, 1992.

125. Ibid.

126. Isaacs interview, May 12, 1992.

5. First Season, 1977–1978

1. Listings in *TV Guide* show that CBS repeated the last episode of *The Mary Tyler Moore Show* on Sep. 3, 1977.

2. "Ed Asner in a New Comedy," cover of *TV Times*, the Sunday television section of the *Los Angeles Times*, Sep. 18, 1977.

3. Julia Inman, "Grant Even Better in Semi-Serious Show," *Indianapolis Star*, Sep. 21, 1977.

4. Shaw to Gene Reynolds, Sep. 21, 1977, property of David Shaw.

5. See Brooks and Marsh, 288; and O'Neil, 214–16.

6. Brooks and Marsh, 718.

7. Reynolds interview, Dec. 4, 1991.

8. Ibid.

9. The title sequence originally aired Sep. 20, 1977.

10. "Cophouse" originally aired Sep. 20, 1977.

11. Asner interview, Dec. 9, 1991.

12. Reynolds interview, Dec. 4, 1991.

13. Ibid.

14. "Hostages" originally aired Sep. 27, 1977; "Nazi" on Oct. 18, 1977.

15. "Hoax" originally aired Oct. 4, 1977.

16. "Scoop" originally aired Nov. 8, 1977.

17. "Christmas" originally aired Dec. 13, 1977.

18. "Henhouse" originally aired Oct. 11, 1977.

19. "Psych-Out" originally aired Nov. 22, 1977.

20. "Barrio" originally aired Nov. 1, 1977.

21. "Housewarming" originally aired Nov. 29, 1977; "Judge" on Nov. 15, 1977.

22. "Aftershock" originally aired Oct. 25, 1977.

23. For details of the incident see Gay Talese, *The Kingdom and the Power* (1966; reprint, New York: Dell, 1981), 431–48. Researcher Michele Gallery described the Talese book as important to series research.

24. Gallery interview, Dec. 5, 1991.

25. Ibid.

26. For details of the incident see Michael Bugeja, "S. Dakotan's Two Lives May Become Movie," *Omaha World-Herald*, Mar. 19, 1977.

27. Shaw to Gene Reynolds, Sep. 21, 1977, property of David Shaw.

28. Ibid.

29. Ibid.

30. Judy Flander, "TV Preview: 'Lou Grant' Was Worth the Wait," *Washington Star*, Sep. 20, 1977.

31. Tom Shales, "First, the Good News: 'Lou Grant' Is Just What TV Needs," *Washington Post*, Sep. 20, 1977.

32. Jay Sharbutt, "Lou Grant Gets Job on Paper," *Kansas City Star*, Sep. 20, 1977. For other reviews of *Lou Grant*, see Rena Pederson, "Lou Grant Deserves to Live," *Dallas Morning News*, Oct. 14, 1977; Katie Kelly, "TV Column," *New York Post*, Nov. 29, 1977; David Eden, " 'Lou Grant' Is TV Season's Headliner," *Minneapolis Star*, Sep. 20, 1977; "Lou Grant," *Daily Variety*, Sep. 21, 1977; Tom Dorsey, "Newsman 'Lou Grant' Comes Up with An Extra," *Louisville Courier-Journal*, Sep. 20, 1977; John J. O'Connor, "TV: CBS Presents 'Lou Grant'," *New York Times*, Sep. 20, 1977; Mike Drew, " 'Lou Grant' Is a Headliner," *Milwaukee Journal*, Oct. 20, 1977; Frank Rich, "Viewpoint: Lou, Carter, CHiPS," *Time*, Sep. 19, 1977, 94; and Harry F. Watters, "Eyeballing the New Season," *Newsweek*, Sep. 26, 1977, 79.

33. See Richard K. Shull, "This Mr. Grant Takes a Paper," *Indianapolis News*, Sep. 21, 1977; Joe Stevenson, "Lou Grant's Desk Lacks Frenetic Look," *Bakersfield Californian*, Sep. 26, 1977; and Roger Wise, "He Even Looks Like a Grump," *Honolulu Star-Bulletin*, Oct. 16, 1977.

34. Marvin Kitman, "Ed Asner: Still the Lou We Know and Love," *Newsday*, Sep. 27, 1977.

35. Mike Drew, "New Fall Shows Forge into Second Week," *Milwaukee Journal*, Sep. 18, 1977.

36. Ray Mariotti, "Lou Grant Gets His Newspaper Facts Straight," *Austin-American Statesman*, Sep. 24, 1977.

37. Gary Deeb, "Genteel 'Lou Grant' Is a Faith-Restorer," *Chicago Tribune*, Sep. 19, 1977.

38. Shooting began on June 23, 1977, according to production notes in Box 40, GRC.

39. Tokatyan interview, Jan. 16, 1992.

40. Reynolds interview, Dec. 4, 1991.

41. Character sketches, property of Daryl Anderson.

42. Rebecca Balding, telephone interview with author, Jan. 14, 1992.

43. Ibid.

44. The episode was filmed between July 14 and July 25, 1977, according to production notes in Box 40, GRC.

45. Balding interview, Jan. 14, 1992.

46. Ibid.

47. Ibid.

48. Ibid.

49. Ibid.

50. Reynolds interview, Dec. 4, 1991.

51. Ibid.

52. Kelsey interview, Dec. 12, 1991.

53. Reynolds interview, Dec. 4, 1991.

54. Kelsey interview, Dec. 12, 1991.

55. Inman, 475.

56. The script "Henhouse" is in Box 40, GRC.

57. Kelsey interview, Dec. 12, 1991.

58. Ibid.

59. Tokatyan interview, Dec. 3, 1991.

60. Adams interview, Feb. 12, 1992.

61. Tokatyan interview, Dec. 3, 1991.

62. Reynolds interview, Dec. 4, 1991.

63. "Sports" originally aired Jan. 10, 1978.

64. Reynolds interview, Dec. 4, 1991.

65. Ibid.

66. Tom Strongman, " 'Animal' Revisited," *News Photographer*, Apr. 1978, 4.

67. Emmett W. Francois, " 'Animal' Revisited," *News Photographer*, Apr. 1978, 4.

68. Tom Warren, "Pan Mail or Fan Mail," *News Photographer*, Sep. 1978, 43.

69. Curt Johnson, "Get Our Act Together," *News Photographer*, June 1978, 43.

70. J. Robert Mantler to Gene Reynolds, Oct. 16, 1978. A copy of the letter is the property of Daryl Anderson.

71. Anderson interview, Dec. 3, 1991.

72. Reynolds interview, Dec. 4, 1991.

73. Anderson interview, Dec. 3, 1991.

74. "ABC's Front Line Rolls Up the Score," *Variety*, Sep. 28, 1977.

75. "A Nielsen Rating," *Variety*, Sep. 21, 1977.

76. "ABC's Front Line Rolls Up the Score," *Variety*, Sep. 28, 1977.

77. "Weekly Rating Scorecard," *Variety*, Oct. 26, 1977.

78. "Weekly Rating Scorecard," *Variety*, Nov. 23, 1977.

79. "Season-to-Date Series Ratings," *Variety*, Nov. 30, 1977.

80. Tinker interview with author, Feb. 26, 1992; and Allan Burns, telephone interview with author, Dec. 17, 1991.

81. Burns interview, Dec. 17, 1991.

82. Ibid.

83. Tinker interview, Feb. 26, 1992.

84. Ibid.

85. Ibid.

86. Ibid.

87. "Network Series Rating Averages," *Variety*, Jan. 4, 1978.

88. Asner interview, Dec. 9, 1991.

89. Ibid.

90. Ibid.

91. "CBS Activates 'Step 2' of Plan to Be No. 1 Again," *Variety*, Dec. 21, 1977.

92. "All Is Usual as ABC Wins Week," *Variety*, Jan. 11, 1978.

93. "Fewer Specials and Minis Planned By CBS' Day," *Variety*, Jan. 18, 1978.

94. "Star of 'Second Season' Sees ABC Running Ahead of Its Pace," *Variety*, Feb. 8, 1978.

95. See Lee Margulies, " 'Lou Grant' Survives Early Ratings," *Los Angeles Times* July 3, 1978; and Peter Rahn, "Asner's 'Lou Grant' Settled In," *St. Louis Globe-Democrat*, May 4, 1978.

96. Lee Margulies, " 'Lou Grant' Survives Early Ratings," *Los Angeles Times*, July 3, 1978.

97. "Airliner" originally aired Jan. 3, 1978.

98. "Scandal" originally aired Feb. 13, 1978.

99. For details of the Foreman controversy see H. Eugene Goodwin, *Groping For Ethics in Journalism* (Ames, Iowa: Iowa State Univ. Press, 1983), 109–14.

100. "Spies" originally aired Feb. 27, 1978.

101. "Hero" originally aired Jan. 17, 1978.

102. For details of the case see Harold J. Nelson, Dwight L. Teeter, Jr., and Don R. Le Duc, *Law of Mass Communications: Freedom and Control of Print and Broadcast Media*, 6th ed. (Westbury, N.Y.: Foundation Press, 1989), 266–67.

103. "Sports" originally aired Jan. 10, 1978.

104. For details of the *Oklahoma City Times* article and its aftermath see Frank Deford, "Fans to Press: Drop Dead," *Sports Illustrated*, Dec. 13, 1976, 24–27.

105. "Poison" originally aired Mar. 6, 1978. For information on the Silkwood case see Howard Kohn, *Who Killed Karen Silkwood?* (New York: Summit Books, 1981).

106. "Sect" originally aired Feb. 6, 1978.

107. "Lou Grant/Hare Krishna Show," *Citizens Freedom Foundation News*, Jan. 7, 1978. A copy of the newsletter is in Box 42, GRC.

108. "Rosenfield Says Pressure Scared 'Grant' Sponsors," *Variety*, Mar. 1, 1978.

109. "Renewal" originally aired Jan. 30, 1978.

110. "Physical" originally aired Mar. 20, 1978.

111. See "Christmas" and "Poison."

112. See "Airliner" and "Sports."

113. See "Takeover," "Airliner," "Christmas," and "Physical."

114. See "Hero."

115. Reynolds interview, Dec. 4, 1991.

116. See "Henhouse," "Christmas," and "Cult."

117. See "Hero."

118. See "Christmas" and "Scoop."

119. "1977–78 Regular Series Ratings," *Variety*, May 3, 1978.

120. Ibid.

121. "Bud Grant Sees a Tight Race as CBS, NBC Chip Away at ABC," *Variety*, Aug. 23, 1978.

122. See "Weekly Rating Scorecard," *Variety*, June 14, 1978; Jay Sharbutt, "Ratings

Pick Up for 'Lou Grant,' " *Dallas Morning News*, Aug. 4, 1978; and "Monthly Rating Scorecard," *Variety*, Aug. 9, 1978.

123. Lee Margulies, " 'Lou Grant' Survives Early Ratings," *Los Angeles Times*, July 3, 1978.

124. For Emmy nominees and winners see Kaplan, 198–207.

6. Second and Third Seasons, 1978–1980

1. Arthur Unger, "An Oasis in TV's 'Summer Silly Season'," *Christian Science Monitor*, June 25, 1979.

2. Ibid.; Greg Moody, "Asner Seeks Other Roles to Avoid 'Lou Grant' Typing," *Milwaukee Sentinel*, July 13, 1979; and Barbara Yost, "Newspapering Rubs Off on Ed Asner," *Phoenix Gazette*, June 21, 1979.

3. The percentage of viewership for *Lou Grant*, a figure known as a "share," was reported at 32 for both seasons. The figures were provided by Arnold Becker, CBS vice-president for television research, letter to author, Jan. 30, 1992.

4. The new credit sequence first appeared with the airing of "Pills" on Sept. 25, 1978.

5. "Pills" originally aired on Sept. 25, 1978.

6. For details of the Farber case see Robert D. McFadden, "An Almost Routine Assignment Led to Historic Case," *New York Times*, Nov. 28, 1978.

7. The Pentagon Papers case involved a newspaper's First Amendment right to publish information in nearly all circumstances. In June 1971 the federal government sought to stop the *New York Times* and the *Washington Post* from publishing a series of articles based on a secret government study of the Vietnam War, claiming national security was at risk. Opponents of the government's action contended that the documents were politically embarrassing but not a national threat. A temporary restraining order issued by a federal judge on June 15, 1971, stopped the *Times* from publishing the articles, an unprecedented use of prior restraint against the press. Another federal judge, however, allowed the *Post* to publish its Pentagon Papers series. Both cases went to the United States Supreme Court, which ruled 6–3 on June 30, 1971, that the government had not proved that national security was involved. The court did not rule, however, that the First Amendment right to publication without prior restraint was absolute. For more on the case see Edwin Emery and Michael Emery, *The Press and America: An Interpretive History of the Mass Media*, 5th ed. (Englewood Cliffs, N.J.: Prentice-Hall, 1984), 597–601.

8. "Conflict" originally aired on Dec. 18, 1978.

9. For a primer on the issues of conflict of interest see Goodwin, 56–84.

10. "Marathon" originally aired on Mar. 19, 1979.

11. Kaplan, 209.

12. "Murder" originally aired on Oct. 30, 1978.

13. Kaplan, 209.

14. "Singles" originally aired on Dec. 4, 1978.

15. "Samaritan" originally aired on Feb. 12, 1979.

16. "Convention" originally aired on Mar. 5, 1979.

17. "Home" originally aired on Feb. 26, 1979.

18. Gary Deeb, "CBS Backs 'Lou Grant' Episode," *Nashville Banner*, Aug. 17, 1979.

19. Richard Starnes, "Nursing Home Groups Fail to Edit 'Lou Grant'," *Cleveland Press*, July 27, 1979.

20. Press release, National Retired Teachers Association and the American Associa-

tion of Retired Persons, July 25, 1979. A copy of the press release is in Edward Asner's papers.

21. " 'Lou Grant' Story Hits Home, Nursing Homes Hit Back," *Long Beach Independent*, July 27, 1979.

22. Tom Hopkins, "Nursing Home Group Attempting to Stop the Presses on 'Lou Grant'," *Dayton Daily News*, July 27, 1979.

23. Joseph McLellan, "Rerun Rumble," *Washington Post*, July 27, 1979.

24. Ibid.

25. Ibid.

26. Howard Rosenberg, "CBS Resists Pressure to Cancel," *Los Angeles Times*, July 28, 1979.

27. Press release, James H. Rosenfield, July 25, 1979. A copy of the press release is in Edward Asner's papers.

28. " 'Lou Grant' Hits Home," *Boston Herald-American*, Aug. 20, 1979.

29. Gerald B. Jordan, "CBS Withstood Move to Shelve Sensitive Show," *Kansas City Star*, Aug. 28, 1979. For similar views of the controversy see Pete Rahn, "Attempt to 'Kill' a 'Grant' Episode Fails," *St. Louis Globe-Democrat*, Aug. 24, 1979; and Cy Brickfield, " 'Lou Grant' Center of Controversy," *Hartford Courant*, Aug. 15, 1979.

30. " 'Lou Grant' Hits Home," *Boston Herald-American*, Aug. 20, 1979.

31. "Prisoner" originally aired on Oct. 2, 1978.

32. Eileen M. Lach to Gene Reynolds, Oct. 3, 1978. A copy of the letter is in the papers of Daryl Anderson.

33. See Kaplan, 209; 383, 389.

34. "Vet" originally aired on Jan. 15, 1979.

35. Barbara Yost, " 'Lou Grant' Show Lauded," *Phoenix Gazette*, April 11, 1979.

36. Allen Williams, telephone interview with author, July 5, 1992.

37. Thomas R. Keating, "The Forgotten Veteran," *Indianapolis Star*, Jan. 17, 1979.

38. Dennis R. Wyant to Gene Reynolds, Apr. 5, 1979. A copy of the letter is in the papers of Daryl Anderson.

39. See Kaplan, 209; and Steinberg, 383.

40. " 'Lou Grant,' 'Taxi' Episodes Honored," *Orlando Sentinel*, July 10, 1979.

41. "Slaughter" originally aired on Nov. 27, 1978.

42. "Schools" originally aired on Nov. 20, 1978.

43. Kaplan, 209

44. "Babies" originally aired on Dec. 11, 1978.

45. The episodes and their original air dates are "Fire," Jan. 8, 1979; "Scam," Jan. 22, 1979; "Sweep," Feb. 5, 1979; "Skids," Apr. 2, 1979; and "Bomb," Mar. 26, 1979.

46. "Mob" originally aired on Oct. 23, 1978.

47. Jerry Patterson to Charles D. Ferris, Oct. 31, 1978. A copy of the letter is in the "Mob" file, Box 45, GRC.

48. A copy of the de Forest Research report is in the "Mob" file, Box 45, GRC.

49. Jerry Patterson, telephone interview with author, Sep. 17, 1992.

50. Jerry Patterson to Charles D. Ferris, Oct. 31, 1978. A copy of the letter is in the "Mob" file, Box 45, GRC. The Personal Attack Rule required broadcasters to give people free access to the airwaves to respond to attacks upon the honesty, integrity, character, or other personal qualities of an identified person or group in the presentation of a controversial issue of public importance. Thus, it was unlikely that the FCC would have considered such a tenuous and debatable connection between Patterson and the drama a personal attack. For more on the rule, see Brown, 422.

51. Gene Mater to Jerry Patterson, Nov. 2, 1978. A copy of the letter is in the "Mob" file, Box 45, GRC.

52. Patterson interview, Sep. 17, 1992.

53. "Dying" originally aired on Nov. 6, 1978.

54. Kaplan, 209.

55. "Hit" originally aired on Feb. 19, 1979.

56. "Hooker" originally aired on Oct. 16, 1978.

57. "Denial" originally aired on Jan. 1, 1979.

58. "Romance" originally aired on May 7, 1979.

59. Kaplan, 207–9.

60. Steinberg, 360.

61. "Network Series Rating Averages," *Variety*, Jan. 3, 1979.

62. "1978–79 Regular Series Ratings," *Variety*, May 23, 1979.

63. "CBS Builds Monday vs. Baseball," *Variety*, Aug. 8, 1979.

64. "Grant Outlines CBS Thinking on New Sked," *Variety*, May 23, 1979.

65. Asner interview, Dec. 9, 1991.

66. Terrence O'Flaherty, "Newspapermen: Real, Unreal," *San Francisco Chronicle*, June 18, 1979.

67. See Julia Inman, "Lou Grant Grouses a Little at the Press," *Indianapolis Star*, July 1, 1979; Dean Huber, "Grant Meets Real Press," *Sacramento Bee*, July 3, 1979; and Arthur Unger, "An Oasis in TV's 'Summer Silly Season'," *Christian Science Monitor*, June 25, 1979.

68. Inman, "Lou Grant Grouses a Little at the Press," *Indianapolis Star*, July 1, 1979.

69. "A Serious, But Not too Serious, Visit to the Real World of Journalism, *The Quill*, Apr. 1979, 20.

70. Resolution, APME, September 29, 1978. A copy of the resolution is in the papers of Edward Asner.

71. Walter Saunders, "Best Newspaperman on TV," *Rocky Mountain News*, June 22, 1979.

72. Greg Moody, "Asner Seeks Other Roles to Avoid 'Lou Grant' Typing," *Milwaukee Sentinel*, July 13, 1979.

73. "Visit to the Real World of Journalism," 20.

74. Moody, "Asner Seeks Other Roles."

75. Tom Hennessy, "Misquote Has Press in a Tizzy," *Detroit Free Press*, Mar. 25, 1979.

76. Bill Giles, "News Notes," *Detroit News*, Apr. 1, 1979.

77. Walden interview, Dec. 5, 1991.

78. Ibid.

79. See Walden Interview, Dec. 5, 1991; Debbi Snook, "Off-Screen 'Rossi' Talks about 'Lou Grant'," *Albany* (New York) *Times-Union*, May 3, 1981; and "A Fine Role Model," *San Diego Union*, May 17, 1981.

80. Kelsey interview, Dec. 12, 1991.

81. Ibid.

82. Steve Otto, "Bay Life Polls a Few Trusted Americans, *Tampa Times*, July 4, 1979.

83. Tom Koch, "Lou Grouch," *MAD*, Mar. 1979, 43–48.

84. Ibid., 44.

85. "Cop" originally aired on Sep. 17, 1979.

86. See Kaplan, 218; and Steinberg, 360.

87. Goodwin, 211–13.

88. "Exposé" originally aired on Sep. 24, 1979.

89. "Hazard" originally aired on Mar. 24, 1980.

90. For a discussion of the Pinto case see Peter Collier and David Horowitz, *The Fords: An American Epic* (New York: Summit Books, 1988), 405–6.

91. Goodwin, 179–80.

92. "Frame-Up" originally aired on Oct. 22, 1979.

93. "Kidnap" originally aired on Nov. 26, 1979.

94. Kaplan, 218.

95. "Lou" originally aired on Feb. 11, 1980.

96. "Charlatan" originally aired on Oct. 15, 1979.

97. "Blackout" originally aired on Feb. 18, 1980.

98. "Andrew, Part 1: Premonition" originally aired on Dec. 3, 1979. "Andrew, Part 2: Trial" originally aired on Dec. 10, 1979.

99. "Inheritance" originally aired on Jan. 28, 1980.

100. For information on DES see Stephen Fenichell and Lawrence S. Charfoos, *Daughters At Risk: A Personal DES History* (Garden City, N.Y.: Doubleday, 1981); and Cynthia Laitman Orenberg, *DES: The Complete Story* (New York: St. Martin's Press, 1981).

101. Kelsey interview, Dec. 12, 1991.

102. Larry McMullen, "The Doctor Who Wouldn't Go Along," *Philadelphia Daily News*, Feb. 6, 1980.

103. The episodes and their original air dates are "Slammer," Oct. 1, 1979; "Indians," Jan. 14, 1980; "Dogs," Mar. 3, 1980; "Censored," Feb. 4, 1980; "Guns," Mar. 17, 1980; "Kids," Dec. 24, 1979; "Gambling," Nov. 5, 1979; and "Hype," Oct. 29, 1979.

104. "Influence" originally aired on Mar. 10, 1980.

105. Kaplan, 218.

106. A. Williams interview, July 5, 1992.

107. Ibid.

108. "Hollywood" originally aired on Dec. 17, 1979.

109. Kaplan, 218.

110. "Brushfire" originally aired on Jan. 7, 1980.

111. Kaplan, 218.

112. "Witness" originally aired on Nov. 12, 1979.

113. "Cover-Up" originally aired on Jan. 21, 1980.

114. See David McClintick, *Indecent Exposure: A True Story of Hollywood and Wall Street* (New York: William Morrow, 1982).

115. "1979–80 Regular Series Ratings," *Variety*, June 4, 1980.

116. Arnold Becker to author, Jan. 30, 1992.

117. Cecil Smith, " 'Lou Grant' Gets 15 Emmy Bids," *Philadelphia Enquirer*, Aug. 9, 1980.

118. Kaplan, 216–27.

7. Fourth and Fifth Seasons, 1980–1982

1. O'Neil, 252.

2. Ibid.

3. Ibid.

4. Mary Murphy, " 'Sometimes I'm So Ambitious I Even Fool Myself,' " *TV Guide*, Apr. 11, 1981, 30.

5. The episode "Nightside" originally aired on Sep. 22, 1980.

6. The episode "Pack" originally aired on Oct. 27, 1980.

7. See Timothy Crouse, *The Boys on the Bus* (New York: Random House, 1972).

8. Among the pack was veteran reporter Flo Meredith, played by actress Eileen Heckart. She was the only character other than Lou Grant to appear in both *Lou Grant* and *The Mary Tyler Moore Show*. In the situation comedy Flo Meredith was Mary Richards's aunt and Lou's one-time love as well as a tough reporter.

9. Kaplan, 230.

10. The episode "Goop" originally aired on Nov. 24, 1980.

11. Goodwin, 135–36.

12. The episode "Libel" originally aired on Dec. 8, 1980.

13. The episode "Strike" originally aired on Feb. 16, 1981.

14. Kaplan, 230.

15. The episode "Business" originally aired on Mar. 23, 1981.

16. The episodes and their original air dates were "Harassment," Sep. 29, 1980; "Sting," Nov. 17, 1980; "Streets," Dec. 15, 1980; "Boomerang," Jan. 19, 1981; "Survival," Feb. 23, 1981; and "Violence," Apr. 6, 1981.

17. The episode "Rape" originally aired on Jan. 12, 1981.

18. Kaplan, 230.

19. The episode "Stroke" originally aired on May 4, 1981.

20. The episode "Venice" originally aired on Mar. 9, 1981.

21. The episode "Catch" originally aired on Jan. 5, 1981.

22. The episode "Depression" originally aired on Apr. 13, 1981.

23. "Generations" originally aired on Jan. 26, 1981, and "Search" on Feb. 9, 1981.

24. "1980–81 Regular Series Ratings," *Variety*, June 10, 1981.

25. O'Neil, 226.

26. Ibid.

27. Kaplan, 228–41.

28. Murphy, " 'Sometimes I'm So Ambitious I Even Fool Myself'," 28.

29. For circulation figures of magazines in 1981, see Hana Umlauf Lane, ed., *The World Almanac and Book of Facts 1983* (New York: Ballantine Books, 1983), 430. At the time, the circulation of *TV Guide* was second only to that of *Reader's Digest*.

30. Ibid., 32.

31. Ibid.

32. Ibid., 31.

33. Kelsey interview, Dec. 12, 1991.

34. Lance Guest, interview with author, Los Angeles California, Dec. 6, 1991.

35. Ibid.

36. Ibid.

37. Ibid.

38. Ibid.

39. The episode "Reckless" originally aired on Nov. 16, 1981.

40. The episode "Risk" originally aired on Nov. 30, 1981.

41. See Goodwin, 109–32.

42. Gallery, interview, Dec. 5, 1991.

43. The episode "Friends" originally aired on Dec. 28, 1981.

44. The episode "Cameras" originally aired on Jan. 25, 1982.

45. The episode "Review" originally aired on Feb. 8, 1982.

46. The episode "Fireworks" originally aired on Apr. 19, 1982.

47. The episode "Suspect" originally aired on May 17, 1982.

48. The episode "Beachhead" originally aired on Apr. 24, 1982.

49. The episode "Blacklist" originally aired on Apr. 15, 1982.

50. Kaplan, 244.

51. The episode "Charlie" originally aired on Sep. 13, 1982.

52. Kaplan, 244. The episode "Hometown" originally aired on Nov. 23, 1981.

53. The episode "Double-Cross" originally aired on Dec. 7, 1981.

54. The episode "Drifters" originally aired on Dec. 14, 1981.

55. The episode "Jazz" originally aired on Jan. 4, 1982.

56. The episode "Ghosts" originally aired on Jan. 11, 1982.

57. The episode "Victims" originally aired on Aug. 30, 1982.

58. The episode "Obituary" originally aired on Mar. 22, 1982.

59. The episodes and their original air dates are "Execution," Nov. 9, 1981; "Immigrants," Feb. 15, 1982; "Law," Apr. 12, 1982; and "Recovery," Mar. 8, 1982.

60. The episode "Hunger" originally aired on Mar. 1, 1982.

61. Aljean Harmetz, "Three Win Humanitas TV Awards," *New York Times*, July 8, 1982.

62. The episode "Unthinkable" originally aired on May 3, 1982.

63. Todd Gitlin, *Inside Prime Time* (New York: Pantheon Books, 1983), 8.

64. Ibid.

65. See Howard Rosenberg, "CBS Yanks 'Lou Grant,' 3 Others From Lineup," *Los Angeles Times*, May 7, 1982; and Suzan Nightingale, "TV's 'Lou Grant' Canceled," *Los Angeles Herald Examiner*, May 7, 1982.

66. Kelsey interview, Dec. 12, 1991.

8. Controversy and Cancellation

1. The newscast aired on Feb. 15, 1982. A tape of the program is in the Vanderbilt Television News Archive, Vanderbilt Univ., Nashville, Tennessee (hereinafter cited as VTNA).

2. "Asner to Send Latin Rebels Medical Aid," *Los Angeles Times*, Feb. 16, 1982.

3. The newscast aired on Feb. 15, 1982. A tape of the program is part of the VTNA.

4. Reynolds interview, Dec. 4, 1991.

5. Ibid.

6. Gallery interview, Dec. 5, 1991.

7. Walden interview, Dec. 5, 1991.

8. Kline interview, Nov. 16, 1992.

9. Sam Merrill, "*Playboy* Interview: Edward Asner," *Playboy*, Apr. 1981, 82.

10. Aljean Harmetz, "Asner Voted President of Screen Actors Guild," *New York Times*, Nov. 4, 1981.

11. Peter J. Boyer, "Candidates Draw Line for SAG Post," *Los Angeles Times*, Oct. 14, 1981.

12. Aljean Harmetz, "Asner Voted President of Screen Actors Guild," *New York Times*, Nov. 4, 1981.

13. Harry Bernstein, "Actors' Union May Tilt Left under Asner," *Los Angeles Times*, Nov. 4, 1981.

14. Sally Ogle Davis, "Battling It Out in Hollywood," *New York Times Magazine*, Apr. 25, 1982, 100–104.

15. Harry Bernstein, "Battle of the Stars: Union Issues Set Asner, Heston at Odds," *Los Angeles Times*, Feb. 11, 1982.

16. "Actors Guild Declines to Give Reagan Honor," *New York Times*, Dec. 20, 1982.

17. Harry Bernstein, "Battle of the Stars: Union Issues Set Asner, Heston at Odds," *Los Angeles Times*, Feb. 11, 1982.

18. Ibid.

19. Merrill, 92.

20. "Echoes of Vietnam: Celebrities Want U.S. Out of El Salvador," *Los Angeles Times*, Mar. 15, 1981.

21. For a discussion of Ronald Reagan's policy in El Salvador see Lou Cannon, *President Reagan: The Role of a Lifetime* (New York: Simon and Schuster, 1991), 195–96; Laurence I. Barrett, *Gambling with History: Reagan in the White House* (Garden City, N.Y.: Doubleday, 1983), 205–10; and Mark Hertsgaard, *On Bended Knee: The Press and the Reagan Presidency* (New York: Farrar Straus Giroux, 1988), 184–204.

22. "Asner to Send Latin Rebels Medical Aid," *Los Angeles Times*, Feb. 16, 1982.

23. Asner interview, Dec. 9, 1991.

24. Ibid.

25. Ibid.

26. "Asner, Wife under Protection after Receiving Death Threat," *Daily Variety*, Feb. 19, 1982.

27. "Heston-Asner Struggle Is Splitting Entertainers," *New York Times*, Feb. 24, 1982.

28. Edward Asner, "We're on the Wrong Side in El Salvador," *New York Times*, Feb. 20, 1982.

29. Harry Bernstein, "Asner Heads Off Guild Recall Drive," *Los Angeles Times*, Feb. 26, 1982.

30. Ibid.

31. Aljean Harmetz, "Screen Actors Panel Stands by Asner," *New York Times*, Feb. 26, 1982.

32. Ibid.

33. "Lou Grant, Demagogue," *Norfolk Virginian-Pilot*, Feb. 23, 1982.

34. "Asner, the Traitor?" *Greensburg Tribune-Review*, Feb. 23, 1982.

35. Patrick Buchanan, "Ed Asner's Political Ideas Belong in the Make-Believe World of 'Lou Grant'," *Los Angeles Herald Examiner*, Feb. 18, 1982.

36. Cartoon by Ed Gamble, *Cleveland Press*, Feb. 21, 1982.

37. Cartoon by Bill Schorr, *Los Angeles Herald Examiner*, Feb. 26, 1982.

38. Cartoon by Steve Sack, *Minneapols Tribune*, Mar. 9, 1982.

39. Cartoon by Paul Conrad, *Los Angeles Times*, Feb. 28, 1982.

40. Luis H. Aguilar, letter to the editor, *Los Angeles Times*, Mar. 2, 1982.

41. Elinor Ashkenazy, letter to the editor, *Los Angeles Times*, Mar. 2, 1982.

42. Sylvie Strauss, letter to the editor, *Los Angeles Times*, Mar. 2, 1982.

43. Sonya Jason, letter to the editor, *Los Angeles Herald Examiner*, Feb. 26, 1982.

44. H. F. Hardy, letter to the editor, *Los Angeles Times*, Mar. 2, 1982.

45. Gary Deeb, "Ed Asner and 'Lou Grant' Hitting the Skids Together," *Chicago Sun-Times*, Feb. 24, 1982.

46. Howard Rosenberg, "Asner and 'Lou Grant'—Keep Them Apart," *Los Angeles Times*, Mar. 1, 1982.

47. Mark Starr, "Asner the Activist," *Newsweek*, Mar. 8, 1982, 23. Actress Jane Fonda visited Hanoi, the capital of North Vietnam, in 1972 and 1974 as part of her controversial antiwar activities. The 1972 visit, which included radio broadcasts to American soldiers and sighting an antiaircraft gun, earned her the nickname "Hanoi Jane" and resulted

in charges of treason from her harshest critics. For more on Fonda's visits to Hanoi see Michael Freedland, *Jane Fonda: A Biography* (New York: St. Martin's Press, 1988), 181–86; and Peter Collier, *The Fondas: A Hollywood Dynasty* (New York: G. P. Putnam's Sons, 1991), 225–28.

48. Anderson interview, Dec. 3, 1991.
49. Gallery interview, Dec. 5, 1991.
50. Ibid.
51. Kelsey interview, Dec. 12, 1991.
52. Bannon interview, Dec. 4, 1991.
53. Walden interview, Dec. 5, 1991.
54. Reynolds interview, Dec. 4, 1991.
55. Asner interview, Dec. 9, 1991.
56. "Boycott of TV Program Urged Over Asner Drive," *New York Times*, Feb. 24, 1982. For decades the threat of economic boycotts had been used to pressure advertisers, networks, and producers. For example, in the early 1950s during the blacklisting era, a Syracuse, N.Y., supermarket executive named Laurence A. Johnson targeted sponsors and networks affiliated with so-called "communist fronters." By the early 1980s religious conservatives such as the Reverend Donald Wildmon of Tupelo, Miss., were organizing campaigns against programs deemed unacceptable. See Erik Barnouw, *The Golden Web: A History of Broadcasting in the United States, 1933 to 1953* (New York: Oxford Univ. Press, 1968), 273–83; and Gitlin, 247–63.
57. David Robb, "Letter to CBS Reveals 'Grant' Sponsor's Concern Over Image," *Hollywood Reporter*, June 3, 1982.
58. Ibid.
59. Ibid.
60. Gitlin,
61. A copy of the letter is among the papers of Daryl Anderson. Used with permission.
62. Mary McGrory, "The Politics of the Firing of TV's 'Lou Grant'," *Washington Post*, June 27, 1982. The eight sponsors cited by the mailing were Ford Motor Company, Noxell Corporation, Keebler Crackers, Ace Hardware Corporation, Emery Air Freight Corporation, Kraftco Corporation, Brown Forman Distillers Corporation, and General Mills Incorporated.
63. Advertisement, *Los Angeles Times*, Apr. 30, 1982.
64. Gitlin, 7.
65. "Donahue" transcript no.05042, provided by Multimedia Program Productions.
66. Reynolds interview, Dec. 4, 1991.
67. Gitlin, 8. CBS eventually replaced *Lou Grant* with *Cagney and Lacey* (CBS, 1982–88), a realistic police drama that for the first time featured two women detectives (played by actresses Tyne Daly and Sharon Gless). CBS canceled the low-rated series after one season, but angry viewers and supportive critics created enough publicity to change the network's mind. *Cagney and Lacey* settled into a six-year run, which included Emmy Awards for Best Drama in 1985 and 1986. For more on the series, see Brooks and Marsh, 136–37, and McNeil, 124–25.
68. Tinker interview, Feb. 26, 1992.
69. Howard Rosenberg, "CBS Yanks 'Lou Grant,' Three Others from Lineup," *Los Angeles Times*, May 7, 1982.
70. Arnold Becker, letter to author, Jan. 30, 1992.
71. Ibid.

72. Larry Reibstein, "The Revenge of the 'Nets'," *Newsweek*, May 16, 1994, 44.

73. Ibid.

74. Ibid.

75. Asner interview, Dec. 9, 1991.

76. Eleanor Blau, "Asner Calls 'Lou Grant' Censored," *New York Times*, May 18, 1982.

77. Suzan Nightingale, "TV's 'Lou Grant' Canceled; Ratings, Politics Blamed," *Los Angeles Herald Examiner*, May 7, 1982.

78. Ibid.

79. Walden interview, Dec. 5, 1991.

80. Reynolds interview, Dec. 4, 1991.

81. Ibid.

82. Ibid.

83. Marchand interview, Jan. 23, 1992.

84. Adams interview, Feb. 12, 1992.

85. Kelsey interview, Dec. 12, 1991.

86. Anderson interview, Dec. 3, 1991.

87. Smith interview, Nov. 18, 1992.

88. Gallery interview, Dec. 5, 1991.

89. See Michael London, "Protesters Seek 'Grant' Renewal," *Los Angeles Times*, May 12, 1982; and David Robb, "600 Protesters Rally in Support of 'Lou Grant'," *The Hollywood Reporter*, May 12, 1982.

90. Ibid.

91. A copy of the leaflet is among the papers of Edward Asner. Used with permission.

92. David Robb, "Labor Turns Out to Support Asner in 2nd Mass Protest," *The Hollywood Reporter*, May 19, 1982.

93. Marilyn Peterson, "In Canceling 'Lou Grant,' CBS Appears to Be Running Scared," *Houston Post*, May 18, 1982.

94. Herb Caen, "Notes on a Frayed Cuff," *San Francisco Chronicle*, May 11, 1982.

95. "Rossi, I Want a Rewrite," *Oakland Tribune*, May 8, 1982.

96. Eric Mink, "Was It Politics," *St. Louis Post-Dispatch*, June 22, 1982. For other views of the cancellation see Phil Kerby, "Artists Should be Distinguished from Their Politics," *Los Angeles Times*, May 20, 1982; Peter Coutros, "Asner, Heston—and God," *Los Angeles Daily News*, May 12, 1982; Gary Deeb, "When It Comes to Politics and Programs, Color CBS Yellow," *Kansas City Star*, television section, June 13, 1982; Sarah Overstreet, "Political Prejudice Interferes with Network TV," *Springfield Daily News*, Aug. 5, 1982; Jimmy Breslin, "Can't Take 'Lou' for Granted," *New York Daily News*, May 20, 1982; Mitch Kehetian, "Ed Asner, a Victim of Bad Journalism?" *Macomb Daily*, May 15, 1982; Steve Emerine, "CBS Buys TV's Best Shows—and Cancels Them," *Arizona Daily Star*, May 12, 1982; Don Freeman, untitled column, *San Diego Union*, May 10, 1982; and Andy Rooney, "Another Great TV Show Canceled," *Arizona Daily Star*, May 12, 1982.

97. "It's-30-for Ed Asner," *Nashua Telegraph*, May 21, 1982.

98. "Ed Asner & 'Lou Grant'," *Los Angeles Herald Examiner*, May 7, 1982.

99. Michael Dougan, "Do You, Too, Mourn for Lou?" *San Francisco Examiner*, May 11, 1982.

100. Mike Duffy, "Fans Hate to See the Old Favorites Go," *Detroit Free Press*, May 10, 1982.

101. Ed Bark, "Why Did 'Lou Grant' Fold?" *Dallas Morning News*, May 10, 1982.

102. "A Clouded Autopsy on 'Lou Grant'," *Milwaukee Journal*, May 12, 1982.

103. Mary Victorine, letter to the editor, "The Readers on 'Lou Grant,' " *San Francisco Examiner*, May 18, 1982.

104. Carlyle P. Johnson, letter to the editor, "The Readers on 'Lou Grant'," *San Francisco Examiner*, May 18, 1982.

105. Ruth Mode, letter to the editor, *Cincinnati Enquirer*, May 21, 1982.

106. James M. Cory, letter to the editor, *Philadelphia Inquirer*, May 13, 1982.

107. John Silvero, letter to the editor, *Philadelphia Inquirer*, May 13, 1982.

108. Harry Bernstein, "Screen Actors Disapprove Asner-Supported Merger," *Los Angeles Times*, May 11, 1982.

109. "He's Victim of Heston Hit Squad, Asner Says," *Los Angeles Times*, May 18, 1982.

110. See "Asner Denies Accusing Reagan of Working to Cancel TV Show," *Los Angeles Times*, May 19, 1982; and "How We See It," *TV Guide*, June 5, 1982, A-2. Note that the headline for the corrected story as it appeared in the *Los Angeles Times* does not accurately reflect the story's content, that is, that Asner had been misquoted.

111. Edward Asner, "Ed Asner Rebuts Criticism, *TV Guide*, Aug. 14, 1982, A-3.

112. Bob Wisehart, "Ed Asner's Poor-Little-Me Act Has Become a Bit of a Bore," New Orleans *Times-Picayune*, May 21, 1982.

113. Gary Deeb, " 'Lou Grant' Cancellation Makes Martyr of Asner," *Chicago Sun-Times*, May 11, 1982.

114. Roger Simon, "Go Back to Rewrite, Lou," *New York Post*, June 4, 1982.

115. Kline interview, Nov. 16, 1992.

116. Anderson interview, Dec. 3, 1991.

117. Smith interview, Nov. 18, 1992.

118. Young interview, July 9, 1992.

119. A. Williams interview, July 5, 1992.

120. Gallery interview, Dec. 5, 1991.

121. Reynolds interview, Dec. 4, 1991.

122. Marchand interview, Jan. 23, 1992.

123. A. Williams interview, July 5, 1992.

124. Freeman interview, May 11, 1992.

125. Asner interview, Dec. 9, 1991.

126. Ibid.

127. Ibid.

128. Edward Asner, telephone interview with author, June 7, 1994.

129. Inman, 57–58.

130. See Harry Bernstein, "SAG Vote Looks Like Referendum on Reagan," *Los Angeles Times*, Oct. 16, 1985; and Harry Bernstein, "Patty Duke Is Elected President of Actors Guild," *Los Angeles Times*, Nov. 6, 1985.

131. Smith interview, Nov. 18, 1992.

132. Peter J. Boyer, "No Finale for 'Lou Grant'," *Los Angeles Times*, June 7, 1982.

133. Kaplan, 241–55.

134. Bannon interview, Dec. 4, 1991.

135. Ibid.

9. The Legacies of *Lou Grant*

1. Tom Brazaitis, "Trib to Miss Sort of Story It Loved Best," *Cleveland Plain Dealer*, May 17, 1982.

2. "Lou Grant: He Was the Kind of Editor Most Journalists Wish They Had," *Detroit Free Press*, May 14, 1982.

3. David Israel, "Requiem For 'Lou Grant'," *Los Angeles Herald Examiner*, Sep. 13, 1982.

4. Andy Rooney, "End of 'Lou Grant' Show Saddens Me," *Los Angeles Times*, May 12, 1982.

5. Steven Reddicliffe, " 'Lou Grant': It's Goodbye to a Favorite," *Dallas Times Herald*, Sep. 2, 1982.

6. For general assessments of *Lou Grant* see McNeil, 448; Brooks and Marsh, 525; Harry Castleman and Walter J. Podrazik, *Harry and Wally's Favorite TV Shows* (New York: Prentice Hall Press, 1989), 297–98; Allan Hunter, ed., *Chambers Concise Encyclopedia of Film and Television* (New York: W. and R. Chambers, 1991), 201–2; 326; and Michael Winship, *Television* (New York: Random House, 1988), 95–96. For detailed discussions of the series see Feuer, Kerr, and Vahimagi; and Grant Tinker and Bud Rukeyser, *Tinker On Television: From General Sarnoff to General Electric* (New York: Simon and Schuster, 1994).

7. Thomas Schatz, " 'St. Elsewhere' and the Evolution of the Ensemble Series," in *Television: The Critical View*, 4th ed., ed. Horace Newcomb (New York: Oxford Univ. Press, 1987), 85–86.

8. Theodore Paul Espinosa, "Text-Building in a Hollywood Television Series: An Ethnographic Study" (Ph.D. diss., Stanford Univ., 1982).

9. Danae Clark, "The State vs. Asner in the Killing of Lou Grant," *Journal of Communication Inquiry* 11, no.2 (Summer 1987): 87–94.

10. See David C. Martin, "Uses and Gratifications Associated with Prime Time Television: Content and Individual Viewer Differences" (Ph.D. diss., Univ. of Oregon, 1981); Ella Taylor, *Prime-Time Families: Television Culture in Postwar America* (Berkeley: Univ. of California Press, 1989); and S. Robert Lichter, Linda S. Richter, and Stanley Rothman, *Watching America* (New York: Prentice Hall Press, 1991).

11. Asner interview, Dec. 9, 1991.

12. Shaw interview, Jan. 28, 1992.

13. Martinez interview, Jan. 14, 1992.

14. Asner interview, Dec. 9, 1991.

15. Murphy interview, Jan. 22, 1992.

16. Zacchino interview, Jan. 16, 1992.

17. Kline interview, Nov. 16, 1992.

18. Asner interview, Dec. 9, 1991.

19. Guest interview, Dec. 6, 1991.

20. Brink interview, Feb. 13, 1992.

Bibliography

Archives

The Gene Reynolds Collection at the University of California at Los Angeles was an invaluable source of information. The collection includes scripts and de Forest Research reports for all 114 *Lou Grant* episodes, CBS Program Practices reports for fifty episodes, files of newspaper and magazine clippings that served as research material for scriptwriters, and production schedule information.

The Vanderbilt Television News Archive at Vanderbilt University in Nashville, Tennessee, provided videotapes of network news programs that reported the Asner-El Salvador controversy and the cancellation of the series.

The Museum of Television and Radio in New York, a repository of thousands of hours of television programs, provided episodes of the early newspaper drama *The Front Page*.

Daryl Anderson, Edward Asner, and David Shaw provided correspondence and other material from their files.

Books

Alley, Robert S., and Irby B. Brown. *Love Is All Around: The Making of "The Mary Tyler Moore Show."* New York: Delta, 1989.

Barnouw, Erik. *The Golden Web: A History of Broadcasting in the United States, 1933 to 1953.* New York: Oxford Univ. Press, 1968.

Barrett, Laurence I. *Gambling With History: Reagan in the White House.* Garden City, N.Y.: Doubleday, 1983.

Barris, Alex. *Stop the Presses! The Newspaperman in American Film.* South Brunswick A. S. Barnes, 1976.

Brenner, Alfred. *The TV Scriptwriter's Handbook.* Cincinnati, Ohio: Writer's Digest Books, 1985.

Brooks, Tim. *The Complete Directory to Prime Time TV Stars, 1946-Present.* New York: Ballantine Books, 1987.

Brooks, Tim, and Earle Marsh. *The Complete Directory to Prime Time Network TV Shows, 1946-Present.* 5th ed. New York: Ballantine Books, 1992.

Brown, Les. *Les Brown's Encyclopedia of Television.* 3d ed. Detroit, Mich.: Gale Research, 1992.

Cannon, Lou. *President Reagan: The Role of a Lifetime.* New York: Simon and Schuster, 1991.

Castleman, Harry, and Walter J. Podrazik. *Harry and Wally's Favorite TV Shows.* New York: Prentice Hall Press, 1989.

Collier, Peter. *The Fondas: A Hollywood Dynasty.* New York: G. P. Putnam's Sons, 1991.

Collier, Peter, and David Horowitz. *The Fords: An American Epic.* New York: Summit Books, 1988.

Crouse, Timothy. *The Boys on the Bus.* New York: Random House, 1972.

Delury, George E., ed. *The World Almanac and Book of Facts 1980.* New York: Newspaper Enterprise Association, 1980.

Dunning, John. *Tune In Yesterday: The Ultimate Encyclopedia of Old-Time Radio, 1925-1976.* Englewood Cliffs, N.J.: Prentice-Hall, 1976.

Emery, Edwin, and Michael Emery. *The Press and America: An Interpretive History of the Mass Media.* 5th ed. Englewood Cliffs, N.J.: Prentice-Hall, 1984.

Fenichell, Stephen, and Lawrence S. Charfoos. *Daughters at Risk: A Personal DES History.* Garden City, N.Y.: Doubleday, 1981.

Feuer, Jane, Paul Kerr, and Tise Vahimagi, eds. *MTM: Quality Television.* London: BFI Publishing, 1984.

Freedland, Michael. *Jane Fonda: A Biography.* New York: St. Martin's Press, 1988.

Ghiglione, Loren. *The American Journalist: Paradox of the Press.* Washington, D.C.: Library of Congress, 1990.

Gitlin, Todd. *Inside Prime Time.* New York: Pantheon Books, 1983.

Goldman, William. *Adventures in the Screen Trade: A Personal View of Hollywood and Screenwriting.* New York: Warner Books, 1983.

Goodwin, H. Eugene. *Groping For Ethics in Journalism.* Ames, Iowa: Iowa State Univ. Press, 1983.

Hertsgaard, Mark. *On Bended Knee: The Press and the Reagan Presidency.* New York: Farrar Straus Giroux, 1988.

Hirshberg, Jack. *A Portrait of All the President's Men.* New York: Warner Books, 1976.

Hubbard, Linda S., and Owen O'Donnell, eds. *Contemporary Theatre, Film, and Television.* Vol. 6. Detroit: Gale Research, 1989.

Hunter, Allan, ed. *Chambers Concise Encyclopedia of Film and Television.* New York: W. and R. Chambers, 1991.

Inman, David. *The TV Encyclopedia.* New York: Perigee, 1991.

Kaplan, Mike, ed. *Variety's Directory of Major U.S. Show Business Awards.* New York: R. R. Bowker, 1989.

Kohn, Howard. *Who Killed Karen Silkwood?* New York: Summit Books, 1981.

Lane, Hana Umlauf, ed. *The World Almanac and Book of Facts 1983.* New York: Ballantine Books, 1983.

Lichter, S. Robert, Linda S. Richter, and Stanley Rothman. *Watching America.* New York: Prentice Hall Press, 1991.

McClintick, David. *Indecent Exposure: A True Story of Hollywood and Wall Street.* New York: William Morrow, 1982.

McNeil, Alex. *Total Television: A Comprehensive Guide to Programming from 1948 to the Present.* 3d ed. New York: Penguin Books, 1991.

Moritz, Charles, ed. *Current Biography Yearbook 1978.* New York: H. W. Wilson, 1978.

Nelson, Harold J., Dwight L. Teeter, Jr., and Don R. Le Duc. *Law of Mass Communications: Freedom and Control of Print and Broadcast Media.* 6th ed. Westbury, N.Y.: Foundation Press, 1989.

Newcomb, Horace, ed. *Television: The Critical View.* 4th ed. New York: Oxford Univ. Press, 1987.

Newcomb, Horace, and Robert S. Alley. *The Producer's Medium: Interviews with Creators of American TV.* New York: Oxford Univ. Press, 1983.

O'Neil, Thomas. *The Emmys: Star Wars, Showdowns, and the Supreme Test of TV's Best.* New York: Penguin Books, 1992.

Orenberg, Cynthia Laitman. *DES: The Complete Story.* New York: St. Martin's Press, 1981.

Ravage, John W. *Television: The Director's Viewpoint.* Boulder, Colo.: Westview Press, 1978.

Reiss, David S. *"M*A*S*H": The Exclusive Inside Story of TV's Most Popular Show.* Indianapolis: Bobbs-Merrill, 1980.

Schatz, Thomas. " 'St. Elsewhere' and the Evolution of the Ensemble Series." In *Television: The Critical View,* 4th ed., edited by Horace Newcomb. New York: Oxford Univ. Press, 1987.

Scheuer, Steven H., ed. *Who's Who in Television and Cable.* New York: Facts on File Publications, 1982.

Schudson, Michael. *Watergate in American Memory: How We Remember, Forget, and Reconstruct the Past.* New York: Basic Books, 1992.

Shanks, Bob. *The Cool Fire: How to Make It in Television.* New York: Vintage Books, 1977.

———. *The Primal Screen: How to Write, Sell, and Produce Movies for Television.* New York: W. W. Norton, 1986.

Shapiro, Mitchell E. *Television Network Prime-Time Programming, 1948–1988.* Jefferson, N.C.: McFarland, 1989.

Steinberg, Cobbett. *Film Facts.* New York: Facts on File, 1980.

———. *TV Facts.* New York: Facts on File, 1985.

Sterling, Christopher H., and John M. Kittross. *Stay Tuned: A Concise History of American Broadcasting.* 2d ed. Belmont, Calif.: Wadsworth Publishing, 1990.

Taft, William H. *Encyclopedia of Twentieth-Century Journalists.* New York: Garland Publishing, 1986.

Talese, Gay. *The Kingdom and the Power*. 1966. Reprint, New York: Dell, 1981.

Taylor, Ella. *Prime-Time Families: Television Culture in Postwar America*. Berkeley: Univ. of California Press, 1989.

Tinker, Grant, and Bud Rukeyser. *Tinker in Television: From General Sarnoff to General Electric*. New York: Simon and Schuster, 1994.

Who's Who in Entertainment, 1989–1990. Wilmette, Ill.: Macmillan Directory Division, 1990.

Wiley, Mason and Damien, Bona. *Inside Oscar: The Unofficial History of the Academy Awards*. New York: Ballantine Books, 1986.

Winship, Michael. *Television*. New York: Random House, 1988.

Journals and Periodicals

Asner, Edward. "Ed Asner Rebuts Criticism." *TV Guide*, Aug. 14, 1982, A-3.

" 'Big Town's' Big Boss." *TV Guide*, Oct. 8, 1955, 8–9.

Braun, Saul. "How Television Cuts the Bleep Out of Shows." *TV Guide*, May 5, 1973, 6–10.

Brill, Steven. "Back on the Beat with Woodward and Bernstein." *Esquire*, Dec. 1983, 497–504.

"Case History of a Star." *TV Guide*, Oct. 13, 1956, 17–19.

Clark, Danae. "The State vs. Asner in the Killing of Lou Grant," *Journal of Communication Inquiry* 11, no. 2 (Summer 1987): 87–94.

"Dateline: Anywhere." *TV Guide*, Mar. 30, 1957.

Davis, L. J. "Looser, Yes, but Still the Deans of Discipline." *Channels*, July-Aug. 1987, 32–38.

Davis, Sally Ogle. "Battling It Out in Hollywood." *New York Times Magazine*, Apr. 25, 1982, 100–104.

Deford, Frank. "Fans to Press: Drop Dead." *Sports Illustrated*, Dec. 13, 1976, 24–27.

Dowie, Mark, and David Talbott. "Ed Asner: Too Hot for Cool Medium." *Mother Jones*, Aug. 1982, 6–13.

Francois, Emmett W. " 'Animal' Revisited." *News Photographer*, Apr. 1978, 4.

Friedman, Mel. "Who Killed Lou Grant." *Madison Avenue*, Oct. 1982, 82–86.

Gage, Nicholas. "Where 'Andros' Hits—and Misses—the Target." *TV Guide*, May 17, 1977, 13–17.

Gelman, Steve. "The Lovable Sourpuss." *TV Guide*, Oct. 15, 1977, 26–29.

Gersh, Debra. "Stereotyping Journalists." *Editor & Publisher*, Oct. 5, 1991, 18–19.

Gitlin, Todd. "The Screening Out of 'Lou Grant'." *The Nation*, June 26, 1982, 772–75.

Goldstein, Steve. "Making of 'Andros'." *More*, Apr. 1977, 49.

Hamill, Pete. "What Does Lou Grant Know about El Salvador?" *New York*, Mar. 15, 1982, 24–30.

Hentoff, Nate. "Who's On First? Free Speech and Doubletalk." *The Progressive*, Aug. 1982, 31–33.

"How We See It." *TV Guide*, June 5, 1982, A-2.

Johnson, Curt. "Get Our Act Together." *News Photographer*, June 1978, 43.

Koch, Tom. "Lou Grouch." *MAD*, Mar. 1979, 43–48.

Levin, Eric. "Censors in Action." *TV Guide*, Dec. 10, 1977, 4–10.

"Location: Europe." *TV Guide*, Aug. 14, 1954, 13–15.

"Making the Rules in Prime Time." *Channels*, May 7, 1990, 23–27.

Mankin, Eric. "Death in the Family." *L. A. Weekly*, May 21–27, 1982, 19–21.

Merrill, Sam. "*Playboy* Interview: Edward Asner." *Playboy*, Apr. 1981, 92.

Murphy, Mary. " 'Sometimes I'm So Ambitious I Even Fool Myself.' " *TV Guide*, Apr. 11, 1981, 30.

Reibstein, Larry. "The Revenge of the 'Nets'." *Newsweek*, May 16, 1994, 44.

Rich, Frank. "Viewpoint: Lou, Carter, CHiPS." *Time*, Sep. 19, 1977, 94.

"Room With a Past." *TV Guide*, Nov. 30, 1968, 26–27.

Rosen, R. D. "A Prime Time for Reporters." *Washington Journalism Review*, Mar. 1982, 42–44.

Russell, Dick. "Leave It to the Merry Prankster." *TV Guide*, Dec. 16, 1978, 39–42.

See, Lisa. "Now the Voice Has Authority." *TV Guide*, Oct. 4, 1980, 26–30.

Seides, Gilbert. Television review. *TV Guide*, Nov. 3, 1962, 14.

Shaw, David. "Actor Wants Byline." *TV Guide*, Jan. 21, 1978, 16–20.

———. "What Killed 'Lou Grant'." *TV Guide*, July 24, 1982, 18–22.

Sklar, Robert. "Viewing 'Lou Grant' Between the Lines." *Television Quarterly*, 15, no. 4 (Winter 1978–79): 39–42.

Starr, Mark. "Asner the Activist." *Newsweek*, Mar. 8, 1982, 23.

Strongman, Tom. " 'Animal' Revisited." *News Photographer*, Apr. 1978, 4.

Swertlow, Frank. "How Jack Bannon Hates His Hot Tub." *TV Guide*, June 12, 1982, 20–22.

Untitled review. *TV Guide*, Dec. 18, 1954.

———. *TV Guide*, Feb. 26, 1955, 14.

———. *TV Guide*, Feb. 11, 1956, 19.

———. *TV Guide*, Feb. 16, 1957, 27.

———. *TV Guide*, June 21, 1958, 27.

———. *TV Guide*, Mar. 4, 1961, 23.

Velie, Lester. "Confessions of a TV Novice." *TV Guide*, June 2, 1962, 4–7.

Warren, Tom. "Pan Mail or Fan Mail." *News Photographer*, Sep. 1978, 43.

Watters, Harry F. "Eyeballing the New Season." *Newsweek*, Sep. 26, 1977, 79.

" 'Wire Service' Brought George Brent Out of Retirement." *TV Guide*, Mar. 16, 1957, 17–19.

"You Can't Go at This Job with a Meat Cleaver." *TV Guide*, Dec. 17, 1977, 18–22.

Zynda, Thomas H. "The Hollywood Version: Movie Portrayals of the Press," *Journalism History* 6, no. 1 (Spring 1979): 16–25.

Dissertations, and Transcripts, and Correspondence

Becker, Arnold. Letter to author. Jan. 30, 1992.

Espinosa, Theodore Paul. "Text-Building in a Hollywood Television Series: An Ethnographic Study." Ph.D. diss., Stanford Univ., 1982.

Martin, David C. "Uses and Gratifications Associated with Prime Time Television: Content and Individual Viewer Differences." Ph.D. diss., Univ. of Oregon, 1981.

Transcript, *Donahue* television program, originally aired May 4, 1982. Transcript no. 05042, provided by Multimedia Program Productions, Cincinnati, Ohio.

Interviews

Adams, Mason. Telephone interview with author. Feb. 12, 1992.

Anderson, Daryl. Interview with author. Los Angeles, Calif., Dec. 3, 1991.

Asner, Edward. Interview with author. Los Angeles, Calif., Dec. 9, 1991.

———. Telephone interview with author. June 7, 1994.

Balding, Rebecca. Telephone interview with author. Jan. 14, 1992.

Bannon, Jack. Interview with author. Los Angeles, Calif., Dec. 4, 1991.

Brinckerhoff, Burt. Telephone interview with author. July 7, 1992.

Brink, Bill. Telephone interview with author. Feb. 13, 1992.

Burns, Allan. Interview with author. Los Angeles, Calif., Dec. 17, 1991.

Cotliar, George. Telephone interview with author. Feb. 13, 1992.

Daly, John. Telephone interview with the author. Dec. 10, 1990.

Damski, Mel. Telephone interview with author. Dec. 10, 1992.

de Forest, Kellam. Telephone interview with author. May 22, 1992.

Freeman, Seth. Telephone interview with author. May 11, 1992.

———. Telephone interview with author. July 8, 1992.

Gallery, Michele. Interview with author. Los Angeles, Calif., Dec. 5, 1991.

Guest, Lance. Interview with author. Los Angeles, Calif., Dec. 6, 1991.

Isaacs, Carol. Telephone interview with author. May 12, 1992.

Kelsey, Linda. Interview with author. Los Angeles, Calif., Dec. 12, 1991.

Kline, Steve. Telephone interview with author. Nov. 16, 1992.

Levin, Peter. Telephone interview with author. Dec. 29, 1992.

Litwack, Sydney Z. Telephone interview with author. July 20, 1992.

Malnic, Eric. Telephone interview with author. Mar. 16, 1992.

Marchand, Nancy. Telephone interview with author. Jan. 23, 1992.

Martinez, Al. Telephone interview with author. Jan. 14, 1992.

Murphy, Mark. Telephone interview with author. Jan. 22, 1992.

Patterson, Jerry. Telephone interview with author. Sep. 17, 1992.

Reynolds, Gene. Interview with author. Los Angeles, Calif., Dec. 4, 1991.

———. Interview with author. Los Angeles, Calif., Dec. 16, 1991.

———. Telephone interview with author. Feb. 14, 1992.

Shaw, David. Telephone interview with author. Jan. 28, 1992.

Singer, Alexander. Telephone interview with author. July 18, 1992.

Smith, April. Telephone interview with author. Nov. 18, 1992.

Thackrey, Ted, Jr. Telephone interview with author. Jan. 10, 1992.

Tinker, Grant. Telephone interview with author. Feb. 26, 1992.

Tokatyan, Leon. Interview with author. Los Angeles, Calif., Dec. 3, 1991.

———. Telephone interview with author. Jan. 16, 1992.

Walden, Robert. Interview with the author. Los Angeles, Calif., Dec. 5, 1991.

Williams, Allen. Telephone interview with author. July 5, 1992.

Williams, Patrick. Telephone interview with author. July 6, 1992.

Yaro, Boris. Telephone interview with author. Jan. 28, 1992.

Young, Roger. Telephone interview with author. July 9, 1992.

Zacchino, Narda. Telephone interview with author. Jan. 16, 1992.

Index